Results-
Based
Leadership

Results-Based Leadership

Dave Ulrich

Jack Zenger

Norm Smallwood

Harvard Business School Press

Boston, Massachusetts

Library of Congress Cataloging-in-Publication Data

Ulrich, David, 1953–

    Results-based leadership / Dave Ulrich, Jack Zenger, Norm
Smallwood.

      p.   cm.

    Includes index.

    ISBN 0-87584-871-0 (alk. paper)

    1. Leadership.   2. Executive ability.   I. Zenger, John H.
II. Smallwood, W. Norm.   III. Title.

HD57.7.U45   1999

658.4'092—dc21   98-42243
                                                 CIP

Contents

Foreword

MY CEO FRIEND WAS GRUMBLING AGAIN about his favorite topic. "With all due respect, Warren, what's missing in your writing and, for that matter, most of the other stuff I've read in your field, is the lack of attention to closure." He looked at me as if I were guilty of the most heinous crime. I came back rather lamely and asked him what he meant by "closure," which he had intoned as if it were something sacred. And he said, "I can tell you what I mean in one word: results." Again, that reproachful look. He then ended his denunciation with a final blow, quoting his venerable management guru, Vince Lombardi: "When all is said and done, more is said than done."

My friend was making an important point, perhaps not sacred, but hugely important. And what makes this book hugely important— and one that human resources experts and executives will turn to again and again—is its relentless emphasis on results. You see, what my friend was really getting at was an area of neglect, something that at times makes us a tad uneasy, even insecure or frustrated. And this is what this book is all about: how organizational capabilities and leadership competencies lead to and are connected to desired results.

I think it's fair to say that most of the books in our field focus on organizational capabilities; you know—agile, adaptable, value based, mission directed, and so on. Or on leadership competencies, such as trust, vision, character, and all manner of exemplary attributes, competencies, and capabilities. All well and good, but what is seriously missing, the authors argue, is the connection between these critical capabilities and results. Ulrich, Zenger, and Smallwood keep asking the "so that" question. Yes to "leadership development" SO THAT . . . *fill in the result.* Yes to "investing in human capital" SO THAT . . . *fill in the result.* Yes, by all means yes to "accountability" SO THAT . . . *fill in the result.* Here is the simple equation that informs virtually every page of this book: *Effective leadership = attributes × results.* As the authors write, "This equation suggests that leaders must strive for excellence in both terms; that is, they must both demonstrate attributes and achieve results. Each term of the equation multiplies the other; they are not cumulative."

Sounds pretty simple, huh? But as Oliver Wendell Holmes once said, "I wouldn't give a fig for the simplicity this side of complexity but I would give my right arm for the simplicity on the other side of complexity." The simplicity of this book is way over on the other side of complexity.

I won't attempt to summarize what's in the book; that's not the purpose of a foreword. But I would like to highlight some of the seminal and original points the book makes and why I think it's "hugely important." First of all, the authors really get down to what desired results are and how they are defined and measured. They focus on four areas of results: employee results (human capital), organization results (learning, innovation), customer results (delight target customers), and investor results (cash flow). Beyond that, the book is refreshingly well organized around the key concepts and how they are measured in relationship to the four results. And finally, they close the circle by providing some fascinating and useful insights about how organizations can develop and retain "results-based leaders."

Shortly after finishing my first reading of *Results-Based Leadership* but before writing this Foreword, I had lunch with two senior executives from a Fortune 500 company and could barely contain my enthusiasm, so rhapsodic, I guess, that one of them raised his eyebrows and essentially asked me the "so that" question (as in "OK, I get you, but what does it get me?"). I can't recall how I responded then, but now, after a few more readings, I know what I should have said. I should have said that the book provides a wise and serious rationale to what we're all about, our raison d'être. It seriously addresses the "so that" question. Those of us interested in making our organizations more adaptive,

effective, creative, and humane are continually asked to justify our existence. Those questions that usually start or end with "At the end of the
day" or the proverbial "bottom line"—those questions practically tat-
tooed on our chests—are one way or another related to my friend's "closure" concern, with how we justify our existence to the enterprise. This
book makes one of the most important statements about the very meaning and importance of leadership.

I started this Foreword with the inevitable Vince Lombardi quote
and would like to end with a quote by a famous Zen master. He said,
"First, enlightenment. . . . Then, the laundry." This book is about both.

WARREN BENNIS
University of Southern California

Preface

WE BELIEVE THIS BOOK emerged from the *Zeitgeist*. That wonderful German word, for which there is no English equivalent, describes ideas that are just "in the air" or that reflect the thinking of an era.

Independently the authors had started thinking about a new way to understand and describe leadership. Each was distraught with the extraordinarily wide range of definitions and descriptions of leadership, and with the inability of investments in leadership programs to produce better leaders. We were dismayed with the quick-fix, "you too can be a leader" Band-Aid being put on leadership problems. Most troubling were the chasms separating contemporary writers and theoreticians from each other. Their disparate theories made rigorous academic research difficult, and their highly diverse views gave little help to the practicing leader.

Pinpointing the very concept of "leadership" felt akin to grappling with a ghost, because no two people saw the same thing or defined it the same way. Leadership development programs that we experienced were amorphous. Sponsors complained that their program did not produce any noticeable change in the attendees' leadership behavior.

At one point, we purchased over 30 books with *leader* or *leadership* in the title to add to the extensive library each of us had collected. Some told inspirational stories of a leader's successes. Others shared secrets of what leaders believed accounted for their achievements. But all had a common dimension. They focused inward and concluded with a "wish list" of attributes possessed by successful leaders. At times, these attributes focused on inner strengths (character, integrity, energy); at other times, they described what leaders knew (technical know-how, strategic thinking) or how they behaved (set vision, flattened the organization, emphasized teams). The more we pondered leadership as merely a bundle of attributes, the more we concluded that the solitary focus on attributes of the leader left something important and obvious out of the leadership equation. We were comforted to read a statement by Peter Drucker to a group of health care executives, saying, "Leadership is all about results."

Each of us discussed our ideas with respected colleagues in the field. After receiving positive encouragement from these friends, we were told, "Well, you should really talk to _____ , because he's talking about writing a book on exactly the same thing you just described." That's how it all began. We were brought together by a common set of ideas whose time we thought had come.

That does not suggest that we were always of one mind. One of us thought we should develop a new theory of leadership, but was talked out of that by his colleagues as being much too grandiose and ambitious. Finally we agreed that our objective was to reframe the discussion about leadership. That led to good debates about the value of the extensive work on competencies and inner characteristics of leaders. As time progressed, we agreed that the research and writing on competencies and inner qualities had great value, and we wanted to be careful not to denigrate that contribution. In fact, after discussions with leading thinkers in the competency movement, we were even more assured that this movement had added value by identifying the knowledge, skills, and behaviors that leaders possess. But the time had come to move beyond this focus.

Our challenge was to balance our respect for that work with our growing discomfort that it was neither sufficient nor complete. The notion that leadership was the result of a multiplication of attributes and results was an important breakthrough. In early presentations describing our ideas, we found that it was easy for listeners to conclude that we were tossing out all prior work. Half of the leadership equation had simply not received much attention. Our challenge was to make that point without trashing the work on attributes.

Our crusade is to create a balance, but not by succumbing to the temptation to swing the pendulum to the opposite end and pretend that results are all that matter. We want to advance both the dialogue about and the practice of leadership. By moving toward greater emphasis on measurement of *results,* we are convinced that the ability to learn leadership will be improved. Our experience is that nearly everything that gets measured gets better in the long run, and if we can help practitioners focus on effective measurements of leadership results, then we will have made a useful contribution.

One of the most difficult steps in this process was to find a descriptor that encompassed all of the work on competencies and inner characteristics of leaders. We flirted with *persona* and used that in early drafts. The reviewers of the original manuscript gave us a variety of valuable comments (many of which were predictably in disagreement with each other), but the one on which they all agreed was a dislike for the term *persona.* So we reverted to a much blander and more traditional term: *attributes.*

Ultimately, we hope we have created a new way to "brand" a company's leadership. Product brand characterizes the firm's product (in taste, look, feel) so that it is quickly identifiable to consumers. A firm's brand characterizes its unique capabilities as seen by customers. Leadership brand describes the distinct results leaders deliver to their firm. Both attributes and results go into a complete leadership brand, and this brand offers significant advantages to a firm. In fact, creating a leadership brand for their organization should become a key challenge for all leaders. Without results, leadership brands remain generic; with results, leadership brands become specific, distinctive, and add value.

Acknowledgments

Many have directly contributed to this work. We want to acknowledge Kurt Sandholtz for his contributions with edits and with employee and customer results; David Altman, for help on investor results; Joanna Howard, for her painstaking work in typing sections of the manuscript, figures, and tables; Bob Eichinger, for continually tweaking and informing us about how competencies matter and how to think about them in a strategic way; Bruce Jensen, for researching cases; Ginger

Bitter, for graciously responding to questions and keeping multiple projects on schedule; Jon Younger, Randy Stott, Vern Della-Piana, Joe Hanson, Mike Panowyk, Courtney Rogers, Ken LeBaron, Kristen Knight, Rebecca Timothy, Sally White, Mark Ellis, Richard Diforio, Tricia Quai, Judy Seegmiller, Brett Stott, Tait Eyre, Katrina Harmon, Libby Carrier, Jack Roddy, and Kathy Buckner. We thank the participants in many of the groups to which we have presented these ideas. Their questions, challenges, and responses have helped to shape our thinking and given us encouragement.

We especially thank Marjorie Williams of the Harvard Business School Press for her enthusiastic support of this project from its conception through publication.

Many other colleagues contributed indirectly. Curt Artis, Warren Bennis, Frank Bordanaro, Janet Brady, Wayne Brockbank, Ron Chrisman, Gerard Closset, Ralph Christensen, Jim Dagnon, Gene Dalton, Peter Drucker, Jill Edelen, Vicky Farrow, Marlene Feigenbaum, Fred Foulkes, Joseph Gallo, Marshall Goldsmith, Hope Greenfield, Carlos Gutierrez, Phil Harkins, Murray Heibert, Irv Hockaday, Syed Hussain, Steve Kerr, John Kotter, Jim Kouzes, Gerry Lake, Ed Lawler, Mike Losey, Arthur Martinez, Bill Mayer, Paul McKinnon, Henry Mintzberg, Thom Nielson, Jeffrey Pfeffer, Joe Pine, Berry Posner, C. K. Prahalad, Ray Reilly, Bonner Ritchie, Tony Rucci, Bob Stemmler, and Rich Teerlink, Jack Welch, and Warren Wilhem are colleagues whose thinking about leadership are woven throughout this book. We have drawn on their work and acknowledge the influence of their ideas.

Finally, we acknowledge our families, who let us use a good portion of holiday and vacation time, plus other valuable periods, in order to complete this work. We dedicate the book to our mothers—Karin Ulrich, Leah Zenger, and Betty Smallwood—who knew all about the importance of combining results with character long before we wrote any of this.

For any errors or omissions, the authors take full responsibility.

DAVE ULRICH
JACK ZENGER
NORM SMALLWOOD

Results-
Based
Leadership

Connecting Leadership Attributes to Results

1

Leaders Matter

THE QUEST TO BECOME a more effective leader will neither begin nor end with this work. However, we want to shift how to think about and become a better leader. It is faddish to think of leaders as people who master competencies and emanate character. While agreeing with this perspective, we believe that it falls short of assuring that leaders lead. Leaders do much more than demonstrate attributes. Effective leaders get results. This book refocuses and reframes the search for effective leadership by connecting attributes to results.

Study after study looking toward the future continues to demonstrate concern about building leadership. One recent Conference Board study found that only 54 percent of companies surveyed felt they had the leadership necessary to respond to change, and only 8 percent of executives rated overall leadership as excellent.[1] The Human Resource Institute found leadership to be the number 1 issue for effective people management. This study asked 312 respondents to rate the most pressing people issues faced in their company. It found that leadership was the most important, with over 70 percent of the respondents saying it is "extremely important."[2] In studies of the future sponsored by the Human Resource Planning Society (called "State of the Art"),[3] by the Society for Human Resource Management,[4] *Workforce Magazine,*[5] and by the McKinsey consulting firm,[6] a similar set of overriding concerns emerged.

Clearly, leadership matters. Successful companies and individuals within companies exhibit leadership depth. The McKinsey study called "War for Talent" found that firms with leadership depth were much more profitable than those without it. Despite this, the gap between required and available leadership talent is widening. When executives are asked how confident they are about their organization's bench strength, they most often respond with increasing negativity.[7] This may be due in part, of course, to the restructuring, consolidation, and downsizing of recent decades which have reduced the number of leadership opportunities available to the next generation of leaders. Even though much has been written about leadership, and even though significant money and time have been expended to improve its quality, significant change has not been forthcoming. A chasm deepens and widens between what is expected of leaders and what they produce.

A simple exercise demonstrates the lure and danger of many current approaches to leadership. In seminars, we ask participants to complete the sentence "In the future, an effective leader at this firm must. . . ." As participants think about this query, they consider market conditions, future strategies, and organizational requirements to compete, then come up with a list of eight to ten attributes of their desired leaders. Off the top of their heads, executives, middle managers, and first line supervisors often come up with items such as sets a vision, understands customers, communicates well, empowers others, has personal passion for the job, relishes change, builds teams, leverages diversity, and so forth. Using this list of leadership attributes, participants specify what effective leaders need to know and do for each item. We then ask, "What is missing from your list?" This causes participants to stop and generally identify more attributes, such as thinks globally, possesses energy and energizes others, tolerates ambiguity, has integrity, and so forth.

When we push even further for what is missing, some participants wonder what point we are trying to make. Eventually, someone almost always notices that the ever-lengthening list of leadership attributes does not include results, or what leaders accomplish because of the knowledge and ability they possess. This simple exercise illustrates the point that is too often overlooked—admired leaders not only learn how to act, but also act in ways that ensure results.

Any number of simple examples illustrates this point. Airline pilots should know the vision of their company, communicate well, manage change, and have integrity, but in addition they must deliver results—in this case, safe travel. Leaders in business, schools, churches, families, and government agencies face the same challenge. It is not enough to have mastered the attributes of leadership; effective leaders must connect attributes to results.

In the search for more effective leadership, something has often been overlooked. Being capable and possessing the attributes of leadership is terrific, but capability must be put to appropriate, purposeful use. Our message to leaders may be put into the simple formula *Effective leadership = attributes × results*. This equation suggests that leaders must strive for excellence in both terms; that is, they must both demonstrate attributes and achieve results. Each term of the equation multiplies the other; they are not cumulative. Therefore, a low score in either attributes or results will considerably lessen the leader's effectiveness. A score of 9 out of 10 in attributes, for example, multiplied by a score of 2 out of 10 on results, yields an effectiveness rating of only 18 out of 100, not 11 out of 20, the score if the two terms were added.

Some leaders and firms have a predisposition to one side of the equation over the other. When this happens, overall leadership effectiveness falls. Some firms focus almost exclusively on "results," driving their leaders to do whatever it takes to make short-term performance objectives. Leaders in these firms care more about what is accomplished than about how it is accomplished, and they risk the lack of sustainable results. In other firms, the emphasis has been almost exclusively on leadership development through attributes, not paying enough attention to results. Both attributes and results matter. They represent the DNA of leadership and, taken together, they create a road map for improving leaders.

Connecting attributes to results and results to attributes becomes the next agenda for building effective leadership. This book focuses primarily, but not exclusively, on results. While tempted to immediately turn attention to the important characteristics and practices leaders use to create results, without appropriate attributes leaders will not be effective over time. Effective leadership requires both attributes and results. Attributes, if done well, matter; and, if done poorly, leaders cannot be effective. This chapter begins with a grounding in leadership attributes so that leaders recognize that who they are and what they know and do matter; then rigorous attention to leadership results follows throughout the rest of the book.

Building Better Leaders through Attributes

The trend in the last decade for individuals wanting to be or build more effective leaders has been to identify and upgrade leadership attributes; that is, the inner or personal qualities that constitute effective leadership. Under our rubric of leadership attributes falls a large array of sometimes confusing and often overlapping terms, including *habits, traits, competencies, behaviors, style, motives, values, skills,* and *character.*[8] These concepts, collectively called "leadership attributes," fall into three broad categories: who leaders ARE (values, motives, personal traits, character); what leaders KNOW (skills, abilities, traits); and what leaders DO (behaviors, habits, styles, competencies). The ARE-KNOW-DO approach to leadership has received enormous attention and investment in the ongoing attempt to upgrade leaders.

An unfortunate consequence of this attribute approach to leadership has sometimes been the oversimplification and reduction of leadership improvement to a shopping expedition. Aspirants or their guides wander through the leadership attribute warehouse, taking from the shelf first one and then another trait, competency, value, and so on, then trying it out through workshops, videos, or books. When one attribute fails or wears out, the shopping recurs, and a new one replaces the old, starting the cycle all over again.

In recent years, the use of leadership attribute models to upgrade leaders has improved dramatically. Using research, more informed shoppers may now acquire the right attributes, given a business strategy, and understand the investments required to improve those attributes. Consulting firms such as Lominger and Personnel Decisions Inc. examine behavioral skills of leaders (for example, analytical thinking and dealing with ambiguity) to identify the competencies necessary for leadership success.[9] Their research-based models have helped many recognize desired leadership attributes.

Many companies have developed more refined and rigorous ways to identify leadership attributes. General Electric provides a good example of a company that makes the most of the attribute model for building and deploying better leaders. GE uses the concept of *competencies,* bundles of leadership behaviors, to improve leaders and has become renowned among the best at developing industry leaders.[10]

GE bases its approach to leadership development on four essential tasks. First, the organization recognizes the importance of leadership to its business success. Senior managers strongly commit to doing what is needed to build the next generation of leadership. CEO Jack Welch, for example, to assure GE's competitive future, claims he spends 40 percent of his time on people issues, much of it on leadership development.

Second, GE has in place a specific process for developing leadership talent. Its thirty-year-old succession planning system guides a large number of firm leaders in their professional development.[11] Culminating with an annual review by the CEO, top GE executives participate in numerous activities aimed at improving their abilities and increasing career opportunities—and aligning both to corporate strategy. These activities include individualized career plans projecting executives' expected growth within the company and extensive investment in their future through workshops and unique job assignments. GE executives are often considered for and offered CEO jobs at other firms, and the company almost always comes out at the top of lists identifying firms with world-class leadership development.

Third, GE defines leadership attributes behaviorally, for the benefit of future leaders. Jack Welch proposed at a meeting of the company's five hundred executives that all GE leaders would be held accountable both for "making the numbers" and for "living the values." Most executives know the meaning of "make the numbers"—annual cash contributions, earnings, and market share gains. "Living the values" was less clear. Participants at the meeting agreed in principle on the importance not only of the numbers but of how those numbers were achieved. They also agreed on the difficulty of specifying how to operationalize "living the values." To find solid ground for this ambiguous concept, GE leaders designed and deployed a pragmatic, measurable tool known as the Leadership Effectiveness Survey (LES). This survey synthesizes GE values into a list of eight categories and then stipulates specific behaviors consistent with each value. The LES serves GE as a standard for leaders at every level, all of whom are expected to reach their numbers the "right way." (See the appendix at the end of this chapter for a copy of the LES.)

Fourth, GE uses the leadership competencies stipulated in the LES to integrate a number of management practices with the purpose of building quality of leadership. These include considering a candidate's abilities on the LES categories when making hiring or promotion decisions; using annual 360-degree feedback from supervisors, peers, clients, and subordinates to rate the extent to which leaders demonstrate the desired LES competencies. This score often affects annual and long-term compensation decisions. LES concepts also guide the portfolio of training courses delivered throughout GE.

Like GE, literally hundreds of companies have now invested in leadership attribute work to build more effective leaders. This work identifies what leaders need to be, know, and do to succeed.

KEY ELEMENTS OF LEADERSHIP ATTRIBUTES

Most of the items (personal character, knowledge, behaviors) found in these attribute models cluster into four overarching categories of what leaders need to be, know, and do: set direction, mobilize individual commitment, engender organization capability, and demonstrate personal character. Figure 1-1 depicts this model. Figure 1-2 synthesizes these categories of ability and their contributing dimensions, behaviors, and actions possessed by most (if not all) successful leaders, as summarized below. (See the notes to Figure 1-2 for a listing of notable work done in this area.)

Set direction.

Leaders position their firms for and toward the future. Anticipating the future involves predicting and juggling numerous influences—among them, customers, technology, regulators, competitors, investors, and suppliers. Into this future state, leaders must position their firms so as to create a unique identity and build value for all stakeholders. Many terms characterize this future state: *vision, mission, strategy, aspiration, destination, foresight, values,* and so forth. Although each of these words means subtly different things, they all point to leaders defining the future of a company in ways that excite participation and allocate resources to make the future happen. Leaders who set direction know and do at least three things: understand external events, focus on the future, and turn vision into action.

Mobilize individual commitment.

Leaders turn vision into accomplishments by engaging others. They translate future aspirations into the day-to-day behaviors and actions required of each employee. Employees thus engaged become committed to meshing their actions with organizational goals, and they are dedicated to investing their mind, heart, and soul to organizational pursuits. Leaders striving for employee commitment must likewise expend valuable resources of time, energy, and focus to fully engage the firm's indi-

FIGURE 1-1

WHAT DO SUCCESSFUL LEADERS DO?
SUMMARY OF LEADERSHIP ATTRIBUTE FRAMEWORKS

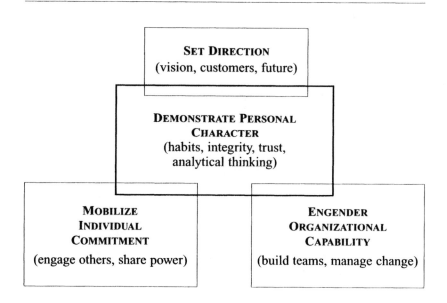

viduals and teams. To do this, leaders must build collaborative relationships; they must share power and authority; and they must manage attention. Leaders must help individuals see and feel how their contributions aid in accomplishing the goals of the organization.

Engender organizational capability.

Leaders build not only individual commitment but also organizational capability. Organizational capability refers to the processes, practices, and activities that create value for the organization.[12] Leaders need the ability to translate organizational direction into directives, vision into practice, and purpose into process. Capability represents the identity of the firm as perceived by both employees and customers. It requires leaders who demonstrate at least five abilities: to build an organizational infrastructure, leverage diversity, deploy teams, design human resource systems, and make change happen.

FIGURE 1-2

SUMMARY OF LEADERSHIP ATTRIBUTES

DIMENSIONS	EXEMPLAR BEHAVIORS OR ACTIONS To what extent do I do the following?
SET DIRECTION	
Understand external events	• Exhibit strong customer orientation.[a] • Think deeply and see new possibilities.[b] • Have the vision, skills, and resources needed to form networks beyond the home base.[c] • Dedicate resources to process innovations that improve customer productivity. • Consistently provide the organization a clear direction. • Demonstrate uncompromising environmental responsibility.
Focus on the future	• Exhibit conviction in creating a vision.[d] • Articulate tangible vision, values, and strategy.[e] • Craft a pathfinding mission.[f] • Operate from a set of inspiring core values and beliefs.[g] • Define, shape, and use core values.[h] • Visualize the business through the customer's eyes. • Claim the future through reconnaissance, technology foresight, conceptual flexibility, vision, and strategic alignment, and by enhancing the company's image. • Think strategically.

a. Arthur Yeung and Doug Ready, "Developing Leadership Capabilities of Global Corporations: A Comparative Study in Eight Nations," *Human Resource Management Journal* 34, no. 4 (1995): 529–548.
b. Rosabeth Kanter, "World-Class Leaders: The Power of Partnering," in *The Leader of the Future,* ed. Frances Hesselbein, Marshall Goldsmith, and Richard Beckhard (San Francisco: Jossey-Bass, 1995), 89–98.
c. Ibid.
d. Edgar Schein, "Leadership and Organizational Culture," in Hesselbein, Goldsmith, and Beckhard, *The Leader of the Future,* 59–70.
e. Yeung and Ready, "Developing Leadership Capabilities."
f. Stephen Covey, "Three Roles of the Leader in the New Paradigm," in Hesselbein, Goldsmith, and Beckhard, *The Leader of the Future,* 149–160.
g. Jac Fitz-enz, survey, Saratoga Institute, 1997.
h. James Heskett and Leonard Schlesinger, "Leaders Who Shape and Keep Performance-Oriented Culture," in Hesselbein, Goldsmith, and Beckhard, *The Leader of the Future,* 111–120.

DIMENSIONS	EXEMPLAR BEHAVIORS OR ACTIONS To what extent do I do the following?

SET DIRECTION *(continued)*

Turn vision into action	• Align performance with vision.[i] • Inspire a shared vision.[j] • Enlist others to attain a future state. • Transform strategy into results. • Inspire a shared purpose. • Create a climate for success.

MOBILIZE INDIVIDUAL COMMITMENT

Build collaborative relationships	• Possess a love of people. • Have the ability to be alone, but also to work with others.[k] • Cheerlead, support, and encourage more than judge, criticize, and evaluate.[l] • Foster collaboration by promoting cooperative goals and building trust.[m]
Share power and authority	• Demonstrate willingness and ability to share power and control.[n] • Listen more than tell.[o] • Possess willingness and ability to involve others and elicit participation.[p] • Exert power through dignity.[q]

i. Kenneth Blanchard, "Turning the Organizational Pyramid Upside Down," in Hesselbein, Goldsmith, and Beckhard, *The Leader of the Future,* 81–88.

j. James Kouzes and Barry Posner, *The Leadership Challenge: How to Keep Getting Extraordinary Things Done in Organizations* (San Francisco: Jossey-Bass, 1995).

k. Charles Handy, "The New Language of Organizing and Its Implications for Leaders," in Hesselbein, Goldsmith, and Beckhard, *The Leader of the Future,* 3–10.

l. Blanchard, "Turning the Organizational Pyramid Upside Down."

m. Kouzes and Posner, *The Leadership Challenge.*

n. Schein, "Leadership and Organizational Culture."

o. Heskett and Schlesinger, "Leaders Who Shape and Keep Performance-Oriented Culture."

p. Schein, "Leadership and Organizational Culture."

q. Heskett and Schlesinger, "Leaders Who Shape and Keep Performance-Oriented Culture."

FIGURE 1-2

SUMMARY OF LEADERSHIP ATTRIBUTES *(continued)*

DIMENSIONS	EXEMPLAR BEHAVIORS OR ACTIONS To what extent do I do the following?

MOBILIZE INDIVIDUAL COMMITMENT *(continued)*

Share power and authority *(continued)*	• Empower and engage employees.[r] • Empower others to do their best.[s] • Strengthen others by sharing power and information.[t] • Use a variety of approaches to get the best out of everyone. • Create opportunities for people to contribute their strongest personal talents to the team effort.
Manage attention	• Manage energy and change people's physical state of being.[u] • Use language to touch the heart.[v] • Create emotion by generating . . .[w] confidence in people who were frightened. certainty in people who were vacillating. action where there was hesitation. strength where there was weakness. expertise where there was floundering. courage where there was cowardice. optimism where there was cynicism. conviction that the future will be better.

ENGENDER ORGANIZATIONAL CAPABILITY

Build organizational infrastructure	• Demonstrate formal leadership capable of integrating, resourcing, and orchestrating activities of various project clusters. • Form ad hoc leadership as required within each of those project clusters.[x]

r. Covey, "Three Roles of the Leader in the New Paradigm."
s. Yeung and Ready, "Developing Leadership Capabilities of Global Corporations."
t. Kouzes and Posner, *The Leadership Challenge.*
u. Blanchard, "Turning the Organizational Pyramid Upside Down."
v. Heskett and Schlesinger, "Leaders Who Shape and Keep Performance-Oriented Culture."
w. Judith Bardwick, "Peacetime Management and Wartime Leadership," in Hesselbein, Goldsmith, and Beckhard, *The Leader of the Future,* 131–140.
x. William Bridges, "Leading the De-Jobbed Organization," in Hesselbein, Goldsmith, and Beckhard, *The Leader of the Future,* 11–18.

DIMENSIONS	EXEMPLAR BEHAVIORS OR ACTIONS To what extent do I do the following?

ENGENDER ORGANIZATIONAL CAPABILITY *(continued)*

	• Align and ensure the match between organization and strategy.[y] • Actively communicate a wide range of information to all employees. • Fully commit to a long-term strategy of building a valuable institution. • Provide encouragement and resources needed for continuous improvement.[z] • Create enthusiastic support for the goals of the business.
Leverage diversity	• Show tolerance of diversity and intolerance of performance, standards, and values. • Not fear the strength in subordinates.[aa] • Integrate different cultures, sectors, and disciplines. • Resolve conflicts diplomatically and find a common cause.[bb] • Advocate partnering and collaboration as preferred styles of behavior.[cc] • Fully utilize people, regardless of race, gender, ethnic origin, or culture.
Deploy teams	• Build self-managing project teams.[dd] • Cross-fertilize and bring the best from one place to another.[ee] • Select the most talented team members available. • Provide specific and frequent feedback that helps improve team performance. • Support the team even during a loss.

y. Covey, "Three Roles of the Leader in the New Paradigm."
z. Jac Fitz-enz, survey.
aa. Peter F. Drucker, "Toward the New Organization," *Leader to Leader* 2, no. 3 (1997): 6–8.
bb. Kanter, "World-Class Leaders: The Power of Partnering."
cc. Jac Fitz-enz, survey.
dd. Bridges, "Leading the De-Jobbed Organization."
ee. Kanter, "World-Class Leaders: The Power of Partnering."

FIGURE 1-2

SUMMARY OF LEADERSHIP ATTRIBUTES *(continued)*

DIMENSIONS	EXEMPLAR BEHAVIORS OR ACTIONS To what extent do I do the following?
	ENGENDER ORGANIZATIONAL CAPABILITY *(continued)*
Design human resource systems	• Build or create culture. • Maintain and sustain culture. • Possess skills in analyzing cultural assumptions.[ff] • Serve as a catalyst and manager of culture change.[gg] • Consciously promote a clearly articulated, stimulating culture.[hh]
Make change happen	• Make change happen and work as a change agent.[ii] • Demonstrate the emotional strength to manage the anxiety caused by change.[jj] • Serve as a catalyst and manager of strategic change.[kk] • Search for opportunities by confronting and challenging the status quo. • Experiment and take risks. • Learn from mistakes and successes.[ll] • Relentlessly seek simpler methods to provide customers with better products or services. • Look for opportunities in change rather than excuses for avoiding change. • Initiate change instead of reacting to external pressures for change. • Vigorously question the status quo. • Use the inputs and ideas of others as stimuli for change.

ff. Schein, "Leadership and Organizational Culture."
gg. Yeung and Ready, "Developing Leadership Capabilities of Global Corporations."
hh. Jac Fitz-enz, survey.
ii. Schein, "Leadership and Organizational Culture."
jj. Ibid.
kk. Yeung and Ready, "Developing Leadership Capabilities of Global Corporations."
ll. Kouzes and Posner, *The Leadership Challenge.*

DIMENSIONS	EXEMPLAR BEHAVIORS OR ACTIONS To what extent do I do the following?
	DEMONSTRATE PERSONAL CHARACTER
Live values by practicing what is preached	• Live the values of my unit.[mm] • Submit myself to the mirror test and find comfort with the person there.[nn] • Lead by example.
Have and create a positive self-image	• Possess a belief in oneself: self-confidence, with humility.[oo] • Demonstrate extraordinary levels of perception and insight into the realities of the world and into group or unit members. • Exhibit extraordinary levels of motivation to enable group members to go through pain of learning and change.[pp]
Possess cognitive ability and personal charm	• Have an open mind and reach out to partners. • Be receptive to information from outside the current framework. • Envision new, mold-breaking possibilities.[qq] • Seek opportunities to learn. • Act with integrity. • Seek broad business knowledge. • Practice insight by seeing things from new angles. • Learn from mistakes. • Remain open to criticism. • Possess learning agility for self-knowledge; think through problems in fresh ways and try new things.[rr] • Meet the challenge oneself to improve. • Deal effectively with complex, ambiguous, and contra-dictory situations. • Urge consideration of counterintuitive alternatives.

mm. Heskett and Schlesinger, "Leaders Who Shape and Keep Performance-Oriented Culture."
nn. Drucker, "Toward the New Organization."
oo. Handy, "The New Language of Organizing and Its Implications for Leaders."
pp. Schein, "Leadership and Organizational Culture."
qq. Kanter, "World-Class Leaders: The Power of Partnering."
rr. Michael Lombardo and Robert Eichinger, "Learning Agility," working paper, Lominger, Minneapolis, 1997.

Leaders who fulfill these functions build organizational capability that outlives them and achieves more for the organization than could any one individual alone.

Demonstrate personal character.

Without doubt, leaders possess character. As scholar Warren Bennis has stated, "Let me state a personal bias that leadership is really a matter of character. The process of becoming a leader is no different than the process of becoming a fully integrated, healthy human being."[13] Followers need leaders they trust, relate to, and feel confidence in. Kouzes and Posner have called this factor "credibility," and they identify a number of contributing attributes such as honesty, ability to inspire, fair-mindedness, and supportiveness.[14] Leaders with character live the values of their firm by practicing what they preach; they possess and create in others a positive self-image; and they display high levels of cognitive ability and personal charm. Max DePree, former CEO at the office furniture company Herman Miller, describes the attributes of a desired leader: spirit, trust, love, grace, warmth, intimacy, and servant leadership. Such well-known leadership frameworks as those by Stephen Covey and Warren Bennis seem to focus on the leader's character as well.[15] Undoubtedly, as leaders develop the personal behaviors, habits, skills, and characteristics collectively known as *character,* they grow into more successful leaders.

Effective leadership requires acquiring knowledge and demonstrating behavior in each of the four categories. A company's ability to field leaders with attributes across the four categories matters more than ever before as competitiveness comes increasingly through the ability to source new talent and build leadership depth. The synthesis of this work in Figure 1-2 allows leaders to identify specific character, knowledge, and behavior required to be a better leader.

In recent years, reflections and research on leadership have improved the quality and use of leadership attribute models.[16] Leadership attributes have also been adapted to different business strategies, geographies, and industries. Leadership attributes have also been defined in behavioral terms which may then be assessed more accurately through 360-degree feedback mechanisms.[17] In many companies, leadership attributes have led to individual development plans in which leaders improve who they are, what they know, and what they do. Leadership attributes have been woven into performance improvement plans that affect compensation and thereby change behaviors.

Through improved leadership attribute models, leaders gain both the broad general qualities shared by all leaders and the particular skills needed to meet the leadership challenges presented by positions at any level and in any function, industry, or location. Clearly, some skills may be taught, others only experienced; some behaviors and attitudes may be learned, others may only be innately part of the leader's persona. Even in the latter cases, however, training often enhances an attribute enough to provide a compensatory balance for the leader's background.

THE PITFALLS OF LEADERSHIP ATTRIBUTE MODELS

Because we have defined effective leadership as *attributes × results,* it is critical that efforts to improve leadership attributes have as much impact as possible. Before presenting a more inclusive leadership model focusing on results and showing how to connect attributes to results, six concerns of many leadership attribute models merit attention. Although an increasing percentage of thoughtful and well-created attribute models overcome these concerns, some firms and leaders continue to fall prey to these attribute pitfalls. Overcoming these traps ensures higher-quality attribute models and overall leadership effectiveness.

Future is more important than past.

Many leadership attribute models emerge by separating high from moderate or lower performers and analyzing the distinguishing character, knowledge, and behaviors of the two groups. Although such work offers valid and reliable distinctions between high and low performers, it may still be flawed. Both groups work in the present, under prevailing conditions and strategies, so the picture derived of desired leadership attributes will be rooted in the present, not the future. Current high performers may be moderate or low performers in the future when the work world changes so quickly and the half-life of knowledge grows ever shorter in most professions, requiring even high performers to unlearn what they know and do. This trap may be avoided by focusing on the future and by anticipating desired attributes rather than relying on past or present attributes.

Tailored attribute models are more important than generic models.

Although many firms deploying leadership attribute models claim to craft unique and tailored leadership models, they often rely on guidance from either the same few consulting firms or a few popular models of leadership. As a result, although firms hope to provide unique models, these models often resemble each other regardless of significant differences in industry and strategy. The attributes derived from a leadership model should reflect the unique challenges of a firm. This may be done by concentrating the modeling effort on business requirements, not on broadly expressed statements of managerial excellence.

Behavior-based attribute models are more effective than theory-based models.

Although many leadership attribute models have focused increasingly on behaviors, not all have. Some models continue to describe attributes generically, in terms of concepts such as "deals with ambiguity" or "possesses integrity." Such concepts may have meaning, but they are useful and measurable only when turned into specific behaviors. Behavior-based leadership attribute models have the power to build leadership excellence and effect change; concept-based ones do not. Creating behaviorally anchored models comes by specifying observable actions that leaders must do more and less of to demonstrate a competence. The concept "possesses integrity" may be recast as the specific behavior "does not give or receive bribes or side payments of any kind for any work."

Line-created and -owned attribute models are more important than HR-created models.

HR-created attribute models have less impact than line-created and -owned models. The task of creating a leadership attribute model often falls solely to an HR professional on staff, a team of HR professionals, or contracted consultants. When they devise and present a finished model to an executive committee for approval, the work, although valid and based on solid research, often lacks the impact of models produced through line management participation. Leaders, managers, and employees usually all relate and commit more to models that bear the stamp of authentic experience. Heavily involving line managers in crafting attribute models increases their commitment to them.

Leadership attribute models need to be used, not just created.

For many leadership attribute models and initiatives, 80 percent of the energy goes into their creation and only 20 percent into their deployment. Deployment deals with how the leadership attributes impact staffing, training, compensation, communication, and other management practices. Too often the leadership attributes, once identified and termed in behavioral terms, fail to impact these managerial practices. This may be overcome by requiring that leadership attributes become the basis for staffing, training, and compensation decisions.

> *Leadership attribute models must define qualities of all leaders, not just those at the top echelon.*

Many, if not most, leadership attribute models focus on the CEO or some other equally visible top leader.[18] The attributes of these senior executives become the basis for what defines good or effective leadership. These models imply that only CEOs (or other top officers) reach the pinnacle of leadership effectiveness, as they have of the hierarchy, and they suggest that these leaders' attributes should be emulated by everyone in the organization. It is, of course, necessary to have effective leaders at the top, but it is not enough for organizational leadership. Effective leadership resides at all levels of the organization. Good leadership models must take into account the kinds of skills and qualities necessary for leaders throughout the organization.

Awareness of these pitfalls improves the validity and usefulness of any leadership attribute model. But even if these concerns were totally resolved for every existing leadership attribute model, they would not produce the quality of leadership necessary for successful, competitive firms. Such models contain a more fundamental, unremediable flaw: they fail to account for the leader's responsibility to produce results, thus dealing with only half of the leadership equation: *attributes* × *results.*

Building Better Leaders through Results

A leader's job requires more than character, knowledge, and action; it also demands results. Even with more refined and empirical models of leadership attributes, such shopping ventures, while seductive in their seeming ease, may mislead leaders and lack sufficient focus on the importance and nature of results.

To move forward on the dialogue about what makes an effective leader, attributes need to connect to results. This means more than positing that a set of attributes might lead to results; it means explicitly focusing on the desired results and linking specific attributes to those results. Attention to leadership results will repay its costs in time and effort many times over in raising the overall quality and effectiveness of a firm's leaders. Such attention will also refine and refocus leadership attributes in ways that ensure that they deliver value.

Major corporations worldwide recognize this and are beginning to implement leadership development programs aimed specifically at bridging the divide between attributes and results, to produce leaders who are thoughtful, sensitive, and supportive, but also productive. Under Human Resources Vice President Vicky Farrow, Lucent Technologies has begun a vigorous campaign to build results-based leaders. Managers at all levels devising personal leadership agendas as part of their career plans are first asked, "What results do you need to achieve?" The leader thus zeros in on business strategy, ways to make the strategy happen, and how to attain balanced results consistent with strategy. Farrow then asks, "On a scale of 0 to 100, how able are you to produce these results today?" The leader thus must examine his or her readiness and ability to deliver the results. Farrow's respondents usually place themselves between 60 and 70 on the scale. Her last question, "What must you learn and do to make these results happen?" helps leaders to recognize the character, knowledge, and behaviors they must pursue if they are to achieve their desired results. By engaging in this process, she ensures that leaders connect who they are, what they know, and what they do to the results they must deliver.

Hewlett-Packard holds leaders throughout the firm accountable not only for the behaviors they exhibit, but also for the results they accomplish. Results cascade from the top of the company through every leader in the company. Each year, Lew Platt, the chief executive officer, articulates the company's priorities through his critical Hoshins, or overarching breakthrough goals for the company. Recently, HP had two corporate Hoshins, one on customers and the other on people. The customer Hoshin works to improve customer loyalty and satisfaction by closing the gap between customer expectations and HP's ability to meet them. The people Hoshin states, "HP's primary sustainable competitive advantage is our ability to create an environment which attracts, develops, and retains highly talented people." This Hoshin focuses on HP's becoming "the best place to work" and the "employer of choice" through valuing diversity, fostering a commitment to continuous learning and career self-reliance, helping employees manage work/life activities, and creating an injury-free work environment.

In one division, HP created an initiative called "bridging the leadership gap," in which the leaders attended to the results they had to accomplish. A group of senior operating managers focused first on the results required for each leader in the division. After discussing the strategy of the business, the leaders converged on the results each had to accomplish for the strategy to happen. To ensure clarity and unity around results, each of the top leaders wrote down an answer to the question: What are the results we must attain for this division to succeed? Without clear unity on this question, they could not have a results orientation. With results specified, then knowledge and behaviors of each leader were stipulated. With this information, investments were made to create better leaders through training courses and development experiences.

At Southern Company, a global electric utility firm, leaders used to work in a regulated environment with a high focus on results, measured in terms of providing reliable service, high safety, and good community relations. As the environment changed to a more competitive market where price and customer service become drivers for success, new leadership results were required, focused on market conditions and more flexibility in the organization. Southern Company has created leaders who achieve results in the right way through courses at Southern Company College on market economics, understanding utility costs, and leadership for results, and through performance expectations in which the focus shifted to shared goals around business results and creating a plan to achieve those results. Its senior leaders felt that if the attributes of leaders did not increase the results required in the new competitive environment, then its leadership models fell short. Southern's management practices have attempted to balance the "what" (results expected of leaders) with the "how" (attributes of leaders).

In nonbusiness settings, a results-based leadership also applies. When Belinda Woodson became principal of Bingham Middle School in Kansas City, the school had a dismal reputation because of lack of discipline, expectations, and goals. As principal, she first identified the results she wanted for the school, including student safety, a learning environment, and a common vision that all students "can behave and can learn." As she hired administrators and faculty, she continually explored their understanding of and commitment to these results. She derived measures of each result which she shared monthly with all staff.

Bimonthly faculty meetings had a "teaching and learning" segment in which progress toward goals was reviewed. When staff met these measures, she awarded prizes (teacher of the month, food certificates, office chairs, and so forth), either individually or collectively.

In each of these cases, leaders' attention focused on both what to accomplish (results) and how to accomplish it (attributes). Now is the time to balance that attention with renewed focus on the definition and accomplishment of results. When leaders fail to exhibit concern for results, however many attributes they possess, they will ultimately be ineffective and their tenures unproductive.

Analysis and research on leadership attributes must, of course, continue. But in themselves, they are incomplete. Yet measuring results without understanding who the leaders are, what they know, and what they do that delivers the results would be equally incomplete. Understanding and measurement of both the attributes and the results of effective leaders are necessary to fulfill the goal of improving leadership quality.

Simply stated, the leadership pendulum, which has in recent years swung too far to the attribute side of the equation and stayed there too long, must start its return swing toward the results term of the equation. But this time leaders need to find a natural connection between attributes and results.

Leaders exhibiting attributes without results have ideas without substance. They teach what they have not learned. They can talk a good scenario and even act on sound general principles, but they fail to deliver. The means—attributes—have become their end. Often popular because of their charm or charisma, they are not long remembered because their leadership depended more on who they are and how they behave than on what they accomplish. Leaders who get results but lack attributes often find their successes short-lived. These leaders achieve without knowing why and can therefore neither replicate their successes nor learn from them. Because for them the end justifies the means, their results often vaporize without a lasting trace. Those lacking attributes may have the raw ability of geniuses, but character flaws inhibit their ability to lead. They repel others, make fatal mistakes, or burn themselves out. Successful leaders get lasting results by aligning attributes with intended outcomes.

Remember: *Effective leadership = attributes × results.*

Benefits of Results-Based Leadership

The positive effects of results-based leadership can be realized everywhere throughout an organization—on the assembly floor and the delivery dock, in the cafeteria and the accounting department, by the planning department and the chief executive. Leaders at all levels need to get results. Results-based leadership frees productivity from the constraints of hierarchy and the limitations of position.

Results-based leaders must continually ask and answer the question—"What is wanted?"—before they decide how to do it. Leaders who act without full knowledge of the results required may work harder but accomplish less. Results-based leaders define results by understanding audience or customer needs and how they can be met.

Results-based leaders define their roles in terms of practical action. They articulate what they want to accomplish and thus make their agendas clear and meaningful to others. Employees willingly follow leaders who know both who they are (their own attributes) and what they are doing (their targeted results). Such leaders instill confidence and inspire trust in others because they are direct, focused, and consistent.

Results-based leaders assess their effectiveness by measuring achievements against goals. Without a results focus, calibration of leadership becomes extremely difficult. Measuring results helps organizations in many ways, from tracking leaders' individual growth, to comparing leadership effectiveness in similar roles, to clarifying the leader selection processes, to structuring leadership development programs. Using results as the standard filters who should enter an organization and how they should be trained. Ultimately, a results focus should help every leader turn attributes into outcomes.

Studies of the link between results and effective leadership have been done before. In one of the most useful, Steve Kerr and his colleagues studied what they called "substitutes for leadership."[19] They began with the assumption that, to get results, two things were necessary among employees in any situation: skills and motivation. Under circumstances where those working to produce results possess both skills and motivation, the leader's job is to do little or nothing; substitutes for leadership exist. But in other settings and for a host of reasons, employees may lack either skills or motivation, so the leader's job in getting results is to provide the skills and motivation to get the job done. Such leaders are results based: they focus on both the results required and on what needs to be done to achieve results, and they get the job done.

This book will help any leader or aspiring leader to find the balance and connection between attributes and results that will open the way to improved effectiveness and productivity. To do so, it helps leaders answer the following key questions:

What personal attributes do I need to be an effective leader?

Successful leaders need to be, know, and do four things: set direction, mobilize individual commitment, engender organizational capability, and demonstrate personal competence. The discussion, figures, and references in this chapter synthesize some of the useful work on leadership attributes and may serve as a starting point for assessing oneself or others. This chapter also suggests traps that must be avoided in many current attribute models.

How do I know if I am an effective leader?

The measure of an effective leader can be found in this simple equation: *Effective leadership = attributes × results*. Tools for assessing and building attributes (Figure 1-2) and results appear throughout the book, but especially in Chapters 2 through 6. Chapter 7 summarizes the tools and actions that can best serve leaders striving to be more effective by focusing on results.

If leadership requires a results focus, how do I determine what those results should be?

Chapter 2 describes desired results, the necessity of aligning them with strategy, and the need to balance them across the four key stakeholders: employees, organization, customers, and investors. To achieve results, leaders must create value in each of these four areas. Serving only employees, for example, yields committed employees, but organizations that fail also to serve customers or to meet investor goals will not be successful.

How do I balance apparently conflicting results?

Balancing the four results requires aligning the results to organization strategy (see Chapter 2). A clear strategy rings like a clarion, signaling to employees, customers, and investors where the organization can best deploy its energy and resources. An equally clear picture will emerge of which results demand more and which results can slide by with less leadership attention.

How can I define, put into operation, and measure my results?

Chapters 3 through 6 offer diagnostic tools for employee, organization, customer, and investor results, respectively, that leaders use to define results and assess their achievements. Each chapter proposes a conceptual framework to describe results, illustrates how leaders achieve these results, and offers specific tools, all of which are of proven usefulness.

Once I know the results I need to achieve, how do I make them happen?

The fourteen specific actions described in Chapter 7 can help leaders make results a major part of their leadership equation, at whatever level they function in their companies.

How can leaders in my organization ensure that other leaders also produce results?

Leaders who get results themselves but fail to pass on the requisite skills and motivation to do so to others coming after them will have failed their companies. Chapter 8 discusses the importance of leaders building leaders. Senior executives, chief learning officers—all leaders in fact—must accept the responsibility and challenge of building the next generation of results-based leaders. Only in this way can corporate vision become stance, goals become achievements, potential become success. Personally qualified leaders who get results while fostering their companies' future, in the form of its people, create strong, healthy, productive, competitive organizations.

Conclusion

Posing and answering these questions shifts the focus on leadership to a balance of, and connection between, attributes and results. By so doing, this book makes a bold statement about the next generation of leadership thinking. This does not mean less attention to the leader's attributes, but it does mean making sure that leaders understand and commit to the results they must produce—and how they are produced.

Appendix A
The GE Leadership Effectiveness Survey

RATING SCALE:
Significant Development Need   **1   2   3   4   5**   Outstanding Strength

CHARACTERISTIC	PERFORMANCE CRITERIA
Vision	• Has developed and communicated a clear, simple, customer-focused vision/direction for the organization.
	• Forward-thinking, stretches horizons, challenges imaginations.
	• Inspires and energizes others to commit to Vision. Captures minds. Leads by example.
	• As appropriate, updates Vision to reflect constant and accelerating change impacting the business.
Customer/ Quality Focus	• Listens to customer and assigns the highest priority to customer satisfaction, including internal customers.
	• Inspires and demonstrates a passion for excellence in every aspect of work.
	• Strives to fulfill commitment to Quality in total product/service offering.
	• Lives Customer Service and creates service mind-set throughout organization.
Integrity	• Maintains unequivocal commitment to honesty/truth in every facet of behavior.
	• Follows through on commitments; assumes responsibility for own mistakes.
	• Practices absolute conformance with company policies embodying GEI&PS commitment to ethical conduct.
	• Actions and behaviors are consistent with words. Absolutely trusted by others.

CHARACTERISTIC	PERFORMANCE CRITERIA
Accountability/ Commitment	• Sets and meets aggressive commitments to achieve business objectives. • Demonstrates courage/self-confidence to stand up for beliefs, ideas, co-workers. • Fair and compassionate yet willing to make difficult decisions. • Demonstrates uncompromising responsibility for preventing harm to the environment.
Communication/ Influence	• Communicates in open, candid, clear, complete, and consistent manner—invites response/dissent. • Listens effectively and probes for new ideas. • Uses facts and rational arguments to influence and persuade. • Breaks down barriers and develops influential relationships across teams, functions, and layers.
Shared Ownership/ Boundaryless	• Self-confidence to share information across traditional boundaries and be open to new ideas. • Encourages/promotes shared ownership for Team Vision and goals. • Trusts others; encourages risk taking and boundaryless behavior. • Champions Work-Out as a vehicle for everyone to be heard. Open to ideas from anywhere.
Team Builder/ Empowerment	• Selects talented people; provides coaching and feedback to develop team members to fullest potential. • Delegates whole tasks; empowers team to maximize effectiveness. Is personally a Team Player. • Recognizes and rewards achievement. Creates positive/enjoyable work environment. • Fully utilizes diversity of team members (cultural, race, gender) to achieve business success.

CHARACTERISTIC	PERFORMANCE CRITERIA
Knowledge/ Expertise/ Intellect	• Possesses and readily shares functional/technical knowledge and expertise. Constant interest in learning. • Demonstrates broad business knowledge/perspective with cross-functional/multicultural awareness. • Makes good decisions with limited data. Applies intellect to the fullest. • Quickly sorts relevant from irrelevant information, grasps essentials of complex issues and initiates action.
Initiative/Speed	• Creates real and positive change. Sees change as an Opportunity. • Anticipates problems and initiates new and better ways of doing things. • Hates/avoids/eliminates "bureaucracy" and strives for brevity, simplicity, clarity. • Understands and uses speed as a competitive advantage.
Global Mind-set	• Demonstrates global awareness/sensitivity and is comfortable building diverse/global teams. • Values and promotes full utilization of global and work force diversity. • Considers the global consequences of every decision. Proactively seeks global knowledge. • Treats everyone with dignity, trust, and respect.

Source: CEO Magazine, July–August 1993, 40. Reprinted courtesy of General Electric.

Defining Desired Results

L EADERS WHO AREN'T GETTING RESULTS aren't truly leading. Or, more specifically, leaders who aren't getting *desired* results aren't truly leading. Every leader does get some results by definition, if only in the sense that every organization is "perfectly designed for the performance it achieves." But the leadership gap described in Chapter 1 occurs when leaders fall short in attaining targeted, expected, hoped for, and planned—*desired*—results.

Leaders must learn to understand and focus on desired results. This chapter offers not a magical (and, alas, mythical) objective-setting tool for guaranteeing attainment of short-term goals, but something almost as useful: the reliable criteria leaders need to consistently pay attention to attaining their short- and long-term objectives, and a set of tests and tools to make sure that leadership attributes translate into the right results.

The following scenario highlights this process in action:

Buzz Nielsen started in the automotive assembly operation right out of college. He liked his job as team leader and had ambitions to move into higher management positions. When promoted to shift supervisor, he excitedly prepared himself to be a successful leader. Following advice from books, cassettes, and leadership conferences, he wrote a personal mission statement, talked with his former peers to get their input, set clear goals, and generally strove to be an effective coach. He formulated his development plan around three specific competencies. It read, "To be a better leader by (1) improving my interpersonal skills, (2) delegating more, and (3) implementing total quality management on my shift." Unfortunately, some of his former peers thought he used big words and fancy phrases but didn't make much of an impact. When this feedback reached him through the grapevine, he was embarrassed. He began to wonder if the leadership position was really worth all the extra effort.

As described in Chapter 1, individuals wanting to be better leaders need a battery of habits, traits, competencies, knowledge, behavior, style, motives, values, and character which we call, collectively, "attributes." But attributes without results are about as valuable as a playbook without playing the game—a mere academic exercise without real-world impact. Results focus on ends, not means. Results-based leadership means achieving outcomes, not just having great character.

Leaders focused on desired results must articulate what they need accomplished. At the heart of results-based leadership, then, lies the simple petition: *So that?* In the course of specifying attributes, leaders must consider the "so that" query. By answering this query, leaders transform mere stated attributes into productive, focused results by making sure that no attribute exists in isolation from a specific *desired* result. This question functions, in fact, as the litmus test for every attribute: does the observable behavior translate into a desired result? Leadership attributes that don't drive or connect to results don't count. It is as simple as that.

Buzz's job as shift supervisor, for example, required not just that he improve his leadership skills, but that he recognize and help accomplish his shift's goals—that his shift produce results. Despite his improved competencies, his failure to achieve results eroded his credibility and leadership success. Buzz made admirable efforts to develop a vision for his shift. But he lacked an answer to the question: So that? Without it, his leadership effectiveness remained incomplete. Restating Buzz's three chosen attributes to incorporate "so that" statements makes the difference plain.

- Improve my interpersonal skills *so that* the people on the shift feel comfortable approaching me when they have suggestions for improvements, allowing our shift to beat its production goals by 5 percent each month.

- Delegate more *so that* people feel committed to the job, as evidenced by a 25 percent reduction in absences and sick days and the elimination of tardiness.

- Implement total quality management *so that* our quality exceeds that of any other shift or line, as measured by defects per 1,000.

This quick, simple example illustrates the basic point: the more clearly leaders state their desired results, the more traction they'll get from their efforts to improve their own attributes and become more effective leaders. This chapter lays out strategy for answering the "so that" query to achieve desired results.

Four criteria exist for assessing whether leaders focus on desired results. These criteria determine how much leaders will achieve within and across each desired result area. Desired results are *balanced.* They don't build success in one dimension by ignoring (or tolerating failure in) another. Desired results are *strategic:* they ultimately contribute to distinctiveness and competitive advantage for their organizations. Desired results are *lasting:* they won't sacrifice long-term success for short-term gains. Desired results are *selfless:* they will work to benefit the larger whole, not just their own group or area.[1] Effective results meet these four criteria; leaders who will strive to be effective must satisfy them. Figure 2-1 presents this results test in summary form. Buzz, for example, needs to consider each of the four criteria (balanced, strategic, lasting, and selfless) in defining desired results. Each of the criteria and a process for dealing with it are discussed below.

Desired Results Are Balanced

A warning about our criteria. The results were not intended to induce guilt. True, the criteria are comprehensive; but a leader achieving truly excellent results in all of these areas would, we recognize, be superhuman. It is axiomatic that any leader evaluating him or herself against these criteria will be found wanting in some areas. However, these comprehensive results criteria provide a standard, making possible an assessment of strengths and weaknesses alike. The clear picture thus attained, vis-à-vis the ideal state, enables leaders and potential leaders to choose how they will improve.

FIGURE 2-1

DEFINING DESIRED RESULTS: A SUMMARY

CRITERIA	QUESTIONS	EVIDENCE OF PROBLEM	EVIDENCE OF SUCCESS
Balanced	To what extent do my results balance across employees, organization, customers, and investors?	Results focus too much on one dimension.	Results balance across the four dimensions.
Strategic	To what extent do my results align with strategy by being linked to one of the following? • Business focus (e.g., product, customer, technology, production capability, or distribution) • Customer value proposition (e.g., low cost, quality, speed, service, or innovation)	Results connect loosely or not at all to the strategy of my business; results fail to create strategic clarity.	Results link strongly to the strategy of my business.
Lasting	To what extent will my results endure over time?	Results will not last; they are short term.	Results meet both short- and long-term goals.
Selfless	To what extent are my results selfless, making the whole more than the parts?	Results do not make the whole greater than the parts.	Results support the whole enterprise, not just my personal gain.

Desired results must serve multiple constituents. Robert Kaplan and David Norton, professors at Harvard Business School and respected consultants, draw on the stakeholder theory of organizations to create what they call a "balanced scorecard."[2] We draw on their work to suggest that leaders' results be balanced across four stakeholders: employees, organization, customers, and investors. Leaders who excel in only one area are not effective leaders. Achieving high employee results, demonstrated by high levels of employee commitment and skills, means little if employees' efforts fail to satisfy customers. In such cases, the leader has failed the balance test. Leaders face a difficult challenge in trying to balance and attain results in all four stakeholder areas. Results-based leaders may, at times, make the deliberate choice of emphasizing one dimension over another, but they cannot afford to ignore any of them for long.

A framework illustrating balanced desired results appears in Figure 2-2. Leaders must balance the results they produce in all four quadrants. If, for example, a leader had to divide 100 attention and energy points across the four results, no one result should receive more than 60 or fewer than 10 points. A leader must identify the intensity and weight appropriate to each of the four results, as well as the activities necessary to achieve each. A worksheet like that in Figure 2-3 can be helpful in making these determinations. Starting with an arbitrary 100 points, the leader identifies the relative weight and attention for each of the four results and shows this by (1) dividing 100 points across the four results (with no one result getting more than 60 or fewer than 10 points) and (2) identifying activities currently under way to achieve each of the results. The completed worksheet provides a baseline, or benchmark, for evaluating the status of desired results.

FIGURE 2-2

A MODEL OF BALANCED OUTCOMES

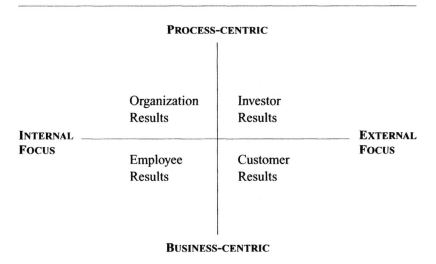

FIGURE 2-3

BALANCED CRITERIA
To what extent are my results balanced across the four quadrants?

RESULTS	ATTENTION (divide 100 points across the four results[a])	ACTIONS TAKEN TO DATE
Employees		
Organization		
Customers		
Investors		
	Total 100	

a. Maximum 60 points; minimum 10 points.

Buzz, for example, might make progress in his quest for leadership by starting with a focus on how to balance the four results. First, he must figure out how much attention his unit has paid to each result. This can be done by dividing 100 points across the four results based on his perception of how much attention has been paid to each. Second, he can figure out what actions support or sustain each desired result. By being more explicit about the results he needs to achieve, he helps ensure that his competencies link to desired results.

Organizations may orient how leaders balance the desired results. For example, McKinsey & Company, a management consulting company, directs new consultants to focus on customers first, employees second, and investors third. Not surprisingly, the McKinsey work ethic demands long hours and frequent travel to ensure that customers are well served. Customer results are king, and successful McKinsey leaders allocate a larger portion of their 100 points to customer results than to employee, investor, or organization results. However, if McKinsey were unable to attract and retain talent (employee results), or if its partners failed to get fat bonus checks each year (investor results), or if McKinsey could not change, learn, and make things happen (organization results), the fault would lie with McKinsey's leadership, for failing to balance results in all four areas.

Arthur Martinez, chief executive officer at Sears, Roebuck, favors a different balance. He places employees first, customers second, and investors third.[3] His viewpoint does not derive from altruism. Sears research has demonstrated a linear correlation leading from employee satisfaction to customer satisfaction to investor results. Sears leaders have learned that the key to increasing customer loyalty comes from improving employee satisfaction; that is, a happy employee correlates to happy repeat customers, which translates into profits. Not surprisingly, then, leaders at Sears spend more time than do leaders of competing retailers working on employee commitment results, without, as their own measures indicate, ignoring customer and investor results.[4] Again, using the terms of the exercise in Figure 2-3, effective Sears leaders allocate more points, or attention, to employee results than to customer, organization, or investor results.

Al Dunlap, the former CEO at Sunbeam, put investor results first. To be an effective leader by our criteria, however, Dunlap should have maintained a better balance across stakeholder needs, allocating no more than 60 percent of his attention and energy to investor results. Allocating too much energy to investor results made him a turnaround leader, but not a results leader. And, in fact, Dunlap's work at Sunbeam created short-term, turnaround results, but they were not sustained. Dunlap's effectiveness as a leader would have been higher had he demonstrated over time an ability to balance results across all four stakeholders.

As these examples show, balanced does not mean equal. Any attempt to place perfectly equal emphasis on each of the four areas would be ill advised and would, in any case, prove impossible. No organization exists in a vacuum. Marketplace dynamics, work force trends, macroeconomic factors, unforeseeable crises—all of these occur beyond the leader's control, yet they directly influence the organization's ability to achieve employee, organization, customer, and investor results. The savvy leader understands that maintaining balance requires constant juggling, the goal being not to let any of the four results areas fall from neglect. By focusing only on internal results—that is, employee and organization capability—companies may neglect pressing customer and investor problems. Too much attention on external issues, on investors and customer results, may lead employees to feel undervalued, thus undermining organization capability.

To take one example, consider Procter & Gamble, a leader in the 1970s and 1980s in creating work environments based on the sociotechnical systems (STS) approach. Pioneering the use of STS to integrate social systems (people and culture) with technical systems (manufacturing equipment layout, and so on), P&G achieved tremendous results in new plant start-ups. These included higher quality, lower costs, and greater job satisfaction.

But engineers later referred to events in the mid-1970s as a learning experience. One plant adopted the new approach early on, and the engineers developing the new plant became enamored of the social systems side of the STS equation, coming to spend nearly all of their attention on internal issues. Workers were promised self-managing teams and a corresponding internal culture. The need to achieve financial or customer results received little mention or attention. Soon, P&G insiders were referring to this plant as the "country club." Employees self-actualized while plant results dematerialized. Eventually, senior management stepped in, stopping the experiment, and employee morale sagged. Some employees felt that, rather than start and then stop the STS program, they wished it had never been started at all. It took several years to turn the situation around and get the plant operating as it should. P&G learned from its mistakes and went on to build a series of successful plants using this technology through the 1980s and 1990s.

Just as an attempt of equality will actually subvert balance, so will the attempt by a single leader to be all things to an organization subvert its efforts to achieve balance. It is unlikely that one person possesses equal skill—or equal interest—in all four results areas. A financial genius may be uncomfortable dealing with people issues. The customer-focused marketing whiz may be totally unskilled at building the capability needed for lasting organization results. Leaders must therefore recognize their areas of strength, weakness, and interest and build a team that collectively covers all the bases. The leadership *team* thus ensures that the organization achieves balance across the four results areas.

Effective leaders keep the four results in balance, striving for dynamic equilibrium. It isn't necessarily bad for an organization to give primary attention to one result over others. What is bad is an organization's failure to address and eliminate weakness in one or more areas. To determine which results should receive more or less attention, leaders must consider the remaining three results criteria.

Desired Results Are Strategic

Leaders must decide which of the four results require the most attention, and which can get by with the least. Desired results must be strategic and must align with the purposes of the organization. If results ultimately determine score, then strategy defines the playing field. Strategy establishes the boundaries for desired results. Effective results-based leaders make it easy for their people to contribute to desired results—what most employees, after all, want to do. When people in an organization know where it is going, how it is trying to distinguish itself, why customers should prefer its products and services over those of its competitors, and how their jobs fit into the whole, they see clearly which results really count and act accordingly.

Unfortunately, leaders who provide clear, straightforward direction are rare. And not just at the CEO level. When was the last time you heard your minister, priest, or rabbi articulate the real purpose of his or her congregation and a vision of how this community of believers could work together to achieve that purpose? Can you tell, the moment you enter a fast-food restaurant, whether the shift supervisor has instilled a clear sense of "why customers buy from us" into the shift's minimum-wage workers? Without knowing the strategy or direction of a work unit, neither leaders nor workers can appropriately balance the four results.

The ability to sustain the right results occurs when a critical mass in an organization agrees to a strategic direction and invests the time, energy, and money necessary to make it happen. Without such clarity, leaders in the same organization may neutralize one another's best intentioned efforts, and individual leaders may invest in too many alternatives, hedging their bets by trying to be the best at everything. The result is often mediocrity.

A story about strategic clarity at Johnson & Johnson illustrates this point. J&J has a well-honed and widely recognized business strategy, which provides a broad set of products for a narrowly defined set of customers: "doctors, nurses, patients, and mothers." A few years ago, the company developed a skin lotion that also happened to be an effective mosquito repellent. Having developed this new and potentially profitable product, J&J leaders faced a dilemma. Did this mosquito repellent lotion fit their customer set? Although doctors, nurses, patients, and parents could, of course, benefit from a mosquito repellent lotion, J&J decided that the product might take focus away from J&J's

core products. In addition, J&J's leaders knew that this sort of "stretch" product would set a precedent for diverting resources and effort into developing other "noncore" products.

So, rather than launch the lotion itself, J&J opted to partner with another company and share royalties. Its leaders' unflinching strategic clarity allowed J&J to benefit financially from its R&D effort, while continuing to push for the fullest possible customer, employee, and organization results.

This story illustrates the single greatest payoff achieved by the results-based leader who attains and maintains strategic clarity: *focus*. The world is full of distractions. With committees, budgets, boards, and unions all competing for a leader's precious time and attention, all too often organizations heed the siren call of *easy* results to the detriment of more-difficult-to-attain *desired* (strategic) results. The common euphemisms—among them, "low-hanging fruit," "gift horses," "slam-dunk projects"—emphasize the seductive "something for nothing" quality of such results. Meaningful results never come packaged that way. They come, rather, from singular, almost fanatical dedication to a chosen and distinctive direction.

To assess your unit's strategic clarity, try the quiz in Figure 2-4. Forgive the cynicism—it's deliberate and warranted, although somewhat tongue in cheek. If you agree with more than two of these statements (or score higher than 40), however, your first leadership task probably should be to spend some serious time clarifying your organization's strategy.

Unless your organization is highly unusual, chances are your score on the Strategic Clarity Quiz was fairly high—higher than you would have liked it to be. To achieve strategic clarity and attain desired results requires clear answers to two fundamental questions:

- At its heart, what is your business about? The answer to this question provides *business focus*.

- Why do your customers buy from you rather than from your competitors? The answer to this question constitutes your organization's *value proposition*.

By answering these two questions, leaders move toward strategic clarity, which in turn leads to an improved definition of the organization's desired results.

FIGURE 2-4

STRATEGIC CLARITY QUIZ

CURRENT STRATEGY	SCORE (1 = seldom, 5 = sometimes, 10 = often)
1. There are multiple, competing visions for where my organization is headed.	
2. At strategy meetings, I hear a lot of motherhood statements about "being the best" or "having the lowest costs and highest levels of service and quality."	
3. The organization leaders talk about having multiple "world-class" functions, reasoning that, if we're the best at everything, we'll have the best overall company (also known as the "Let's be super!" strategy).	
4. Our organization practices "budgetary socialism," investing time, money, and other resources equally across projects, divisions, departments, and so on.	
5. Our strategy statements are expressed primarily in financial terms: net earnings, ROI, stock price, and so on.	
6. When asked the question—What does this organization need to do really well over the next five years?—most employees respond, "I don't know," or the answer varies from group to group.	
7. Our strategy is recorded in a thick binder, somewhere.	
8. Management readily changes its guiding principles. We've already done Business Process Reengineering, Total Quality Management, Principle-Centered Leadership, and High-Performing Teams; this year we're doing Strategy.	
9. After the senior management team devises a new strategy, it is ratified, copied to fancy paper, matted, framed, and hung on every conference room wall, but otherwise largely ignored.	
10. We tend to follow the strategies set by the industry leader.	
Total:	

BUSINESS FOCUS

You'd be surprised to discover how many leaders can't answer the simple question: What is your business about? They respond with an industry affiliation: We're in the chemicals business. They come up with a high-level activity report: We make and sell vacuum cleaners. What they fail to produce is an insight derived from paring the business down to the core of viability. Business focus describes what makes the organization tick at the elemental level. And, as in the characterization by Empedocles of all matter as rooted in earth, air, water, or fire, businesses must fall into one of relatively few elemental forms of business focus: product, customer, technology, production capability, or distribution.[5]

Organizations with a *product focus* concentrate on making a product or line of products and finding as many customers as possible for those products. Of the six foci, this approach may be the easiest to understand. Design a product, manufacture it, sell it. The steps to product focus seem simple, and some businesses perform them extremely well—Ford Truck, for example, makes the highest-selling vehicle in the United States: the F-150 pickup. Ford Truck has a business focus. It won't anytime soon come out with a line of sports cars, travel trailers, or fly-fishing equipment. It will keep on doing what it has been doing so successfully: finding ways to sell its single product to ever-greater numbers of consumers.

The product of a product-focused business may not always be quite so obvious. Take Harley-Davidson, for example. It maintains a product business focus, but the product isn't motorcycles. "What we sell," as one company insider expressed it, "is the ability for a 43-year-old accountant to dress in black leather, ride through small towns, and have people be afraid of him." A bit overstated, perhaps, and deliberately humorous, but not far off the mark. The "rebel lifestyle" has become the Harley-Davidson product, and motorcycles constitute only one component of a product suite that includes apparel, road rallies, accessories, and (above all else) the Harley mystique.

Organizations with a *customer focus* concentrate on learning the needs of a specific set of customers extremely well, and then finding ways to fulfill those customers' needs through a wide variety of products and services. Johnson & Johnson, already cited above, represents a prime example. Many other successful businesses take this approach, although some of them might at first seem surprising, even counterintuitive. Nike, for example, might be easily mistaken as having a product focus. After all, doesn't Nike try to find ever more customers for its single product, sports shoes? Not at all. Nike targets a specific customer: the high-performance athlete. It aggressively pushes into new product lines (outerwear, apparel, luggage, game equipment, and so on) that meet the needs (and flatter the egos) of its athlete (or athlete wannabe) customers. And because it isn't product focused, Nike doesn't own or operate a single manufacturing plant except those that make its proprietary components (such as air soles). Its strategic partners in Asia do 99 percent of Nike's manufacturing. Owning manufacturing would only slow Nike down.

Organizations with a *technology focus* typically control a unique and valuable idea or process. Their business strategy involves finding as many products as possible to which to apply their technology and as many customers as possible for these products. One example of a technology-focused firm is 3M, with its unique know-how in coating and bonding processes. Using these techniques, 3M provides a staggering array of products for an incredibly diverse pool of customers: adhesive tape, Post-It notes, Scotchguard fabric protector, sandpaper, weatherstripping, surgeon's tape, furnace filters—you get the idea.

Companies with *production capability focus* strive to keep existing assets running at full capacity. Airlines provide a good example of this. When one of Delta's planes flies from Chicago to New York, many of the costs are fixed, regardless of the number of passengers on board. The flight crew—pilot, copilot, attendants—remains the same, for fourteen or forty or one hundred forty passengers. Even the amount of fuel required remains approximately the same. For Delta to profit from a given flight, it must fill its seats with fare-paying passengers. Hotels, paper mills, steel mills, and similar enterprises all typically share the production capability focus.

The final strategy approach is to take a *distribution focus*. Firms with such a focus build distribution channels as the heart of their businesses. Using these, they then attempt to sell products and services appropriate to their distribution system. Many multilevel marketing companies are distribution focused. Nu Skin has become a billion dollar company by recruiting distributors to market their health and skin-care products. Nu Skin's leaders pay considerable attention to rewarding their distributors well for bringing in new members to help sell Nu Skin products in ever-increasing volume.

CUSTOMER VALUE PROPOSITION

A business focus draws an organization's attention inward and shows its leaders where they need to build organizational capability. Building capability, however, should not be an end in itself. Getting in shape by running, weight lifting, and eating a proper diet is fine, but the payoff comes from using that hard-won strength to enjoy life.

The value proposition turns a company's attention outward. The five potential value propositions are low cost, quality, speed, service, and innovation. Every organization must offer all of them, but should specialize in one. The subsidiary value propositions need only reach the industry average or attain industry parity. The anchor value proposition, however, must be sufficiently strong to lend the organization distinctiveness in the eyes of its desired customers. Customers buy one company's products or services rather than those of its competitors because they prefer its value proposition.

Businesses concentrating on a *low-cost* proposition usually promise their customers the lowest price available. Champion International, a paper company, uses the low-cost value proposition to distinguish itself. This does not mean that Champion can get by with low quality or poor service. On the contrary, Champion must provide quality and service as good as those of any other business in its industry. Champion's customers then choose it and feel they are getting service and quality comparable to that at other firms—but at a lower price.

Mont Blanc produces writing instruments and maintains a value proposition of *quality*. Mont Blanc pens and pencils cost upwards of $75. Customers pay the price because they value the look, feel, and function of Mont Blanc products.

Speed constitutes the third value proposition. Organizations with a speed anchor get their products to their customers faster than do their competitors. Federal Express, for example, competes on speed, promising to deliver letters or packages faster than its competitors.

Service provides the competitive anchor of companies such as Caterpillar, the farm equipment manufacturer. Its credo emphasizes its value proposition: "Twenty-four-hour parts service anywhere in the world." Service-anchored businesses provide flexibility and services that their customers value.

Innovation-anchored companies promise their customers cutting-edge products unavailable from their competitors. Hewlett-Packard, for example, uses an innovation value proposition to distinguish its printer business. HP will go to any lengths to stay ahead of the field, even to the point of cannibalizing its own products, continually introducing new features to attract and keep customers who use its laser printers and other products.

Having a clear business focus and value proposition helps leaders to define their strategy and to set priorities, which then achieve desired results. Effective leaders then communicate their strategy to stakeholders.

Figures 2-5 and 2-6 offer a methodology for gaining strategic clarity and using that clarity to balance desired results. To assess your strategic criteria, begin by completing the worksheet in Figure 2-5.

STEP 1: Allocate 100 points across the five business focus options. This may be done by the leader working alone or by a team assigned to help define the unit's business focus. The point is to identify a primary driver to which to allocate energy, so one of the five options must be accorded at least 60 points.

STEP 2: Allocate 100 points down the column of value propositions. Again, this may be done by the leader working alone or by a team charged with defining the unit's competitive anchors. You are identifying a primary proposition, remember, so at least 60 points must be placed on one of the five anchors.

STEP 3: Identify the cell with the highest business focus and value proposition scores. This cell, which represents the unit's primary strategy focus, defines both where the business aims to build internally—its business focus—and what the business uniquely offers its customers externally—its value proposition.

STEP 4: Using Figure 2-6, you may now begin to determine your unit's desired results, as clarified by and to be given emphasis under the revealed focus and proposition.

FIGURE 2-5

STRATEGIC CRITERIA FOR RESULTS

BUSINESS FOCUS

VALUE PROPOSITION	PRODUCT	CUSTOMER	TECHNOLOGY	PRODUCTION CAPABILITY	DISTRIBUTION	TOTAL
LOW COST	+	+	+	+	+	= 100
QUALITY						
SPEED						
SERVICE						
INNOVATION						
TOTAL	= 100					

Primary strategy (convergence of top business focus and top value proposition):

FIGURE 2-6

STRATEGY AND BALANCED RESULTS

	PRIMARY STRATEGY (business focus + competitor focus)	
RESULTS	GIVEN STRATEGY, ATTENTION REQUIRED (divide 100 points across the four results)	ACTION REQUIRED
Employees		
Organization		
Customers		
Investors		
	Total 100	

Begin by dividing 100 points across the four results—employee, organization, customer, and investor—according to how much attention each should receive, given the primary strategy chosen. No one result should get more than 60 points or less than 10 points. This allocation may be done by the leader alone or by a team, but often teams make more insightful and sensitive assessments. You may find it useful to compare the scores assigned here to those derived for Figure 2-3, where you calculated current balanced results without regard to strategy. As a last step, after allocating the points, consider what actions you can take to ensure that your group achieves each result. Chapters 3 through 6 offer dozens of suggestions for increasing employee, organizational, customer, and investor results, but this exercise allows you to explore your instinctual, even automatic responses to the problem of attaining desired results.

Using the Buzz case study presented earlier, he could work to gain strategic clarity by defining the business drivers and competitive anchors for his work unit. This exercise alone offers enormous focus on what the business must do to win. Buzz may then begin to get clearer about the relative importance of each of the four results and initial actions to begin to make them happen by using the worksheet in Figure 2-6.

Desired Results Are Lasting

Western businesses are often criticized as being too oriented toward short-term gains.[6] To the extent that such criticism is justified, these companies focus on near-term priorities, such as increasing stock price rather than building long-term value. One criterion for successful results leadership, however, must be the ability to balance short-term results without inhibiting or preventing longer-term results.

Kevin Hall, an industry unit leader at Savage Industries, a materials management and transportation systems company, faced a quandary. During renegotiations for a multimillion-dollar contract with a valued customer, the customer, although satisfied with Savage's work on previous contracts, sought several competitive bids "just to keep the process honest." Hall worried that some of the competitors would underbid him. He wrestled with the issue of losing the business outright, which would drive up overhead costs for other industry units, versus "buying" the business, which even if unprofitable at least contributed to the company's overall immediate results—a classic short- versus long-term results dilemma.

Because he was new to the company, he solicited advice from several other people in the company, including the president, Alan Alexander. Alexander said the decision was Hall's, but that he should use both long- and short-term criteria. For Hall, that made the answer clear immediately. Meeting the competitor's bids would undermine the long-term value of the "Savage System." The customer pressed him for a low bid, claiming that the work was his if he could meet a lowball competitor's bid that would not permit Savage to provide the "worry-free service" that differentiated it from competitors. Hall was unwilling to put that reputation at risk. The customer gave the work to the competitor.

What followed is revealing of Savage as a company. Alexander and others came to Hall and expressed their support of his actions. The seemingly insolvable dilemma became Savage's touchstone for effective leadership. Leaders and employees alike know, accept, and act on the lesson: "We don't bid on price only, and our customers must value our service and be willing to pay for it. If not, they shouldn't be our customers. Customers who make a mistake and go to a competitor will soon be back, giving us the work at a price that allows us to be a valued supplier. In a world that pressures us to take short-term action, we are determined to build our long-term capability by making sound day-to-day decisions."

Balancing short- and long-term results becomes trickiest when facing an emergency. Two well-known stories about Exxon and the *Valdez* accident and about Johnson & Johnson and the Tylenol-tampering incident show how similar emergencies may elicit very different responses—with very different consequences—for the companies affected.

The general public believes that Exxon handled the *Valdez* oil spill in a manner that showed it didn't care about the environment. Virtually all Exxon "insiders" know that this is untrue. Even if untrue, the perception, which Exxon failed to avoid or alter, has done long-term damage to its image as a "caring" business. Johnson & Johnson's public response to the incidents of tampering with its Tylenol product, on the other hand, had the opposite effect. The company responded quickly and nondefensively to the emergency, improving the public's view of the company and hence preserving its reputation, a long-term value.

When the Exxon *Valdez* started spilling oil over a pristine wilderness, Exxon leaders publicly waffled. Senior managers met to discuss options, accountabilities, and blame. They really wanted to do the right thing, but Exxon had always been somewhat "press shy," trying to avoid making its mistakes public, and the emergency unfortunately didn't dislodge this attitude. Employees, customers, and investors were shaken and disappointed at Exxon's inability to take quick action and handle the situation. Eventually, Exxon did the right thing. Thousands of employees trekked to the disaster area, donating thousands of hours to the cleanup. Exxon spent billions of dollars to rectify its mistake. Even though Exxon eventually managed the situation, its slow action in the short term damaged its reputation in the long term.

Johnson & Johnson handled the Tylenol-tampering disaster very differently and much more effectively. When the first tampering reports appeared, senior J&J managers went immediately to the press to accept responsibility for the failure in product safety and to describe how they would eliminate it. Millions of dollars worth of products were recalled and then replaced with new products in tamper-resistant packaging. J&J's short-term actions increased the public perception of the integrity of the company. The Tylenol tampering incident left people with the belief that they could trust J&J in the long term.

Although it is easy to advocate balance of short- and long-term values, it is more difficult to do so. The following approaches—achieve clarity, "satisfice," connect, link to values, accept change, and communicate—help leaders establish and maintain criteria for managing this juggling act.

ACHIEVE CLARITY

Leaders can't balance what they don't understand and can't articulate. They must be clear about which results should receive short- and long-term emphasis. The worksheet in Figure 2-7 may help by eliciting a list of short- and long-term results for each stakeholder. By specifying the short- and long-term results for each stakeholder, leaders may begin to see the trade-offs necessary to ensure lasting results.

"SATISFICE"

Herb Simon, a professor of management and decision making, won the Nobel prize in economics for developing the concept of "satisficing."[7] In essence, this theory suggests that, in many cases, when faced with decisions or choices, people do not or should not attempt to achieve the optimal or best solution, but a minimally acceptable one. Not all things worth doing are worth doing equally well. Satisficing involves recognizing that some results are more important than others and that, in some cases, a minimum standard of achievement may be sufficient.

In weighing short- against long-term goals, some results will stand out as more important than others. The lesser goals may, in some cases, be well enough served by meeting minimum standards; other goals will require the highest-level results. Hall at Savage recognized that, by not making a low-cost bid, he risked losing a customer, which would in turn cause a fall in short-term profits to minimally

FIGURE 2-7

TIME HORIZON AND BALANCED RESULTS

	TIME HORIZON	
RESULTS	SHORT TERM	LONG TERM
Employees		
Organization		
Customers		
Investors		

acceptable levels (satisficing both customers and short-term profits in the short term), but allow the firm to maintain its identity and reputation for service over the long term. Leaders make short- versus long-term trade-offs all the time. Recognizing that minimally acceptable results can sometimes be sufficient, while optimizing others, makes results more lasting.

CONNECT

Desired results often connect to one another. Sears found, for example, that short-term employee morale affected long-term customer commitment. Using this finding, it focused substantial attention on engaging employees and increasing their commitment to the company. All Sears employees received instruction in economic literacy to learn how the company made money, involving participation in "town hall meetings" where they could share suggestions for improving how work is done. Sears also invested in training through which first-line supervisors became more able to lead a diverse work force. These initiatives considerably improved short-term employee morale, leading to longer-term gains in customer satisfaction.

Leaders who identify and reinforce the connection between one result and another may then focus their attention on the antecedent result in the short term, knowing that longer-term results will follow.

LINK TO VALUES

When faced with short- versus long-term results choices, leaders with an articulated set of values make choices more easily. Jim Collins and Jerry Porras, professors at the Stanford University Graduate School of Business, found that a strong set of values helped companies survive. Leaders who understand their company's and their personal values build lasting results. In the Tylenol-tampering incident, J&J executives were willing to absorb short-term reduced investor results because of their overriding commitment to producing ethical drugs. Lacking clear values, rudderless leaders constantly shift from goal to goal. With values, while actions may change, the overall direction and focus stay clear. Values inform desired results when leaders ask the question: What is the *right* thing to do in this case? When they find a clear answer to this question, leaders produce lasting results.

ACCEPT CHANGE

Business is dynamic and constantly changing; so, too, must be desired results. Phelps Dodge is one of the world's largest copper-mining firms. For a decade, the price of copper remained steady, which enabled Phelps Dodge executives to make long-term decisions. Within a three-month period, however, new mines opened and demand eroded, cutting the price of copper in half. This price cut meant that Phelps Dodge executives had to shift their priorities. They now had to tailor their investment strategy, building new operations more slowly than planned, reducing operating costs, and managing investor expectations. Bucking industry trends, which saw competitors reducing headcount, Phelps Dodge executives worked to achieve high financial performance and operating efficiency through investment in their people. They adopted the mantra "pioneering the creation of value" and challenged each employee and team of employees to create value in the difficult business environment they faced. Their short-term investment in employees has resulted in lasting results for all stakeholders.

COMMUNICATE, COMMUNICATE, COMMUNICATE

Managing short- and long-term results requires leaders who communicate. Leaders need to communicate effectively about trade-offs, priorities, values, and connections. They need to reveal to employees the trade-offs required to balance short- and long-term results. They need to discuss priorities and the implications of optimal versus satisficing results. They need to clarify values so that employees making hard choices can rely on those underlying values. They need to explain how choices favoring one result connect to other results. They need to acknowledge the dynamic and changing nature of the effort to achieve lasting results.

One executive shared with us his belief that the debate over short-versus long-term results is a false one. For him, both short- and long-term results must be achieved for all stakeholders. A debate that emphasizes one over the other masks the challenge and necessity of attaining both.

Desired Results Are Selfless

Real leadership doesn't consist of beating your peers to the next rung on the ladder. It means getting results that benefit the entire organization and accomplishing these results in ways that build greater capability.

Real leadership usually involves a high degree of collaboration with others, both leaders and followers, to make the trade-offs that move the entire organization ahead. Leadership requires selfless results, and these come only from the appropriate use of power and from making the whole more that the sum of the parts.

APPROPRIATE USE OF POWER

Leaders, by definition, have power or influence over others, and in many organizations that power is often used for personal rather than organizational purposes. Morgan McCall and Michael Lombardo, who studied "derailment" factors at the Center for Creative Leadership, have found links between two of the top four factors in managerial failure and the misuse of personal power. These factors are betrayal of trust and excessive ambition (exhibited, for example, in frequent thoughts about the next job and in playing politics).[8] In later work, Morgan McCall found evidence that successful leaders used power to benefit others and the organization more than themselves.[9]

When leaders spend their time working on their own personal agendas—their careers, their schedules, their territory—they believe they are gaining power, but in fact they are losing. Increasing influence and power requires putting institutional ends first and insisting that everyone play by the same rules. Leaders who act to stop abuses give employees reassurance that they can trust the system's integrity: the leader gains power. Gene Dalton and Paul Thompson share a scenario that compellingly illustrates this process.

> Kerry Jensen, a sales executive at an electronics firm, was transferred to take over the management of the company's southern sales division. Not long after he came into the division, he heard rumors that the supervisors in two of the leading sales districts were neglecting to report returned machines, thus inflating their sales figures and entitling them to win special bonuses and rewards. Jensen spent a year establishing himself in his new position, getting to know the people, and gathering data about what was being done in these two districts. When he had fully determined that the practice was deliberate, ongoing, and dishonest, he took action. He went to each of the two supervisors and told them what he knew. He also told them that he realized how difficult it was to get someone fired in their company. But he vowed that he would spend every effort for as long as it took to have them fired if they didn't resign. Both resigned within a month.

The story of what Jensen had done quickly spread throughout the division. Other supervisors and salespeople came to Jensen and told him that they had known of the practice and were relieved to know that something had been done about it. Jensen's credibility increased. The southern sales division, which had been among the sales leaders in the country, rose to the number one position in sales and service.[10]

MAKE THE WHOLE MORE THAN THE SUM OF ITS PARTS

In an old training exercise, NASA, participants rank-order a list of items they would need if stranded on the moon. Individuals do the ranking, then teams do the ranking. In most cases, comparisons of these rankings with those of an expert panel composed of astronauts found that team rankings matched more closely with the experts' than did individual rankings. The exercise illustrates the synergistic principle that the value of the whole should be more than the sum of its parts. This principle has been applied to show how effective teams outperform individual efforts,[11] and organizations as a whole should create more value than subunits.[12]

Such synergy may also apply to leadership. Leaders who seek personal gain at the expense of peers or of institutional results generally lose over the long run. They focus on their part and lose sight of the whole. In one downsizing company, for example, at a meeting to decide the numbers by which each function would have to be reduced, the head of human resources took an unusual and bold stand. Her department, she said, should absorb a larger percentage of the overall downsizing effort because it was the right thing to do for the business. In the traditional world of corporate politics, at first blush, this act seems naive. On further examination, it was politically brilliant—and right for the company. In the short term, the company benefited because the marketing and engineering units required more resources and attention in the new, difficult environment they faced. In the long term, this HR director gained enormous credibility because she did what was right for the business.

Leaders who achieve results must be selfless about their role. Organizations entrust people with leadership roles. Leaders gain stature as they promote trust and confidence in how they operate. People must believe that their organization is fair. This belief develops when good performance is rewarded and abuses of trust or performance are not tolerated. It also grows when leaders act to align or match results with those required of other individuals or the organization as a whole. In Figure 2-7, write down your personal desired results and the desired results of your organization as a whole. Examine the worksheet to make sure these match or at least harmonize. If they don't, reexamine your leadership principles. True leaders meet the criterion of selfless results.

Conclusion and Implications for Results-Based Leaders

Results matter. Desired results matter more. Balanced results form the foundation of desired results. To achieve desired, balanced results, leaders need to understand strategy enough to achieve strategic clarity, duration enough to make results lasting, and synergy enough to make the results selfless.

Leaders with a results focus must satisfy these four criteria for effective results: balanced, strategic, long lasting, and selfless. Once these criteria are satisfied, results may be specified that enable a leader to be more than just personally credible. Figuring out what to do to achieve each of the four results will be the focus of the next four chapters.

Buzz, the leader at the beginning of the chapter, may now begin to turn his competencies into results. The answers to the "so that" query will lead to the desired results when he takes into account the four criteria: balanced, strategic, long lasting, and selfless.

Employee Results: Investing in Human Capital

3

CHAPTER 1 COVERS the leader's need for attributes and Chapter 2, the need to turn attributes into four types of desired results, each tied to stakeholders the leader must serve: employees, organization, customers, and investors. The next four chapters will take these four stakeholder areas in turn to explore ways leaders define, achieve, and sustain desired results, beginning here, with employee results.

Our understanding of employee results draws on an emerging body of inquiry treating issues variously termed "intellectual capital,"[1] "human capital,"[2] "knowledge management,"[3] and "the learning organization."[4] Although these concepts subtly differ, all converge around the importance of employees as producers and users of the information and knowledge that allow organizations to compete. Leaders achieve employee results when human capital increases over time and consistently meets the needs of the organizations. As used in this book, "human capital" refers, collectively, to intellectual capital or individual employee knowledge.

How can leaders get more out of their employees? The old adage remains true: The company, in the form of its people, walks out the door at the end of every workday. As business becomes increasingly knowledge and service driven, employee results will continue to become more, not less, important. Leaders must recognize and foster the link between successful employee results and the process of building human capital. We define human capital in this chapter in both traditional economic and more current managerial terms and by showing its importance for leadership. We then focus on how to build employee capability, followed by how to build employee commitment.

What Is Human Capital and Why Does It Matter?

Human capital from an economist's perspective consists of a company's market value (that is, the firm's value in the marketplace, calculated by multiplying stock price by shares outstanding) divided by the replacement value of its fixed assets.[5] Some firms with relatively few hard marketable assets (for example, plant, equipment, inventory, and so on) may have much more market value than book value. Microsoft, for example, currently has a market value about nine times its book value. This represents the market's valuation of Microsoft's human capital. Other firms with extensive facilities, capital equipment, and other hard assets may have replacement values closer to their market values. In these cases, the market places less value on the firm's human capital.

This definition makes calculations and comparisons of value across firms relatively easy. It does not, however, adequately measure human capital in a way that leaders can use on a daily basis. High market value may be due to brand success, dominant market share, innovation, an exclusive technology, or some other factor, any or all of which can create extraordinary market value.

Human capital can also be defined in terms of what is inside the heads and hearts of the people who work in an organization. In economic terms, this approach puts a value on the knowledge, education, experience, and creativity of the work force.[6] Although desirable, accurate measurement of such employee qualities and contributions remains elusive.

If leaders are to make the most of their organization's human capital, a clearer, more applicable definition is required. A useful distinction here is the one between what employees *can* and what they *will* do. Some analysts apply the term *human capital* only to what employees *can* do for an organization. Far more useful, realistic, and promising, from the leader's point of view, is an inclusive assessment of human capital, one that includes *willingness,* or commitment, along with capability.

The lack of a clear and accepted definition leaves the concept of human capital relevant, timely, and important, but vague and soft. This chapter proposes a simple, yet useful and measurable definition: *Human capital = employee capability × employee commitment.* As this equation suggests, within a given unit, overall employee capability should increase with experience, but capability alone will not guarantee a high level of human capital. Units with high capability but low commitment possess talented employees who stand around the water cooler; firms with high commitment but low capability have intellectually challenged employees who work hard and quickly. Both extremes are dangerous; building human capital requires both employee capability and employee commitment.

Thus measured, human capital can be assessed at the firm, unit, or individual level. A restaurant chain, for example, may measure the human capital at each of its restaurants, using an index based on employees' average skill level (capability) multiplied by employees' average length of service (commitment). The resulting human capital index would likely be a useful predictor of other positive outcomes for the given unit, including customer loyalty, employee productivity, and profitability.

Knowing how to increase human capital will become ever more valuable to firms as human capital continues to increase in importance as an element of organizational success. Leaders who want to increase employee results can do so by increasing both the capability and the commitment of their employees.

Human capital can be seen as a problem or as an opportunity. To make it work for you, keep in mind the following principles and cautions.

Human capital is underutilized.

In countless private discussions with executives, we have heard them readily acknowledge that they could do more with the knowledge, creativity, and experience of the people in their organization. One executive lamented, "We just don't know what we know." What has been true historically will only be more so in the future: knowledge work is increasing, not decreasing. In his excellent work on the intelligent enterprise, James Brian Quinn observes that the service economy grows

both directly, in service industries such as retail, investments, information, and food, and indirectly, with service becoming more critical in
traditional manufacturing industries such as automotive, durable goods,
and equipment.[7] As the service economy grows, the importance of
human capital increases. Service excellence derives from solid customer relationships, which are made possible through the capability and
commitment of individual employees forging the relationships.

Human capital is one of the few assets that can appreciate.

Most firm assets (building, plant, equipment, or machinery, for
example) begin to depreciate the day they are acquired. Human capital,
on the other hand, an asset embedded in the minds and hearts of
employees, can and must grow if a firm is to prosper. The leader's job is
to make employee knowledge productive and to turn human capital into
customer value.

Human capital is portable.

Employees with the most human capital have essentially become
volunteers.[8] Because they can find work opportunities in many firms
and thus have a choice about where they work, they can be said to volunteer to work in any particular firm. Volunteers give commitment
when they feel an emotional bond with a firm. Economic return matters
less to them than creating meaning. The human capital of employees as
"volunteers" matters more because increasingly employees may leave
for other firms. Leaders can no longer invoke "role power" to get things
done; they must find new ways to elicit commitment.

Human capital has been both mismanaged and undermanaged.

Especially in the past decade, many management initiatives have
overlooked the role of human capital in organizations. In the name of
downsizing, delayering, and restructuring, many valuable employees,
repositories of substantial amounts of organizational experience and
knowledge, have been jettisoned. These actions have most often been
taken with little or no thought given to the long-term consequences of
the loss in human capital. In addition, downsizing has coincided with
increasing global competition, customer requirements, fewer layers of
management, increased employee obligations, pressures on productivity, and every other modern management practice. Small wonder, then,

that employees feel bruised and scraped by their workplace experiences. Pay, too, adjusted for inflation, has actually declined over the past decade. Worse yet, upper management is often oblivious to this fact because the executive's personal quality of work life has generally improved, as evidenced by skyrocketing executive compensation.[9]

Human capital requires a different way of thinking about careers.

The difference will most affect the next generation of a firm's leaders. In a recent workshop, sixty high-potential managers from a very successful global company engaged in a discussion of careers. Half of these managers (most of whom were in their thirties or early forties) did not think that they would retire from that company, citing not lack of opportunity but high levels of stress and company demands. Ninety percent personally knew someone who had, in fact, voluntarily left the company within the preceding six months for those reasons. A member of the group shared these issues with an executive the next day, who tellingly responded that a job at the company was a good job, that backups were in place for anyone who did not want to work hard, and that discussions of work/life balance did not serve business results.

Human capital within a firm correlates with customer perception of the firm.

Firms often seem to appreciate least and to make the least investment in employees whose human capital most directly affects customers. A number of studies have demonstrated the link between the attitude of front-line employees and customer attitudes about a firm.[10] Customers' opinion of McDonald's, Sears, or the Ford Motor Company, for example, relates directly to the service they receive from the local store or dealer, not to the public relations campaigns scripted by corporate headquarters. Companies may invest millions in training executives to think strategically and act globally, but customers' impressions of the firm come from the employees who serve them when they buy food, clothes, or cars. Too many firms allow these employees to be transient, uncommitted workers, often incompetent to answer questions and unable to meet customers' needs. As a result, the overall image of an organization falls. Rather than investing in the training and development of this group, most training is focused on top executives, salespeople, and professionals.

Human capital draws everything else together.

Investments in physical plant, technology, new products, distribution systems, and marketing collectively function thanks to an organization's human capital. This obvious, but often unacknowledged, point should become every leader's mantra.

The net result of the statement above is simple: human capital matters. Leaders seeking results must create, build, and sustain human capital within their work units. Douglas Iverster, the president and chief operating officer of Coca-Cola, recently said, "People are our defining assets." He has staked his career on creating a learning culture throughout Coke.

Human capital is like muscle tone: "Use it or lose it." Firms that want to succeed need leaders who encourage the use of human capital. Unused or underutilized, human capital withers. People don't keep up with changes in their professions; their commitment sags.

Unfortunately, most current responses to the failure to build human capital have been misguided or inadequate. Under the rubric "corporate citizenship," many senior executives now talk about dealing with work/life issues. Although undertaken with the best intentions, corporate citizenship initiatives often devolve into feel-good exercises and public relations. The message seems to be "After you have done all the real business, spend time with these nice-to-do, citizenship concerns of employees." Wrong. Human capital is *the* business issue of the day.

Using our definition of human capital as *employee commitment* × *employee capability*, we can now shift attention to creating the case for leaders paying attention to it and focus on how to increase it.

What Is Employee Capability?

The term *employee capability* represents the knowledge, skill, ability, and motives of each individual employee in his or her position. At one level, this means that leaders should be concerned about whether their employees have the *technical* know-how, the skills needed, to get their work done. A sales and marketing leader in a multinational corporation's China office, for example, would naturally expect employees to understand the product information, business practices, and customer relationships appropriate to that market.

At another level, leaders should be concerned about employees' *social* know-how, or how they work together, as part of their overall employee capability. Working together focuses less on technical know-how and more on interpersonal skills and sensitivity to how work gets done; the patterns of influencing, decision making, collaborating, and communicating that move a group effort forward.

Employee capability simply suggests that when employees have both technical and social know-how, they are more able to accomplish work. A leader's job is to clarify what employees need to know and do, then to figure out how to make sure employees do what is needed.

HOW TO MEASURE EMPLOYEE CAPABILITY

There have been both overly simplistic and complicated methods of assessing employee capabilities. At the simplistic level, leaders ask the general question: Do my employees have the technical and social ability to get work done? This general question usually generates equally generic responses, such as "Suppose so," "Sure," "Why not." If leaders do not go beyond such responses, they will fail to elicit the kind of detailed, specific information they need to adapt and spread what works or to change what doesn't.

Some highly sophisticated and complicated methods for measuring employee capability have been developed. Unfortunately, these often amass employee capability data—skills inventories, performance reviews, career aspirations, career histories—which, for want of a concrete connection to present work and needs, are simply warehoused. These expensive-to-produce employee data warehouses often cost more to create, update, and maintain than they are worth.

Most leaders need detailed, but not complex, assessments of their employees' capabilities. The simple, robust methodology proposed here constitutes a "big meter" which, like an automobile's speedometer, can be always before the leaders' eyes, ready for constant monitoring of its basic yet essential information.

Leaders have four ways to effectively measure employee capability, as illustrated in Figure 3-1. Employee capability may be assessed for either individuals or groups and either quantitatively, using numbers, or qualitatively, using descriptions. Whatever the approach, leaders need to be both rigorous with empirical assessments and inquisitive with probing and relevant questions. The figure gives examples of the precision

FIGURE 3-1

MEASURES OF EMPLOYEE CAPABILITY

	QUANTITATIVE FOCUS	QUALITATIVE FOCUS
INDIVIDUAL ASSESSMENT	**Cell 1: Quantitative Individual Measures** Using the scale below, create a weighted performance index by rating the capabilities of the people in your work group, using qualities such as education, training, talents, intelligence, and the following point scale: Raw novice, 50; average new hire, 100; highest possible, 150	**Cell 2: Qualitative Individual Measures** • How valuable is this employee for the business results? If this employee left, how great would be the loss? • Who uses the output from this employee? Which customers outside the firm? Which other employees inside the firm? • How comfortable would you be with the employee's representing your unit to senior management, customers, potential employees, or investors? • If you had an unexpected pool of money to use as bonuses for the employees, what percentage would you give this employee? • How able is this employee to make things happen? • How much respect does this employee have among peers?

Person	Rating	Last Year
Monika	135	130
George	130	120
Frank	125	130
Cindy	115	115
Stuart	95	80
Kristy	90	60
Franklin	80	85
Mean average	110	101

Alternately, use 360° feedback to determine each individual's overall standings

	QUANTITATIVE FOCUS	QUALITATIVE FOCUS
COLLECTIVE ASSESSMENT	*Cell 3: Quantitative Collective Measures[a]* • Employee training and development expenses as a percentage of total expenses. • Reputation of company employees with headhunters. • Years of experience in profession. • Employee satisfaction index. • The proportion of employees suggesting new ideas, including the proportion implemented. • Position backup ratio: percentage of key jobs for which backup is ready and available. • Overall backup ratio: number of people qualified to move into key jobs. • Ratio of offers to acceptances overall and in key positions.	*Cell 4: Qualitative Collective Measures[b]* • What employee skills do your customers value most? • Why do recruits come to your unit? What skills do you look for in them, and what skills do they look to acquire for you? • Which managers have the reputation for developing future leaders? What do these future leaders seem to know and do? • Where do high-potential managers want to work? Why? • When competitors hire, do they hire from you? • Why do people leave you for jobs elsewhere? • What are the technical and social know-how required of the employees in the future? What percentage of current employees will likely be able to acquire those skills? • If you had to start your business over again from scratch, what percentage of the current employees would you hire?

a. See Jac Fitz-ens, "The Truth about Best Practices: What They Are and How to Apply Them," *Human Resource Management Journal* 36, no. 1 (1997): 97–104; and Thomas Stewart, *Intellectual Capital: The New Wealth of Organizations* (New York: Doubleday, 1997).

b. See Stewart, *Intellectual Capital*, 232.

and specificity that leaders will find most revealing. No one approach excludes the use of others. By mixing and matching approaches according to prevailing needs and conditions, leaders will find one that is flexible, adaptable, and reliable for them.

To take one example, consider cell 1 of Figure 3-1. Here, a leader derives an empirical assessment of employee capability using as a baseline the education, training, and experience of the average new hire during the previous year. With this standard of human capital in place, the leader assesses, relative to it, the experienced work force.

The new-hire measure is the most revealing and flexible yardstick because it acknowledges that the qualifications needed change constantly. What constituted "technically qualified" years ago will often not pass muster today. Ten years ago, for example, administrative assistants didn't need to know how to use a word processing program, a spreadsheet program, or a program that integrated text, data, and graphics into a presentation on disk ready to go with a few hours' notice. They may not have been required to know how to use a computer at all. Today, needless to say, they are.

The baseline measure thus reflects ever-changing standards of capability for a specific function or position. Other revealing measures include those tracked by the Swedish firm Celemi:[11] employees' average number of years' experience in their professions; turnover among experts; seniority among experts; percentage of capability-enhancing customers, that is, those who bring projects that challenge the capability of Celemi's employees; and rookie ratio, or the percentage of employees with less than two years' experience measured against the total work force.

The leader and others (peers, subordinates) charged with assessing the achievement of objectives (including, perhaps, an HR representative) gather or consider the targeted information and measure each individual in the group against that standard. This cumulative assessment helps leaders to determine whether an individual's human capital continues to improve from year to year. The other approaches demonstrated in Figure 3-1 can, if woven together, provide a highly credible index of employee capability.

Leaders who want employee results must have capable employees. Unless they track their capability through both quantitative measures and qualitative dialogues, these results may not occur.

HOW TO BUILD EMPLOYEE CAPABILITY

Leaders whose groups lack adequate levels of employee capability have many options for overcoming the problem. The basic alternatives, the "six B's" are to *buy, build, benchmark, borrow, bounce,* and *bind* needed talent. Each of these is described more fully below. Figure 3-2 provides a worksheet to assess the effectiveness with which you employ these strategies, and to plan changes, additions, or improvements to your approach to building employee capability in your group.

Buy.

Leaders may go outside their unit for new people when they want to grow or replace current with higher-quality talent. In addition, many executives seeking rapid transformation rely on buying new talent. Larry Bossidy replaced 90 of the top 120 executives at AlliedSignal, bringing some from inside but most from outside, thus clearly indicating a change in the firm's culture and direction. Buying new talent brings in new ideas, breaks old cultural roadblocks, and creates human capital by shaking up the firm.

A *buy* strategy works—when talent is available and accessible—but it carries great risks. External talent may turn out to be no more qualified than the internal talent. Wholesale replacements risk alienating internally qualified employees, who may resent management carpet-baggers who come into the firm without having paid their dues. The effort to integrate diverse external talent into a working, credible team with a solid grasp of the firm's intricacies can be a minefield of lurking disasters. Companies who go this route often find their progress slower and more erratic than they had expected.

The *buy* strategy only works when the new talent creates an "aha!" effect among existing employees. This happens when the acquired talent is so qualified that the other employees both feel and express their delight with the hire, putting aside jealousy at the thrill of working with the new employee. We envision "buy" being a less viable employee capability approach, given that the demand for qualified employees often exceeds supply, making it increasingly expensive to attract external talent.

Build.

Leaders using the *build* strategy invest in the development of their current work force, helping them find new ways to think about and do

FIGURE 3-2

STRATEGIES FOR BUILDING EMPLOYEE CAPABILITY

STRATEGY	DEFINITION	SCORE (1 = low, 10 = high)	LEADER ACTIONS TO IMPROVE
Buy	Acquire new talent by recruiting individuals from outside the firm or from other departments or divisions within the firm.		
Build	Train or develop talent through education, formal job training, job rotation, job assignments, and action learning.		
Benchmark	Visit organizations that excel in work processes targeted for improvement.		
Borrow	Partner with consultants, vendors, customers, or suppliers outside the firm to garner new ideas.		
Bounce	Remove low-performing or underperforming individuals.		
Bind	Retain the most talented employees.		

their work. Many firms—for example, Motorola and General Electric—invest heavily in programs that help employees unlearn old technical and managerial skills and learn new ones. In addition to such formal training programs, structured on-the-job development experiences facilitate skill improvement. These programs build human capital when employees learn to couple inquiry with action, when new ideas replace old, and when on-the-job behavior changes.

For a *build* strategy to accumulate human capital, senior executives must ensure that real development, not academic exercises, takes place; that training is tied to business results, not theory; that action learning occurs; and that employees learn steadily and systematically from their job experiences. The risk of a *build* strategy lies in spending enormous quantities of money and time on training for its own sake and failing to build the human capital that can create business value.

One powerful technique for building capability is finding star performers inside the organization and determining how their approaches to their jobs differ from those of their colleagues. Almost every work group possesses a member who has figured out the best and most efficient ways to get a job done. These techniques can often be learned—but only through careful observation. Once the technique has been analyzed and understood, others in the organization can be taught to follow the pattern.

Benchmark.

The *benchmark* technique for increasing human capital involves sending front-line people and executives to visit other organizations that excel in a given work process. By seeing the successful group in action, the observers learn what can be done and how to do it. Benchmarking can utilize organizations both inside and outside the observer's industry; such visits can even be made to competitors. The power of the technique comes from its tendency to free employees from complacency and arrogance, which naturally build up inside most successful organizations, as well as from the powerful teaching mechanism of seeing an excellent example in action. Although benchmarking may be considered a subset of a build strategy, it differs in that it enables targeted executives to see how other companies do business, an eye-opening experience. The risk is that those benchmarking will try to merely copy, not extend what they observe, and that what is benchmarked today may not work tomorrow.

Borrow.

Managers using outside vendors to bring in new ideas, frameworks, and tools to strengthen their organizations are employing the *borrow* strategy. The use of consultants is no longer a luxury, but a business reality. When consultants are used to good effect they partner with clients, by sharing knowledge, creating new knowledge, and designing work processes with a fresh perspective and lack of bias unavailable to those more closely involved.

Many firms must, however, make an effort to use consultants without becoming dependent on them. We call this "adapt, don't adopt." Adapting focuses on changing the consultants' approach based on the need of the business and on transferring the knowledge of the consultant into the client organization so that the consultants essentially "work themselves out of a job." Leaders who use consultants will "lease to own, not rent." Clients must unravel the processes and tools consultants offer, making them their own, to be replicated and deployed by employees after the consultants leave.

As do the other methods, borrowing external input to increase human capital has risks. Large amounts of capital and time may be expended with little return. A company may become dependent on consultants, failing to make the knowledge transfer that would grant it ownership of improved processes. It also risks using answers from another setting without making appropriate adaptations.

Bounce.

In the *bounce* strategy, leaders remove individuals who fail to perform up to standards. Sometimes this means that individuals who were once qualified may have failed to keep up with and are not qualified for current work practices. Other times, this means removing individuals who simply are not capable of changing, learning, and adapting at the rate required by today's volatile economic and technological conditions.

Firms seeking to increase their average human capital systematically and courageously remove the bottom percentiles. To use this technique effectively requires careful, responsible planning and management courage so that difficult personnel decisions are made decisively. Clearly defined standards and expectations must prevail so that both those leaving and those staying understand why. Finally, the procedure for bouncing the unproductive must be fair and equitable and meet all legal requirements.

Bouncing, or removing marginal talent as a means of increasing human capital, carries risks, of course. Management must guard against seeing downsizing as a panacea, which it definitely is not. It must be careful not to lose the wrong individuals, and it must avoid demoralizing those who stay. Above all, firms must not make these personnel decisions on perception rather than fact, thereby losing management credibility.

Bind.

The *bind* technique concentrates on retaining employees critical to a firm's success. Retention matters at all levels. Success requires retaining both the senior managers whose vision, direction, and capability guide the firm's course and the technical, operational, and hourly workers who produce the products or offer the services that attract and keep customers. Companies must remember that investments in individual talent often take years to pay back, which makes retention critical.

Retention works two ways. Consider the situation of a large bank where the managers were frustrated with their excellent credit training program. It finally dawned on them that it was *too* good, because after providing trainees with three years of formal classroom training coupled with tailored job assignments, the graduating qualified loan officers were regularly recruited by competitors. The bank's buy and build strategies were working, but it lost in overall human capital because it failed to retain those in whom it had invested.

Another firm, facing high labor costs and the possibility of layoffs, decided to focus, not on the 7 to 10 percent of workers who might have to be let go, but on the 20 to 25 percent whom it could not afford to lose. Firm managers identified these critical employees, interviewed them to explore what would keep them attached to the firm, and then devised individual employee contracts with them to encourage them to stay. The firm was thus able to retain its critical employees and increase its human capital, despite cutbacks.

What Is Employee Commitment?

Commitment represents how people in an organization *will* behave, rather than how they *could* behave (that is, their capability). Committed employees devote their emotional energy and attention to their firm.[12]

Commitment can be detected in how employees relate to each other and in what they feel about the firm. In many cases, the competitive pressures that demand even greater employee commitment actually undermine it. The unrelenting, very real competitive pressures demand more of employees—to be more global, more customer responsive, more flexible, more learning oriented, more team driven, more productive, and so on. These competitive demands require more committed employees who give their emotional, human, and physical energy to firm success.[13]

Recent work on mass customization in marketing provides a new way to think about employee commitment.[14] Mass customization recognizes the uniqueness of every customer and fine tunes market segments to the individual or, at most, the family level. Levi Strauss, for example, now offers custom-made jeans; customers are measured for size, the information is sent electronically to the manufacturing site, and the pants are tailored and then shipped direct to the customer. Some grocery stores have frequent-shopper programs where customers use frequent-shopper cards to get better service (for example, shorter lines, discounts). Over time, these programs allow the retailer to know individual consumers' buying patterns. Some stores will then deliver goods directly to customer homes.

Employee commitment develops where employees perceive their firm as mass-customizing employment relationships. Firms that have the capacity to do so—and employee customization runs counter to ingrained ways of dealing with employees—will increase employee commitment.

Historically, our industrial society viewed people as machines. Scientific management operated on the premise that work should be simplified as much as possible so that workers need have only minimal skills and education. By structuring work in this way, employers came to see their employees as interchangeable. If one failed to perform, the company simply substituted another person in that place.

In consequence, many of the labor relations policies, too, were structured on the assumption that everyone was treated exactly alike. Much of the thrust behind the labor movement encouraged this, by focusing on equal treatment for all employees—no management favorites. Workers sought the guarantee that all would be treated exactly the same way.

Clearly, the demand for and attainment of equal treatment resulted in many valuable gains for labor. But like many good ideas that get carried too far, negative consequences, too, arose. Workers felt they were—and resented being—treated as part of a herd. Individual differences in learning and working were ignored; so, too, were differences in personal or family needs and conditions. The individual was expected to conform to the needs of the organization, in its working hours, its demands for or acceptance of overtime, its vacation schedule, its dress code, and its culture.

These conditions and expectations led to increasingly adversarial relations between labor and management. Along with the adversarial spirit came an even worse consequence: apathy. Workers didn't care about the organization. When the corporation failed to attend to their needs as individuals, employees reciprocated by shutting down any feelings of loyalty or commitment which they might have had for their employers.

Companies today can no longer consider workers interchangeable. With most developed countries facing record low unemployment, companies desperately need qualified people. Every organization needs smart, computer-literate, creative, adaptable people. Yet corporate America, because of the widespread downsizing and layoffs of recent years, has forfeited worker commitment and abrogated the old contract between workers and companies. The expectation that loyalty and hard work would guarantee lifetime employment was totally erased. Companies must now earn employee commitment by entirely new means. Generation X employees (that is, workers born between 1965 and 1981) value autonomy, flexibility, and individualism more than they do any traditional, one-size-fits-all management practices.[15]

The only way firms can recapture commitment is by treating workers in ways that respect their individuality. Workers want flexibility in working hours and assignments. They want the opportunity to help create the content of their jobs. They want to control their career progression. Workers want, in other words, a strong voice in everything they do. Companies must now work with employees in a partnership to design their future, helping them to understand and appreciate the opportunities the organization provides. Individuals commit to firms where they see possibilities for learning and growth. When the individual feels part of a community of people for whom he or she has respect and caring, commitment follows. To create these conditions, organizations must foster an environment that develops and enhances these qualities, and to do so they must foster a complementary management style, which we call "mass-customizing the employee deal."[16]

HOW TO MEASURE EMPLOYEE COMMITMENT

Three "large gauges" can help leaders measure employee commitment: work force productivity, organizational climate, and employee retention (see Figure 3-3). Leaders should constantly watch each of these dials.

Work force productivity.

Productivity may be the single most important measure of a leader's results with his or her employees. Improvements in productivity constitute the major determinant of a country's living standard. Productivity creates a pool of resources for paying rising salaries and improved benefits. Without productivity improvement, wage increases come only from returns, which would otherwise go to shareholders or owners. Higher wages during periods of high inflation are illusory, simply reflecting the inflation rate.

Firms that demonstrate aggressive productivity improvement have been rewarded in the marketplace. GE has shown 5 to 6 percent per annum productivity increases, as compared with an overall 1.2 percent for the economy in general. Cisco Systems targets a 10 percent annual productivity increase—and has consistently hit that number. Firms with such high productivity gains enjoy a significant competitive advantage. But less than 20 percent of firms have any organized productivity improvement process. One reason may be the lack of a measurement procedure.

Productivity represents output per unit of input. One measure of productivity might therefore be firm revenues divided by direct employee costs (salaries and benefits). This provides a more accurate measure than merely dividing revenues by the number of employees, because it measures the return on dollars spent for people. Profits divided by employee costs can be another useful productivity measure. EBIT (earnings before interest and taxes) should be used, to avoid muddying the calculation of employee productivity, with the company debt, or the tax structure. Obviously, these measures function most

FIGURE 3-3

MEASURES OF EMPLOYEE COMMITMENT

MEASURE	DEFINITION	LEADER'S APPLICATION
Work force productivity	Ratio of output per unit of input. Output may be revenue, volume, profits, cash, people hired, etc.; input may be number of employees, employee costs, etc.	Plot productivity on a time line and compare to that of other groups.
Organizational climate	Ways in which work is done within a company. Measures may include how work is governed, how people are treated, how information is shared, and how decisions are made.	Assess using periodic surveys of key indicators.
Employee retention	Work force stability. Comes from the percentage of employees leaving the firm in a given time period (generally a year).	Plot percentage of turnover, year to year, comparing with industry and community figures. Also show turnover by departing workers' tenure and performance quartile.

powerfully when they are taken over time, so that trends can be observed. Also valuable are comparisons between organizations in the same industry.

Parts of organizations can develop unique measures of productivity. Sales force productivity can be measured using total dollars spent for sales force compensation (including bonuses and commissions) divided into total revenues. Manufacturing plants can look at output measured by dollar volume of units divided by dollar costs of all manufacturing employees. Human resource departments may calculate cost per hire or cost per employee. Accounting departments may measure the cost to process travel expense forms or accounts payable transactions.

Organizational climate.

Organizational climate (or, more popularly today, culture) serves as a second useful gauge of commitment. Culture provides a key link between a company and its employees' motivation to do their best work, unleash their creativity, work with intensity, act with a sense of urgency, and put forth extra effort when required.

Organizational culture combines many factors, including the perceived quality of management and supervision, the clarity of the firm's mission and vision, the fairness of its compensation and benefits policies, employees' relationships with coworkers, the quality of communication within the organization, the way decision-making processes are used, the quality of facilities and equipment provided, and the mechanisms for feedback to higher management. Culture determines an organization's adaptability, and in the long run, has a tremendous effect on its ability to compete while adapting to new circumstances and to changes in customer requirements.

Many organizations have long been making an effort to measure climate or culture and conduct periodic audits of work force practices and employee attitudes. Most such audits are relatively broad in scope, assessing most or all of the dimensions noted above. IBM, for example, regularly performs culture audits, at least once every eighteen months. Managers are held accountable for any downward trends revealed by these measures, because IBM has learned that these provide early warning signals of problems to come. If your organization hasn't already started this process, start now.

To use climate data effectively, leaders must compare their firm's or group's data year to year as well as comparing them to broader-based normative data to see how they stack up with industry or other cross-country standards.

Most leaders make no apologies for holding employees responsible for how they use company money or how they treat a company car. Leaders must similarly demand adherence to a standard for responsible treatment of people. Condoning anything less is a serious mistake. How managers treat people and build the culture and climate in their groups should be monitored as closely as, even more closely than how they spend money.

To garner honest and revealing climate assessments, follow these general principles:

- Assure respondents of their absolute anonymity or confidentiality.

- Provide specific feedback that takes account of trends in responses.

- Train leaders to conduct sessions with their employees to share information and enhance leaders' understanding of what the climate data mean for their groups.

- Make appropriate changes in response to issues surfaced by this process.

- Let people know what policy changes derive from the climate assessment process, to make the explicit link between their participation and workplace improvements.

- Repeat the surveys regularly; their value will increase as more data accumulate, revealing trends, and as employees increasingly trust the process.

- Focus on the general direction of the scores' movement, not the absolute starting point or the current numbers.

Employee retention.

The final dimension essential for measuring employee commitment is retention.[17] Companies that constantly lose good people in large numbers may have a leadership problem. When the best people churn through an organization and the mediocre ones stay, the organization is headed downhill. When highly effective people cannot see a good future by staying in the organization, and competitors can easily pull away the top people, leadership has failed the group.

Understanding employee retention and loss at a given company requires examination of a number of measures. First, the absolute levels of turnover should be measured and evaluated. The ideal number is not zero; some turnover is usually healthy. But, in general, healthy turnover should be no more than 10 percent annually. A group experiencing higher turnover should set off an alarm bell. Leaders should, in addition, be aware of turnover trends over time, comparing current measures to those taken in past years.

Turnover rates should be compared with those in benchmark organizations used to assess other areas of company effectiveness. How does turnover at one company compare with that in the surrounding community?

Companies need to know not just how many people are leaving, but who they are. An 8 percent turnover rate may not seem excessive, but if it includes mainly top performers and few middling or low-performing people, a problem exists that requires immediate attention. To resolve it, the company must know why its people are leaving. Turnover due to retirement or the relocation of a spouse differs significantly from turnover due to employees' finding better opportunities elsewhere. Finally, companies should examine when people leave. Within the first six months? This points to weaknesses in how new hires are assimilated and acculturated. After three years? This indicates an entirely different set of problems.

Quantitative and qualitative turnover measures both serve to reveal the nature of the impact leaders have on employees. Studies in manufacturing and sales organizations consistently show a high positive correlation between productivity and reduced turnover: a stable, low-turnover work force produces significantly more.

HOW TO BUILD EMPLOYEE COMMITMENT

Employee commitment, given today's economy and today's worker, will demand utmost flexibility from every organization. The five dimensions outlined below—work arrangements, work impact, growth opportunities, rewards, and community—can help organizations and groups within organizations to move toward productive flexibility. When leaders tailor individual employee contracts around each of these five dimensions, they customize the employee relationship, which increases employee commitment.

Work arrangements.

Flexibility may be built into where, when, and how work is done. Traditionally, time clocks marked the beginning and end of the workday in a specified workplace. New technologies, however, such as the Internet, allow extremely flexible work arrangements. Technology enables workers to control where work is done, as well as when. For example, a large bank offering its customers twenty-four hour call-in service found staffing the call center from 6:00 to 9:00 A.M. and from 6:00 to 10:00 P.M. difficult: Workers wanted to be home with their families. The bank solved the problem by allowing employees to put call centers in their homes so that they could respond to customer calls without being out of the home. The bank made the commitment clear that customer service had to exceed minimum standards, but employees who wanted to could work from home. The result? After one year, customer service, employee morale, and retention of "at-home" call center representatives exceeded bank averages. Allowing employees to work at home, through hoteling relationships where they share an office, or flexible hours (for example, four days at ten hours per day versus five days at eight hours per day) increased employee commitment. These arrangements allow for the work/life balance that is crucial to many employees.

Flexible work arrangements can also include special policies and physical settings. Changing policies around uniforms, dress codes, and prescribed vacation days appeals to employees who are more interested in results than in regulations. The creation of campuslike physical settings, which provide employees with comfortable environments of open spaces, casual areas for conversation, sports and physical facilities, and on-site child care centers, has also become an element in some employees' commitment to their organization.

Work impact.

Some of the recent studies of generation X employees have shown that they prefer work that requires creativity and welcomes innovative solutions. Allowing employees the flexibility to choose their projects and to define how those projects will be done increases work impact and employee commitment. Pride in work comes when employees can see their work to completion, when those who use their work give them credit for what they have done, and when they feel they have created outcomes useful to others. By creating work settings where employees can see and feel the impact of their work, leaders increase employee commitment.

Growth opportunities.

Commitment increases when employees do work that they can learn from. Employees' opportunities for growth come when leaders provide them with skill training, job assignments requiring new skills, feedback on performance, the chance to work in cross-functional teams, and relevant educational experiences. Employees become increasingly committed to jobs where they can learn new skills, and to jobs they find personally challenging. Allowing employees to customize their growth opportunities provides them with further opportunities to learn and shifts responsibility for that learning to the employees themselves.

Rewards.

Commitment increases when employees receive public affirmation of a job well done. In work settings, endorsement can come in part from recognition, but part may also come from compensation and benefits. Giving employees choices about the form of their compensation helps create commitment. At one northeastern bank, for example, a woman in the organizational effectiveness department had recently completed her Ph.D. After putting in fifteen years at the bank, she was looking forward to a good career there. Somewhat to her chagrin, however, her husband was transferred to the Southwest, where she could not find a comparable job. Her boss in the bank offered her a deal: if she would put 30 percent of her salary into a travel fund, the boss would match it. Using this fund, the employee would travel back and forth, spending twelve to fifteen days per month on site at the bank and working at home the rest of the time. The employee accepted, thus maintaining her seniority at the bank and applying her knowledge in a challenging job. To the bank's benefit, she was more committed to her employer than ever—and to the unique financial and work arrangement package.

Community.

A worker's relationship with peers, supervisors, and executives remains one of the biggest predictors of commitment. When community replaces hierarchy, employees feel they work for people who care about and respect them as individuals—and they reciprocate with increased commitment. Community can be fostered by giving employees the luxury of helping to select their teammates, of forming relationships of trust with supervisors, and of connecting with customers.

Figure 3-4 illustrates how such customization might work. It shows how four employees weigh each of the dimensions. The logic is that the firm provides each employee with 100 units of value, then lets the individual specify the relative weight that each dimension receives, thus tailoring his or her employment contract to personal interests and values. Michael, for example, cares most about flexible work arrangements, so he might opt for a contract that permits adaptable work hours and locations. Helen, more interested in whom she works with than in money, career opportunity, or advancement, should have a strong voice in selecting team members. Joe, most interested in acquiring more skills and talents, should be given development and training experience. Jana values all five dimensions equally. In this case, all four employees had 100 points to divide. In fact, given that some employees give a firm more value than others, the total number of points to divide may vary by employee.

By knowing employees' preferences, leaders can tailor the company-employee relationship and increase employee commitment. Key to this flexibility, of course, is continuing employee productivity: employees must meet and exceed performance standards. As employees meet ever higher standards, they gain further flexibility and authority over the five dimensions; employees who fail to meet standards lose ground on flexibility.

Customizing the employee relationship in each of the five dimensions increases employee commitment. When employees receive from the work setting what is meaningful to them, they will give back to the firm commitment and service. Leaders of small firms or local work units who have been able and willing to adapt all five dimensions to meet individual employee needs have already begun to reap the benefits in commitment. As leaders in large firms recognize the importance of human capital and the centrality of employee commitment to building and maintaining it, they, too, will find ways to customize the contracts of talented employees along these five key flexibility dimensions.

FIGURE 3-4

BUILDING EMPLOYEE COMMITMENT

DIMENSIONS OF EMPLOYEE CONTRACT	ILLUSTRATIVE CHOICES	EMPLOYEE			
		MICHAEL	JANA	HELEN	JOE
Work arrangements	Where work is done (e.g., home, hotel, office) When work is done (e.g., hours) What policies govern how work is done (e.g., dress code)	40	20	20	10
Work impact	What projects are done What creative challenges are taken on What career ambitions an employee may have What ways employees can see the impact of their work	20	20	10	20
Growth opportunities	What skills an employee wants to acquire What feedback an employee receives What job assignments, task forces, etc., an employee does What training or educational opportunities are available to an employee	20	20	10	40

Dimensions of Employee Contract	Illustrative Choices	Employee			
		Michael	Jana	Helen	Joe
Reward	What short- and long-term cash rewards are available What stock and other deferred incentives are available What flexible benefits may be sustained	10	20	10	20
Community	Who employee works with What teammates the employee has How the employee relates to a boss	10	20	50	10
Relative importance of each element of the contract		100	100	100	100

Implications for Leaders of Employee Results

Human capital derives from the capability and commitment of employees. Capability without commitment constitutes untapped insight. Commitment without capability results in sometimes-dangerous action. Both capability and commitment are necessary if human capital is to grow. The appreciation of human capital has rightly become a dominant agenda for executives in many firms.

Leaders interested in investing, leveraging, and expanding their human capital should spend time raising standards, setting high expectations, and demanding more of their employees. They cannot stop here, however. They must also provide resources that help employees meet these higher demands. One insight derived from work with a number of companies has been that leadership need not be the font of all resources, but should involve employees in deciding what resources they need to meet the high demands placed on them. If leaders can approach employees with both high demands, and the methods for acquiring resources needed to meet those demands, employees become engaged, and they flourish. The organization's human capital becomes a defining asset, and leaders accomplish their stretch goals.

Leaders must not wait for people to leave, for innovation to wane, or for productivity to falter. Leaders must produce in the arena of employee results because it so profoundly affects all other areas of corporate achievement.

Organization Results: Creating Capabilities

4

ORGANIZATIONS DON'T THINK AND DO; people think and do. Leaders seeking results thus need to focus their attention on people and on increasing human capital, the subject of the preceding chapter. But because leaders lead organizations, not just people, and because organizations constrain how people think and what they do, this chapter helps leaders figure out how best to achieve organization results.

The importance of leaders in creating organization results can be demonstrated with a simple case of an athlete changing teams and improving performance. One organizational setting may be more able to leverage an athlete's skill than another. When Isaac Austin, for example, first played basketball in the NBA with the Utah Jazz, he was a talented athlete, but not a particularly dedicated one. After being cut from the team, he played for a year or two in Europe before being acquired by the Miami Heat as a backup player. With Miami, Austin changed. While he may have played for other NBA teams, something changed in his capacity because of the team's expectations. He lost weight, worked out regularly, and became a leading scorer. Much of the credit for this successful transformation should go to his increased commitment, but some also belongs to his new team and to Coach Pat Riley, who established high expectations for the team and required that all members meet them. Pat Riley, as team leader, created a high-achieving organization through reasonable but high standards for work and performance. His leadership not only helped individuals develop their talents, but it brought the organization a new attitude and commitment to success that in turn elicited the best from the athletes.

Similar examples can be found in many settings. When leaders succeed, they generally create something different throughout their organization. Most of these differences show up in how individuals think and what they do, but others show up in the organization itself and in the way expectations are set and results produced. In essence, organizations have personalities, often established and modeled by their leaders.

Leaders can and should deliver organization results and help others develop the skills they need to make that happen. This chapter answers the questions: Do I have the right organization? and What can I do to ensure my organization has the capabilities required to achieve results? This chapter also clarifies the process of defining results as capabilities and proposes the essential capabilities that leaders should create in their organization, offering leaders specific suggestions they can use *now* to create more capable organizations.

Defining Organization Results

HUMAN CAPITAL VERSUS ORGANIZATIONAL CAPITAL

The leadership challenge of attaining organization results lies in ensuring that the whole is more than the sum of its parts. Individuals are parts. They bring their skills and commitment to an organization in the form of human capital. Without talented people committed to using their talents to benefit the organization, businesses will generally fail.

The leader's job, however, goes beyond building human capital to creating organizational capital. Organizational capital represents what the whole organization does beyond the talents of individual members. When a sports team playing well together can outperform an all-star team of better individual athletes, when a choir or orchestra as a whole sounds better than any individual soloist, when a work unit creates an innovative product or outperforms expectations, organizational capital exceeds human capital.

Consider this example. In the early 1990s, Eastman Kodak's black-and-white film business underwent a dramatic transformation. The group was losing money and draining company assets. The dated product line aroused little enthusiasm among group employees, and results were awful. At that point, a new leadership team, chaired by Stephen Frangos, came into the division with the intention of transforming the business. Rather than try to change the individual employees, many of whom had been with Kodak for decades, Frangos's new strategy was to create renewed enthusiasm and excitement for the work. Under the rubric Team Zebra, this leadership team worked to convert the operation from a losing to a winning enterprise. It involved employees in decisions, organized work as a team effort, shared information about (and learned from) successes and failures, focused on competencies and results, and celebrated achievements incessantly. In a three-year period, the operation turned around. Not only were profits up, but workers also felt the organization was a fundamentally different place to work. A new set of organizational capabilities had supplanted the old, and individuals with years of experience found themselves thinking and behaving differently.[1]

Leaders who get organization results ensure that the organization produces more than do the individual parts; that achievements outlive the energy and actions of any one individual; that organization accomplishment takes precedence over individual performance; that the organization operates with an internal culture, shared among all employees, about how to accomplish their work; and that an external identity or culture distinguishes the organization to its customers, potential customers, suppliers, and competitors.

Organization results clearly matter, and they function at many levels. They can be used to screen potential employees, as when recruiters warn job seekers that a firm's culture requires extensive travel or long hours or frequent transfers, thus dissuading some from taking the job. A church might advise potential new members that it requires active commitment and community service, discouraging those unwilling to contribute their time to church goals. Among established members of an organization, commitment to organization results helps maintain high levels of performance. Southwest Airlines, for example, which measures productivity by aircraft time in the air per employee revenue, has the highest productivity in the industry. A company culture focused on results and high performance lets employees know they are expected to work hard to maintain those performance standards, and to fit in, they regularly do.

Successful leaders shape organization results so that long-term success depends not on any one individual, but on the overall organization.

ORGANIZATION AS A STRUCTURE OR AS A SYSTEM

Leaders seeking organization results must answer this question: Do I have the right organization? Traditionally, leaders have found the answer by viewing their organization either as a structure or as a system.

Organization as structure has been encapsulated in the adage "Structure follows strategy." Leaders trying for the right organization would tinker with the structure in one of a number of ways. They might try shifting organizational structures using different dominant logics for organizing. At times this means focusing on business units (product lines or businesses), functions (for example, marketing, sales, engineering), locations (for example, country or regional structures), or a matrix (using for structure at least two of the above). Other times, structure changes might shift organizational decision making and control from a centralized (corporate) to a decentralized (by business unit, function, or location) format.

At still other times, leaders tinkering with structure undertake reengineering, downsizing, or consolidation. The implicit assumption behind these efforts is that the smaller or more efficient an organization, the more effective it will be.

Recently one company announced a major organizational shift involving a move from a geographic to a product-line organization. This global company, which had country managers responsible for all products sold within their territories, shifted to a structure giving business unit managers responsibility for representing the product worldwide. Within the company, the announcement of the structural change was met with cynicism. C. K. Prahalad characterizes such restructurings as the equivalent of someone swinging twelve birds in a cage around his or her head ten times. Each bird lands on a new perch, and the result is called a restructuring, but those in the organization experience basically the same view upon looking up and still seeing the same twelve birds in the cage. In the organization described above, employees wondered, "What's really new?" beyond the new titles and organization charts.

Work on organizational diagnosis yielded a new approach: organization as a system. In this approach, organizations were depicted as integrated systems, not just structures. Numerous systems models have arisen since the original insight, including 7-S,[2] "star",[3] and other models which aligned strategy to organization systems.[4] Leaders aligning strategy to organization systems assess their organization's strengths by the extent to which they align and integrate their systems.

Organization as a system routinely arouses cynicism. One company tried more than thirty new programs in the preceding decade, in a restlessness that indicated management's attempts to improve systems. Among employees, these initiatives became a joke: they often promised more than they delivered and were replaced by new programs before they could produce any results. Defining an organization by its systems or actions has the same drawbacks as trying to describe an employee only by his or her behavior at only one point in time. Photographs are more often staged than real representations of how people behave. Likewise, system assessments of organizations often fail to fully represent how organizations actually operate.

In recent years, an emerging and converging view of the nature of organizations has evolved. This view suggests that an organization cannot be equated with its structure, its systems, or its management practices. An organization can be accurately defined only by enumerating the capabilities it possesses and the management practices that create those capabilities. The leader who seeks organization results must create an organization imbued with capabilities to win.

ORGANIZATION AS CAPABILITIES

Regardless of the lens or discipline used to examine an organization (the possibilities include, for example, quality, HR, or strategy), the ultimate definition increasingly rests on its capabilities. Figure 4-1 summarizes the various elements, derived from a number of disciplines that have converged in this new approach to understanding organization.[5]

Leaders following this approach spend less time debating the relative merits of these contributing perspectives (for example, how *core competence* differs from *culture* differs from *high-performing work system*). Rather, they work to create competitive organizations by recognizing the similarities inherent in these views. Each of the six perspectives stresses that organizations constitute more than either structures or systems. Organizations' capabilities meet the following criteria:

FIGURE 4-1

A CONVERGING AND EMERGING THEORY OF ORGANIZATION

STRATEGY	ORGANIZATION THEORY	QUALITY	ORGANIZATION DEVELOPMENT/ CHANGE	HUMAN RESOURCES	CONSULTANTS
Core competence What are the core competencies necessary to accomplish our strategy?	Organization types What types of organizations exist (e.g., market, bureaucracy, clan, adhocracy)?	Processes What processes need to be managed to ensure customer quality (e.g., order to remittance, customer interface)?	Culture What culture do we need to accomplish our strategic goals?	High-performing work systems How do our HR practices coalesce to create high-performing work systems?	Disciplines, critical success factors What are the disciplines or critical success factors for us to succeed?

UNDERLYING MESSAGE:

ORGANIZATION AS A BUNDLE OF CAPABILITIES . . . ACROSS BOUNDARIES

- Capabilities must offer integration; capabilities mean not individual competence or management systems, but an organizationwide commitment.

- Capabilities add value to customers; capabilities derive from how those outside the firm define value.

- Capabilities maintain continuity; capabilities remain stable over time.

- Capabilities offer uniqueness; capabilities must be difficult for competitors to copy.

- Capabilities engage employees; capabilities create meaning for an organization's employees.

- Capabilities establish identity; capabilities delineate the organization's identity for customers, employees, and investors.

Successful organizations often become known by the capabilities they possess. Southwest Airlines, for example, has embraced the capabilities of productivity as its trademark, and workers keep aircraft in the air through a rapid turnaround at the gate. This is made possible by a positive work environment that encourages creativity and fun on the job. The Eastman Kodak black-and-white film group members established capabilities of innovation while exploring new uses for their products, and by collaborating as they worked in teams to get work done.

Capabilities serve as a key to the transition from formulating a mission, vision, or value to taking action. As shown in Figure 4-2, leaders often try to shift their strategy from a current state (cell 1) to a future state (cell 4) through strategic planning workshops, vision-creating exercises, and the drafting of mission statements. Unfortunately, many of these future strategic states fail to deliver anticipated results because of two common mistakes.

First, leaders who try to implement a new strategy with old capabilities (cell 2) or actions (cell 3) will have trouble achieving their future strategy goals (cell 4). When the Southern Company, a utility, invested heavily in China by purchasing CEPA, its leaders quickly learned that their Chinese investment required a management approach different from any of those they had used successfully in the southeast United States. The capabilities required to win in China were different from those in the United States. Success in Chinese markets depended on

FIGURE 4-2

STRATEGY/CAPABILITY/ORGANIZATION ASSESSMENT

	CURRENT	**FUTURE**
STRATEGY	1	4
ORGANIZATION CAPABILITY	2	5
MANAGEMENT ACTIONS	3	6

relationships of trust with key decision makers and adapting quickly to local markets, more than on reducing costs and gaining economics of scale that were critical to success in the domestic markets. As leaders at Southern recognized the required capabilities, they invested in new management actions (cell 6) to instill these capabilities in the company. Among the actions required were: partnering with local agencies to attract employees who knew the Chinese markets, training sessions to understand how to do business in China, and extensive communication to all Southern employees about the new organization capabilities required to succeed in China.

Second, leaders try to implement a new strategy (cell 4) by investing in the latest management fads and initiatives (cell 6). Research by Mark Huselid and Brian Becker has shown that disconnected management actions undermine the potential for organization performance. For example, when staffing decisions are made using one set of competencies, training using another, and compensation yet another, employees become more confused than focused, and organization results languish. Huselid and Becker recommend "bundling" management actions so that congruent and aligned decisions follow.[6] The bundles that integrate management actions represent the capabilities a firm needs to succeed. At Eastman Kodak, Steve Frangos in the black-and-white film division chose to focus on the capabilities of innovation and collaboration, and he initiated dozens of management actions that reinforced and sustained those capabilities.

Results-based leaders must meet the challenge and obligation of turning future strategies (cell 4) into future capabilities (cell 5) and then into future management actions (cell 6). They do so by answering the question "Do I have the right organization?" differently.

Traditionally, leaders focused on the organization as a hierarchy and tried to change the number of levels; currently, leaders focus on capabilities and try to instill those capabilities throughout the organization. Traditionally, leaders tried to build better organizations by changing boxes on organization charts or altering processes through reengineering; currently, leaders invest in activities that engender capability. Traditionally, leaders diagnosed organizations by examining how well systems aligned; currently, leaders diagnose organizations by the extent to which capabilities exist. Traditionally, leaders achieved organizational results if the firm had clear roles, understood rules, and efficient routines; currently, organizational results come from leveraging capabilities.

Today's leaders must meet the challenge of creating organizational results by identifying and leveraging critical capabilities.

Common Critical Capabilities

In work with Mike Lombardo and Bob Eichinger, we distilled the research and writing on capabilities and identified sixteen possible organization capabilities.[7] Further assessment and synthesis of these capabilities suggests that results-based leaders most often focus on four of the most common and critical capabilities: learning, speed, boundarylessness, and accountability.[8] Figure 4-3 illustrates how these relate to primary leadership functions (managing systems and change, generating ideas, maintaining stability) and Figure 4-4 summarizes them in terms of key questions and activities, measures, and so on.

Each critical capability is essentially simple in concept. *Learning* means the ability to innovate, generate new ideas, and leverage knowledge. *Speed* means the ability to act with agility and to have the capacity for change—moving quickly, reducing cycle time, being responsive, and acting flexibly. *Boundarylessness* means the ability to collaborate in teams and across organizational units and to act as a virtual organization. *Accountability* means the ability to have discipline, to reengineer work processes, and to create employee ownership—all for results.

By focusing on and creating these four capabilities, leaders answer the question, What can I do to ensure that my organization has the capabilities it requires to reach strategic goals? They, in fact, achieve organization results in the process.

LEARNING

Learning is the ability of an organization to generate and generalize ideas with impact.[9] Organizations differentiate learning by generating new ideas in the form of innovation. Learning also means that ideas originating in one part of the organization are codified and shared throughout the other parts, thus avoiding repetition of mistakes and guaranteeing replication of successes.

Coca-Cola, for example, is becoming a learning organization. Coke has hired talented individuals for each geography and product line who have the responsibility to synthesize keys to winning and to share this information throughout the organization. Knowledge transfer

FIGURE 4-3

COMMON CRITICAL CAPABILITIES

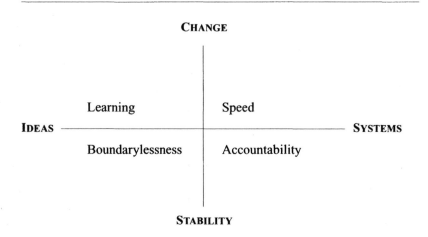

FIGURE 4-4

SUMMARY OF FOUR COMMON CRITICAL CAPABILITIES

CAPABILITY LABEL	LEARNING	SPEED	BOUNDARYLESSNESS	ACCOUNTABILITY
RELATED TERMS	Knowledge, ideas innovation	Change Agility Cycle time	Teams Collaboration Virtual coordination	Reengineering Continuous improvement Quality
KEY LEADERSHIP QUESTION	How critical is it for my unit to learn and share knowledge?	How critical is it for my unit to move quickly, change, and adapt?	How critical is it for my unit to work in teams, across boundaries, and collaboratively?	How critical is it for my unit to have clear processes and accountabilities for getting work done?
MEASURES	Vitality index Learning index	Capacity for change index	Boundarylessness index	Accountability index
KEY ACTIVITIES TO CREATE	Generate ideas Generalize ideas	Turn what we know into what we do	Team assessment/ boundarylessness assessment	Responsibility grid
EXAMPLE COMPANIES	Coca–Cola Lucent Technologies Motorola	3Com Quantum	Champion General Electric	Medtronic

takes place through technology, forums, best-practice studies, and workshops, helping Coke leaders leverage their global position. Coke leaders believe that by being better than their competitors at moving good ideas from one region of the world to another, they will gain market share.

Learning at Lucent Technologies focuses on innovation. Lucent Technologies separated from AT&T and positioned itself as the technology leader in the telecommunications products and services field. Lucent leaders in this rapidly changing market recognized that only continuing innovation would enable them to compete effectively. They began pilot projects, invested in new ideas, and formed relationships with university and other research facilities that incubate future technologies.

Organizational learning may be measured as either an end or a means. The vitality index used at 3M measures the percentage of revenue from products that it created in the preceding five years. This innovative ends measure tracks learning output and indicates the extent to which 3M leaders have created a learning culture. Measuring learning *means* requires focusing on the leadership behaviors and organization practices that encourage learning. The learning index shown in Figure 4-5 and tested in more than one hundred companies provides a useful assessment of an organization's learning capability.[10]

Leaders who want to create an organization result around learning need to encourage constant experimentation. They must look outside their organization continually for new ideas. They must dare to hire individuals who think differently from the organization's norm. They must ensure the quality of thinking and ideas. They must encourage the sharing of knowledge from site to site in the organization. They must work to reduce fear of failure. They must facilitate dialogue on ideas. And, finally, they must create rewards for sharing knowledge.[11]

SPEED

Most organizations face an unpredictable, uncontrollable, and unforeseeable business environment. Rather than spend enormous amounts of resources creating strategies that may or not succeed under such uncertainty, leaders obtain organizational results by moving with speed. Organizations with speed demonstrate a capacity for change, agility, flexibility, and reduced cycle time. The future looms uncertain for all— both losers and winners. While those destined to lose form task forces to study change, winners will have already adapted. Organizations display varying degrees of speed. Some once-agile organizations have grown rigid, inflexible, and unable to change; others, perhaps equally venerable, maintain their flexibility.

The computer industry represents an especially rapidly changing, dynamic industry. The field is littered with companies whose good products became single events, where rapidly changing conditions undermined promising new products. At Sun Microsystems, Scott McNealy, the chairman, CEO, and president, claims that 85 to 90 percent of what the company ships in a given year was created within the preceding twelve months. McNealy believes that many computer firms will not survive the ongoing industry shakeout because they will fail to adapt quickly enough to rapidly changing technology. Strategies in his world constitute visions and images of the future, not elaborate mathematical projections that become outdated by the time they are refined. Similarly, Bill Gates, founder and CEO of Microsoft, often expresses the fear that at his company, complacency and arrogance will replace commitment and action. Speed keeps organizations alive and fresh.

The leadership team at 3Com, a firm in computer connections, places a premium on speed and constantly thinks of ways to change and govern work differently. Even when these efforts lead to success, however, the process of undoing and restructuring the organization gets management attention. Deborah Engel, former chief human resource officer at 3Com, had the task of continually recommending ways to reorganize that would help 3Com move quickly into new markets. They strove to increase speed by constantly scanning their environment and seeking new opportunities, planning for a future that would differ from the past, and maintaining a relentless discomfort with the status quo.

Quantum, a disk drive manufacturer headquartered in San Jose, California, finds speed critical to its competitive position. The cycle time for new disk drives coming to market can now be measured in months. New products arriving late to market not only lose market share, but can be fatal to the business. To act with speed, Quantum leaders share knowledge with all employees about the importance of moving quickly. They have established research, engineering, and manufacturing centers around the world, connecting them through technology, and they have created many teams throughout the organization where decisions can be made and implemented quickly.

As with learning, speed can be measured and assessed as an end or a means. Speed's end result shows up in reduced cycle time for products and services. Quantum, for example, tracks the time required to bring

FIGURE 4-5

A LEARNING INDEX

ABILITY TO GENERATE NEW IDEAS		ABILITY TO GENERALIZE IDEAS WITH IMPACT	
SPECIFIC STRATEGY	SCORE (0–10)	SPECIFIC STRATEGY	SCORE (0–10)
Competence acquisition: To what extent do we demonstrate public commitment to learning by constantly seeking new ways of working and by having learning as a part of our business strategy?		**Culture:** To what extent is our culture focused on learning?	
Boundary spanner: To what extent do we learn by going outside our boundaries to learn what other companies do?		**Competence:** To what extent do we have individual, team, and organizational competencies for learning?	
Continuous improvement: To what extent do we learn by constantly improving on what has been done before; that is, by mastering each step in a process before moving on to new steps?		**Consequence:** To what extent does our performance management system encourage learning for individuals and teams?	

ABILITY TO GENERATE NEW IDEAS		ABILITY TO GENERALIZE IDEAS WITH IMPACT	
SPECIFIC STRATEGY	SCORE (0–10)	**SPECIFIC STRATEGY**	SCORE (0–10)
Experimenter: To what extent do we learn by trying new ideas and by being willing to experiment with new ideas?		**Governance:** To what extent do our organization structure and communication processes encourage learning?	
		Capacity for change/work systems: To what extent do our work processes and systems encourage learning?	
		Leadership: To what extent do leaders throughout the organization demonstrate a commitment to learning?	
Total generate: *(sum the above and divide by 4)*		**Total generalize:** *(sum the above and divide by 6)*	

Total learning score *(generate × generalize):* _____ × _____ =

new products to market, an *ends* approach. *Means,* too, may be calculated, using an index like that in Figure 4-6 (used in such firms as General Electric and Sears[12]), which helps assess the extent to which an organization's practices make things happen faster.

Results-based leaders create organizations that act with speed. These leaders manage by looking to the future; expressing discomfort with the status quo; acting without complete knowledge; sensing customers' future expectations; communicating directly with employees; and using their personal credibility to make change happen.[13]

BOUNDARYLESSNESS

Growing organizations often create categories differentiating individuals, teams, and units. Hierarchical levels (for example, executive versus employee), functional specialties (for example, marketing versus manufacturing), businesses (product line 1 versus 2), geographical location (Asian versus European operations), and scope (corporate versus field) exemplify common boundaries that exist in organizations. A leadership imperative to remove boundaries means paying less attention to the category in which an individual works and correspondingly increased attention to the competencies the individual possesses. In boundaryless organizations, talented individuals provide needed expertise—regardless of hierarchy, function, business, or position. Teamwork, relationships, and horizontal organizations have created a new standard for how to get work done.

General Electric, for example, works systematically to reduce boundaries of all types throughout the organization. Leaders at GE encourage what they call "town hall meetings," at which employees share ideas with managers, who then respond on the spot. GE leaders also use cross-functional teams to serve similar customers, and they involve customers and suppliers in their training programs. The corporation moves talent globally to ensure global thinking, and it spreads information, authority, competence, and rewards throughout every group and location.[14]

Figure 4-7 provides an index for measuring boundarylessness. This index suggests management practices and actions for improving an organization's ability to achieve boundarylessness. As illustrated, four boundaries—vertical, horizontal, external, and global—can be traversed through the simple expedients of sharing information, emphasizing competence, disseminating authority, and reapportioning rewards. Using this index, you can pinpoint ways to increase boundaryless behavior throughout your organization.

Results-based leaders who create boundaryless organizations ensure the widespread sharing of information, the enhancement of individuals' skills through training and development, the delegation and sharing of authority, and clear rewards to encourage sharing across all boundaries. Such leaders encourage collaboration over competition; sharing over hoarding; lifelong skill building over single-event training; flexibility over territoriality; and relationships built on trust, not roles.

ACCOUNTABILITY

Organizations may learn, change, and remove boundaries, but if they lack accountability and discipline, success will elude them over time. Accountability comes from discipline, processes, and ownership. Discipline requires getting work done with rigor and consistency, meeting scheduled commitments, and following through on plans and programs to deliver promises. Process accountability may require reengineering how work gets done, reducing redundant efforts, and driving down costs at every level. With accountability comes ownership, as individuals feel responsible for accomplishing work. Leaders who foster accountability continuously improve how work gets done, deliver high-quality products and services, and ensure commitment from all employees.

Accountability as an organizational capability does not imply a hierarchical organization structure. Firms with flat structures may have high accountability, if and when employees share a commitment to goals and processes to achieve goals. Leaders may build accountability as a capability through many means.

Sears leaders, for example, worked hard to build accountability among all employees. After discovering the high positive correlation between front-line employees' commitment and customers' commitment, Sears executives focused on improving employees' sense of personal accountability for customer service. Sears began a series of development experiences for its 230,000 store employees. These efforts included town hall meetings at which employees could share concerns and solve problems alongside their immediate supervisors and extensive training sessions using learning maps, where employees began to understand such

FIGURE 4-6

A Capacity for Change Index

Key Success Factors for Change	Questions to Assess and Accomplish the Key Success Factors for Change	Score (1 = low, 10 = high)
Leading Change *Who is responsible?*	Do we have a leader • who owns and champions the change? • who makes a public commitment to making change happen? • who will garner resources to sustain change? • who will put in personal time and attention to following change through?	
Creating a Shared Need *Why do it?*	Do employees • see the reason for the change? • understand why the change is important? • see how the change will help them and/or the business in the short and long term?	
Shaping a Vision *What will it look like when we are done?*	Do employees • see the outcomes of the change in behavioral terms (what they will do differently as a result of the change)? • get excited about the results of accomplishing the change? • understand how the change will benefit customers and other stakeholders?	

MOBILIZING COMMITMENT *Who else needs to be involved?*	**Do the sponsors of the change** • recognize who else needs to be committed to the change to make it happen? • know how to build a coalition of support for the change? • have the ability to enlist support of key individuals in the organization? • have the ability to build a responsibility matrix to make the change happen?
MODIFYING SYSTEMS AND STRUCTURES *How will it be institutionalized?*	**Do the sponsors of the change** • understand how to link the change to HR systems; for example, staffing, training, appraisal, rewards, structure, communication, and so on? • recognize the systems implications of change?
MONITORING PROGRESS *How will it be measured?*	**Do the sponsors of the change** • have a means of measuring the success of the change? • plan to benchmark progress on both the results of the change and the process of implementing it?
MAKING IT LAST *How will it get started and last?*	**Do the sponsors of the change** • recognize the first steps in getting started? • have a short- and long-term plan to keep attention focused on the change? • have a plan for adapting the change as necessary over time?

These processes were developed in 1992, during work at General Electric by a design team that included Steve Kerr, Dave Ulrich, Craig Schneier, Jon Biel, Ron Gager, and Mary Anne Devanna (GE outsiders) and Jacquie Vierling, Cathy Friarson, and Amy Howard (GE employees).

FIGURE 4-7

MEASURING THE BOUNDARYLESSNESS OF ORGANIZATIONS

HOW BOUNDARYLESS IS YOUR COMPANY?
Score each cell 1 to 5

	INFORMATION	COMPETENCE	AUTHORITY	REWARDS
VERTICAL BOUNDARY	Information is shared from top to bottom. Employees at all levels know what is happening in the organization and why.	Employees at each level have the talent and skills they need to do their jobs.	Decision making is pushed down to the lowest possible level at which competent decisions can be made.	Rewards (financial and nonfinancial) are shared widely throughout the organization.
HORIZONTAL BOUNDARY	Information is shared across all organization units.	Talent moves from one unit to another in the organization, as needed.	Cross-functional decisions are made through teams, horizontal organizations.	Rewards encourage cross-functional work and collaboration.

	INFORMATION	COMPETENCE	AUTHORITY	REWARDS
EXTERNAL BOUNDARY	Information moves across the value chain (including suppliers and customers). ___	Talent inside the organization meets the requirements of the value chain. ___	Decision making includes members of the value chain. ___	Rewards focus on meeting the goals set by those in the value chain. ___
GLOBAL BOUNDARY	Information moves around the world. ___	The organization's talent can compete globally. ___	Decision making takes account of any impact on the global organization. ___	Rewards encourage global thinking and action. ___
				Total score: ___

Source: Ron Ashkenas, Dave Ulrich, Todd Jick, and Steve Kerr, *The Boundaryless Organization: Breaking the Chains of Organizational Structure* (San Francisco: Jossey-Bass, 1995), 28–29. Reprinted by permission.

issues as the economics of the business, customer buying patterns, and competitive trends. The company trained store managers to improve their ability to coach and encourage employees and initiated a total performance index for all managers which held them accountable for meeting financial, customer, and employee results. The culmination of the initiatives instilled accountability throughout all Sears employees.

The accountability index in Figure 4-8 lists ways in which employees experience discipline, ownership, and responsibility, the cumulative effect of which is to ensure accountability. When employees achieve accountability, the organization benefits from the resulting high percentage of on-time projects, completions, productivity, and quality delivered to customers.

FIGURE 4-8

ACCOUNTABILITY INDEX

ACCOUNTABILITY ITEMS To what extent do my employees do the following?	SCORE (1 = low, 10 = often)
1. Follow disciplined processes in getting work done.	
2. Feel ownership for the goals of the organization.	
3. Work to remove bureaucracy.	
4. Drive out costs at every level.	
5. Eliminate redundancies.	
6. Meet commitments.	
7. Commit to quality in all work activities.	
8. Accept responsibility for getting the work done.	
9. Receive rewards tied to meeting goals on time and within budget.	
10. Experience clear expectations for who has to do what to get work done.	
Total score:	

Leaders who build accountability first make sure that employees know what is expected of them and then follow up to ensure that employees perform according to those expectations. As a result, they create ownership among all employees who commit to a disciplined, continuously improving, and responsible organization.

So far, this chapter has covered how results-based leaders can create capable and competitive organizations. To do so, leaders must shift their thinking about organizations away from structure, forms, rules, and roles and move more toward a focus on capability. To sustain the winning organization of the future will require leaders who possess and master *learning, change, boundarylessness,* and *accountability.* Are these four the only empirically defined capabilities of the competitive organizations of the future? Not necessarily. However, these are the capabilities that will enhance opportunities for and the likelihood of success.

Leaders Who Attain Organization Results

Results-based organization leaders striving to make these four capabilities a priority might consider using the four-step process outlined below.

STEP 1: Align capabilities. To create organizational results, leaders must ensure that their organizations have the capabilities required for success. The four critical capabilities explored above—learning, speed, boundarylessness, and accountability—have proven to be fundamental for this process. Figure 4-9 illustrates one method for determining whether an organization has an appropriate mix of these capabilities. To use the figure, divide 100 points across the four capabilities, according to the organization's strategy. Our rule of thumb is that no one capability should receive more than 60 or less than 10 points. These scores can then be plotted on Figure 4-3 to create a profile of the capabilities your organization requires.

Scores will vary according to an organization's business strategy. A firm in a rapidly changing industry requires flexibility and change to compete, for example, and its score might reflect that by allotting more points to speed and learning than to accountability; other firms in cost-driven industries might focus more attention on accountability. None of the four capabilities is inherently more important than

FIGURE 4-9

ASSESSING THE FOUR COMMON CRITICAL CAPABILITIES

GIVEN MY ORGANIZATION'S STRATEGY, HOW CRITICAL IS EACH OF THE FOLLOWING FOUR ORGANIZATION CAPABILITIES?	SCORE (none more than 60 or less than 10)
Learning: The ability to innovate, generate new ideas, leverage knowledge.	
Speed: The ability to act with agility, have the capacity for change, move quickly, reduce cycle time, be responsive, act flexibly.	
Boundarylessness: The ability to collaborate in teams, across organization units, and act as a virtual organization.	
Accountability: The ability to have discipline, reengineer work processes, and create employee ownership for results.	
Total:	100

any of the others; their deployment in a given organization depends on the strategy of the business. The points and their distribution represent management attention in both time and resources allotted to each of the four capabilities, thus demonstrating the alignment of organization capabilities with organization strategy.

STEP 2: Improve capabilities. This chapter has offered a number of approaches leaders can use to improve the capabilities their organization requires. As leaders invest in actions that improve their organization's ability to learn, to move with speed, to be boundaryless, and to ensure accountability, they create competitive organizations.

STEP 3: Measure capabilities. The indices provided in Figures 4-5, 4-6, 4-7, and 4-8 offer results-based leaders the mechanisms they need to track each of the four critical capabilities. As they employ and monitor these indices, the results-based leader will gain the same information and control over the status of organizational capabilities that they now depend on to track financial and other corporate measures and results.

STEP 4: Take action. Ultimately, the results-based leader who creates a winning organization thinks differently about the fundamental nature of organization. Organization becomes less a matter of structure and systems and more a matter of capabilities. Such thinking shifts the dialogue about organization away from roles, rules, and responsibilities, and toward the capabilities needed to win. Figuring out which of the four capabilities matters most begins a process that aligns capabilities with strategies and integrates management actions with capabilities.

With capability as the architecture for organization, results-based leaders can devote their resources to creating and enhancing capabilities. Such leaders concern themselves not only with employee, customer, and investor results, but with shaping their organizations to achieve results over time. Their legacy to the organization is leaving greater capability than existed before their coming.

Customer Results: Building Firm Equity

BOTH TYPES OF RESULTS discussed thus far improve overall performance. Employee results improve performance by leveraging human capital (Chapter 3) and organization results increase performance by building organizational capability (Chapter 4). Both types of results focus on stakeholders *inside* a firm. The subject of this chapter—customer results—shifts the focus *outside* the firm. No matter how much human capital and organizational capability a leader creates, if a firm's customers don't appreciate or value what the firm offers, customer results will fall short.

Leaders with a customer emphasis create *firm equity,* a concept woven together from two strands of thinking. Marketing, the first source, has shown unequivocally that products with strong brand identity (for example, Coke, Kodak, McDonald's, and Nike) not only sell more, but receive a price premium. A liter of Evian bottled water, for example, would likely sell for as much as 25 to 30 percent more than a liter of an unknown or generic spring water.[1] This research has been applied in airports where the food providers shifted from unknown to well-known brands (for example, McDonald's, Taco Bell, Chili's, Burger King, and Pizza Hut), with a subsequent increase in food purchases. Product brands have a remarkable impact on how customers respond to a firm's products.[2]

The second strand of thinking on firm equity comes from studies examining a firm's culture.[3] A corporate culture generally represents the norms, assumptions, values, and artifacts within a firm. Cultural statements become operationalized when executives articulate and publish the values of their firm, which provide patterns for how employees should behave. Firms with strong cultures achieve higher results because employees sustain focus both on what to do and how to do it.[4]

The concept of firm equity combines ideas from product brand equity and corporate culture. Equity represents the value of an asset as determined by the potential buyer of that asset.[5] For example, home equity represents the market value of a home (what a current buyer would pay for it) as compared to the original purchase price. In firms, customers may value a firm's product brand, giving that brand its equity or value, but they may also value doing business with the firm, not merely for the sake of a particular product, but out of an allegiance born of service, trust, and a number of other factors. This allegiance constitutes what we call "firm equity." In other words, *brand* equity focuses on products; *firm* equity focuses on the firm. Firm culture, too, then shifts in definition from a focus on the *values* of the firm to more of a focus on the *identity* of the firm in the minds of its customers. Firm equity results from successfully executing a business strategy that integrates product brands into the cohesive whole known as culture.

The retailer Nordstrom, for example, has been justly lauded as a firm with a strong culture. Generally, this has come to mean that Nordstrom employees feel a strong commitment to a shared set of values, norms, and assumptions, which yields benefits to the company in the form of high employee commitment and unity, as well as reduced governance costs (their employee-to-supervisor ratio is unusually high). As a result, Nordstrom enjoys the highest revenue per square foot in the industry. Nordstrom reinforces its culture through such management practices as hiring only certain types of employees and offering high commission rates. This is where most discussions about Nordstrom's culture end.

However, the story goes deeper. Although employee unity has been an important element in the company's culture, so, too, have been its high levels of firm equity. Nordstrom's firm equity comes from customers' thinking of Nordstrom as a whole, not as a source of any specific product. Ask someone wearing apparel bought at Nordstrom to name the brand of the skirt, blouse, slacks, or shoes they are wearing, and more often than not, they will not know—or care—about the clothing brand. They *will* know and care about Nordstrom's identity as a firm. To these devoted customers, Nordstrom stands for service and quality. This identity, when shared broadly among customers, constitutes firm equity.

The current leadership approach at Kellogg, led by new president Carlos Gutierrez, emphasizes firm equity as well. Kellogg's brand equity includes such ready-to-eat cereal products as Corn Flakes and Rice Krispies, as well as convenience foods such as Pop Tarts and Eggo Waffles. The company has historically managed these and other similar products as separate brands. Leaders at Kellogg now pursue a more integrated approach in the way that they think about how all these products work together. If new Kellogg products and existing products can be successfully integrated to form a single, coherent identity of value to consumers, Kellogg will have achieved a firm equity that can take its customer results to new levels.

Customer results follow from high firm equity. Leaders must meet the challenge of understanding and influencing their customers to create firm equity. When leaders achieve firm equity, customers are not only satisfied, but committed,[6] customer intimacy increases,[7] and unity occurs between the employees and customers.[8]

The firm equity concept has implications for leaders who must balance internal employee and organizational requirements with external customer expectations. Consider this example. About a year previously, Chuey Castaneda, vice president for a global automotive parts supplier, weathered with his company yet another round of business process reengineering initiatives that they hoped would finally put them in a more profitable position. Just as it seemed the company had finally stabilized, Castaneda received a call from one of his top customers complaining about the effects of the cost-cutting measures.

As part of its benchmarking efforts, Castaneda's company had determined that its deliveries were faster than those of its competitors, but that this speed raised costs. The reengineering team decided to ship fewer times each month, resulting in a delivery schedule equal to that of their competitors. Unfortunately, the top customer now complained to Castaneda that there was no difference between his company and his competitors. If things didn't change back to the way they were before the cost cutting, this customer warned that his company would start considering other suppliers. As Castaneda pondered the situation, he began to think he faced a no-win situation. Either his company failed to make a profit, or it started losing customers.

Castaneda's dilemma is not uncommon. In the search for greater efficiency, his company cut both fat and muscle, leaving customers with an overall perception of the firm as mediocre. The escape from this trap requires a clear understanding of firm equity. When reengineering efforts or any other change in management initiatives inside a firm help create positive images among customers outside the firm, an increase in firm equity results. Castaneda's company, in the process of cutting costs, should have been sensitive to its equity, identity, or image held by its key customers. Had this firm realized that alteration of its delivery policies would undermine the firm identity and erode customer commitment, the cost cutting might have been managed very differently. To correct the problem and to forestall similar problems in the future, company leaders must pursue change initiatives consistent with building and maintaining a firm brand; this effort will, in turn, give rise to a culture that will reinforce future actions to also be consistent with preserving firm brand identity. This mutually reinforcing loop builds firm equity.

This chapter explores ways to create customer results through firm equity, demonstrating how to maintain a distinctive relationship with customers while remaining profitable. To achieve this customer equity, leaders must replace three common myths about customers with three new realities.

Myth 1: The Customer Is Always Right

RECOGNIZE THE "NOT" CUSTOMERS

Adhering to the myth "The customer is always right," that anything and everything should be done to keep any and all customers happy, paradoxically undermines customer results. In fact, not all customers are right all the time. Some customers can be dead wrong. If leaders listen to the wrong voices, they risk not getting desired results. Leaders need to know how *not* to pay attention to the "not" customers.

One revealing cautionary tale involves Harley-Davidson, which several years ago began making and selling dirt bikes, the motorcycles used for racing and jumping in mud and desert conditions. Dirt bikers dress tough, in helmets, chest protectors, padded pants, and high boots. At first, it made perfect sense for Harley to sell dirt bikes. After all, a motorcycle is a motorcycle, isn't it? No. Today's Harley has a strong, distinctive image for its customers. A Harley is a big bike with a certain look and feel and sound. To drive a Harley means to dress up in leather and a bandanna and head out on a long, curving highway. A Harley keeps low to the ground and has a deep rumbling sound: When a Harley "Fat Boy" idles, it sounds throaty, growling, ominous. A Harley is a "grown-up's" bike.

A Harley does not sound at all like a dirt bike from Honda, Suzuki, or Yamaha. A 250 cc, two-stroke Honda buzzes at a high pitch like a swarm of bees. A dirt bike is a "kid's" bike. You bounce on a dirt bike; you cruise on a Harley. For these and other less meaningful reasons, Harley got out of the dirt bike business. It had been profitable, but it had sent a confusing message to Harley's "real" customers. However fine the Harley dirt bikes, however many customers bought and would continue to buy them, Harley could retain its distinctive image with its primary customer base only by pulling back to what it does best.

Anyone who does not fit the profile of a company's primary or target customer is a "not" customer. For Harley, both dirt bike buyers and highway bike buyers are potentially primary customers. However, by focusing on one customer group, rather than both, Harley achieved distinctiveness. "Not" customers seduce leaders into mediocrity. They appear ready to buy products, but they're not "lifetime" customers. When a company consistently provides a clear image and delivers reliably on that image and promise year after year, it can develop a following of lifetime customers.

To achieve great customer results, therefore, companies must define their target lifetime customers and then work very hard to deliver the outstanding products and services those customers expect and require. Some customers more than others thus generate firm equity. Harley wants and works to create firm equity among its targeted customers, those who want to experience the Harley lifestyle.

Current viewpoints on customer focus most often suggest spreading risk across a broad spectrum of potential customers to allow a business to survive economic vagaries. Not so. Every organization can, at least in theory, serve customers, but for an organization to build potential firm equity, it must serve some customers better than they can be served by competitors. The idea that a customer is anyone who will pay money for a product or service leads to poor business decisions.

DON'T CHASE TWO RABBITS

A second threat inherent in the myth "The customer is always right" can be encapsulated by the old Chinese proverb "When you chase two rabbits, you catch neither." The same adage applies to business. A company can't chase two rabbits and succeed with both of them. The now-defunct airline People Express provides an apt example. Started by Donald Burr as a regional airline providing inexpensive flights between major East Coast cities, People Express originally had a clearly defined customer set: East Coast travelers willing to give up the perks offered by conventional airlines in exchange for much lower fares. People Express originally targeted Greyhound buses as its primary competition—not other airlines—because it aimed to provide buslike, low-cost, no-frills service.

The People Express concept of a low-cost airline was an unprecedented success, but that success also fueled the company's demise. Instead of sticking to its established customers, People Express started wondering about all of the travelers choosing other airlines, especially business travelers with bigger budgets. So People Express began chasing these other customers, offering costly frills such as real lunches and dinners, first-class seating, and so on. Obviously, People Express could not offer these extras at its former low prices, so it raised them. Its prices, although still lower than those of its competitors, were nonetheless higher than before, and as its customer base grew, its costs grew, and its prices continued to rise. Before long it was competing directly with United, American, and Delta. Unfortunately for People Express, because it had an image as a low-priced regional airline, if it cost about the same to fly People or United, most people chose United. People Express soon declared bankruptcy.

The story of Southwest Airlines has a different ending.[9] Southwest steadfastly maintained its interest in the same customer base as People Express, but in a different part of the country. Southwest sees its main competitor as, not another airline, but car travel. Southwest has evolved a system for delivering cost-efficient, no-frills travel, and it remains one of the most successful airlines in the world.

Trying to be all things to all customers prevents leaders from creating firm equity. More attention paid to targeted customers, on the other hand, builds firm equity in the right customers.

Reality 1: Some Customers Are More Right Than Others

Leaders face the challenge of picking the right customers in whom to build firm equity. Firm equity in the wrong customers does not create customer results. Picking the right customers is akin to a home buyer's picking the right home to buy, with the hope of increasing home equity. Not all home equities rise equally; house architecture, neighborhoods, school districts, community reputations, taxes, access to shopping, and layout of the rooms in the house all have an impact on which house will increase in equity. Leaders need similar criteria for determining those customers who will prove more right than others, who will create more firm equity than others, and who will commit to the company for the long haul. Divining this customer and beginning to build stable firm equity takes place in two stages: segmentation and customization.

CUSTOMER SEGMENTATION

Customer segmentation involves defining the customers of most value to a firm. Leaders must begin by segmenting their customers if they want to learn why different groups buy their products and to capitalize on that knowledge. Harley chose the "macho" customers over the dirt bikers. Southwest chose bargain hunters over the comfort conscious. Leaders often must pick among a large array of customers those few who will respond to company targeting by ensuring the lasting loyalty that leads to customer results.

To identify a customer segment, a firm clusters customer needs and its offered benefits into categories. The firm then chooses which groups of customers it will serve. Various segmentation categories exist; the following are among the most useful:

- **PRICE.** Like Southwest Airlines, a firm may use price to bring a set of customers into focus.

- **IMAGE.** Like Harley-Davidson, a firm may use image to create an identity with a set of customers. Firm equity of this type often leads customers to buy multiple products congruent with the firm's equity image. Harley's clothing and restaurant businesses, for example, leverage its overall firm equity.

- **GEOGRAPHY.** Wal-Mart began with a focus on serving customers in rural areas, opening stores where there were no other large competing retailers. As the company expanded, it maintained its geographic focus by opening many stores in one city rather than by opening one store in many geographic areas. The approach gave Wal-Mart a geographic segmentation.

- **TASTE.** Coca-Cola has learned that customers develop very strong loyalties to the taste of a product; hence its range of offerings, including regular Coke, Diet Coke, caffeine-free Coke, and Cherry Coke. Coke now has sixteen taste segments, each of which represents a group of customers passionate about a particular product's taste.

- **TECHNOLOGY.** Dell Computer has learned that many buyers prefer ordering through the Internet. It has created easy-to-use order forms for those who buy directly from Dell. Other computer firms, like Compaq, rely more on in-store distribution and catalog sales.

- **CHANNEL.** Across product lines, some customers buy in person, others through distributors or third parties, and others through technology.[10] Many companies concentrate in one or another, the better to build strength of service to their chosen market segment.

One electronics firm examining its customer base using segmentation made the remarkable (to them) finding that 20 percent of its customers produced 80 percent of its revenue. In planning to achieve their goal of 25 percent growth per year for the next four years, the firm's leaders realized that, by targeting just ten customers and gaining share from each of them, they could reach their goal faster than if they tried to serve all customers. Figure 5-1 shows the segmentation they used to target their customers. On one axis, they showed the overall size of the customer by revenue, and on the other axis, the current amount purchased from their firm.[11] This segmentation exercise helped the firm identify those customers they should retain (keep at any cost), attain (focus on, go after), contain (keep, but not at any cost), and abstain (not

FIGURE 5-1

CUSTOMER SEGMENTATION MATRIX

OVERALL REVENUE IN MARKET AREA

	HIGH (purchases a lot in market/product area)	LOW (purchases relatively little in market/product area)
HIGH (purchases a lot from the target company)	**1 Retain** Work to keep these customers at any cost.	**3 Contain** Keep the customers, but not at any cost.
LOW (purchases little from the target company)	**2 Attain** Focus, go after, attack, and get these customers.	**4 Abstain** Don't put much energy into these customers.

PURCHASES FROM TARGET COMPANY

work hard to keep). After targeting the customers who were most critical to attaining its growth rate, the firm then justifiably invested time and energy to know and serve those customers, even at the risk of losing others.

Segmentation helps leaders identify which customer groups to protect, which to pursue aggressively, and which to leave behind.

CUSTOMIZATION

Customization goes beyond segmentation.[12] Segmentation identifies groups of customers of value to a firm; customization brings the firm's attention to bear on each individual customer of value. Segmentation and customization may be used together to separate the right from the "not" customers.

Levi Strauss, for example, designed their Dockers line for a specific customer segment: middle-aged, relatively affluent men who wanted pants more dressy than blue jeans, but not as dressy as formal slacks, and which would not sacrifice comfort. This segment strategy was a hit, and Dockers has become a successful product. Now Levi's has moved toward customization. Using technology to measure customers for an exact fit, it transfers the data electronically to a manufacturing plant anywhere in the world, makes the custom-size pants, and ships them directly to the individual customer. Segmentation led to a new product line; customization focuses on the individual drawn to the product line.

Many companies have the ability to customize products or services. Customers can pick a unique paint color or decorative design and have this applied at the factory prior to delivery. Airlines customize services to suit their best customers through frequent-flier programs, which allow them to build a customer profile and supply the customers with preferred seats, special meals, and so on.

Using such data, many firms are beginning to build mass customized relationships with their targeted customers. Sears, for example, through its credit card database, has quantities of information on customer purchases. Sears can search this information for patterns that can help it anticipate customer needs. If a customer buys a crib, blue baby clothes, and newborn-size diapers, Sears can conclude that this customer had or will have a child within a month. The growing child becomes the focus of planning and marketing for the next eighteen years. When the child begins school, he will need school clothes and supplies; he will want certain types of toys. He will accumulate sporting goods and, later, automobile supplies. Sears can transform its warehoused data into customized information that will help it mass-customize to better meet patrons' needs.

Leaders who achieve customer results realize that not all customers are equal. Some are more right than others. Using segmentation and customization, leaders can both identify the customers central to their success and target those customers for the special attention through which leaders create firm equity.

Had Castaneda's automotive parts supplier firm done segmentation-customization analysis, it would have recognized that, even though facing necessary reengineering, it could not afford to lose a top customer. Although reengineering helped cut costs, it undermined customer value, and top customers should have been consulted during the process to prevent that from happening. Only the key customer was in a position to point out early on in the reengineering effort that it would hurt, not help, firm equity.

Leaders should constantly assess the extent to which they build firm equity in the right customers. The right customers may easily be determined by plotting current and potential customers against the segmentation matrix in Figure 5-1. The leader learns a great deal from the exercise, but two cells are of particular significance. Cell 4 shows where a firm expends too much attention on customers whose overall business and business with the firm does not justify it. Cell 2 allows leaders to identify, by name, the key or target customers whose business with the company promises potential increases. Firm equity with these customers must be increased.

Myth 2: Delight All Customers

Another difficult-to-absorb lesson of the business world is that a company gets into trouble by trying to "delight" all of its customers. In fairness, this myth hinges on how leaders define "delight." But leaders who define it to mean that all customers want to be pampered, coddled, and so on are walking on dangerous ground. Leaders need to understand exactly what "delighted" means to targeted customers. Clark Equipment Company, for example, once had a reputation for building the "Cadillac" of forklifts. During the 1960s and 1970s, Clark enjoyed dominant market share in the forklift industry. By about 1977, however, a Japanese company entered the market on a global scale, producing not another Cadillac forklift, but the Honda Civic version of the forklift— reliable, without frills, and inexpensive.

Unfortunately for Clark, its customers preferred the no-frills, less expensive forklift. They tried to convey that preference to Clark Equipment leaders and promised to "buy American" if Clark would build an inexpensive forklift competitive with the Japanese product, but Clark leaders during this crucial period of time refused to believe the feedback. They wanted to continue to "delight" customers with better and better—and more and more expensive—forklifts. Slowly but surely they nearly went out of business.

Leaders often undertake such misguided initiatives, intending to "delight" their customers but in fact wasting money and missing the mark on customer needs and concerns. In another example, an international maker of commodity paper began offering a money-back guarantee: customers dissatisfied with their paper could return it and receive a full refund. When it made the guarantee, the company was selling all the paper it could make at the price set industrywide by demand. In this industry, companies win when they keep manufacturing costs low for a paper of a predetermined quality standard. The logic of offering a guaranteed service proposition to a group of customers who buy on the basis of the cheapest paper available failed to motivate customers. The guarantee probably sounded good to well-intentioned leaders inside the company—it just didn't matter to the customers. The administrative cost of the money-back guarantee eroded the firm's profitability.

Debunking myth 1 revealed that not all customers are equal; this myth suggests that even targeted customers may have different buying criteria. As Harley customizes its bikes, it may find that targeted customers have different buying criteria. One will pay more for the bike if it comes with a long-term service contract; another might like Harley clothing included in the bike purchase; and another might like membership in a bikers' group. Understanding what targeted customers value builds firm equity.

Reality 2: Delight Targeted Customers

Leaders obtain customer results and build firm equity, first, by understanding—and making sure employees understand—why customers buy products or services and, second, by ensuring that customers have experiences consistent with their intent. To accomplish this, employees must be ready to do more than respond to current orders; they must understand customers' buying patterns and know how the organization has delivered and intends to continue to deliver what the customer values. Again, firm equity results from maintaining a vision of the firm's distinctive culture in the minds of its best customers. Understanding targeted customers thus provides the foundation for culture building and for positioning the firm as a brand.

To do this successfully requires that firms clearly represent one of the five "value propositions" for customers (previously discussed in Chapter 2):

- **COST.** It costs us less to make our products than our competitor, so we can price our products less expensively. Or, we make more money than competitors because the price for our product is fixed while our operating costs are lower.

- **QUALITY.** Our products or services are better than those of our competitors.

- **SPEED.** We can get our products or services to our customers faster than our competitors can.

- **SERVICE.** We are more convenient and easier to access, and we have ways of doing business that our customers prefer.

- **INNOVATION.** Our products are newer, more innovative, or more on the cutting edge than those of our competitors.

Every organization should stand out from its competitors on one of these value propositions. This distinction represents the primary reason why target customers buy a firm's products or services. Firm equity grows when customers receive the value they desire from the firm, and employees know how customer value affects their behavior.

Because delivering outstanding values to target customers distinguishes a firm in their eyes, firms should invest in one such value to the point of becoming world class and should be very careful about tarnishing their reputation in that area in any way. Yet the other value propositions remain competitive necessities; they must not be ignored. A firm's performance in these other competitive areas should always be "as good as" the industry average. If a firm falls below industry parity in any one of the key value proposition areas, customers would perceive the business as unfit, creating competitive disadvantage for the firm, no matter how strong it remained in its primary value offering.

The pizza industry illustrates well the dynamics of customer value propositions. Domino's Pizza has staked out speed as its competitive anchor. Domino's claims it will deliver pizza within thirty minutes or the pizza is discounted. Domino's primary customers want their pizza "right now." Obviously, though, Domino's cannot make low-quality pizza or employ rude order takers or delivery drivers. The competitive necessities other than speed must be "as good as" the industry average, or Domino's customers will buy elsewhere. If it delivered fast pizza that tasted like cardboard, it would be in trouble. However, when it delivers fast pizza that tastes "about as good as the average pizza," Domino's wins big.

Little Caesar's pizza competes on low price, aiming to provide the lowest-priced pizza on the market. Little Caesar's primary customers become anyone needing to feed a crowd, satisfy simple tastes, or eat on the run when lacking time to savor a pizza or anything else. Again, even though Little Caesar's competes foremost on price, it cannot ignore the other necessities. The pizzas maintain reasonable quality, and customer service is adequate, or better. Little Caesar's wins its niche in the pizza industry by offering the lowest prices while maintaining parity on other value necessities.

Sbarro's, an Italian restaurant located in upscale malls throughout the country, sells to customers wanting high-quality pizza (or other Italian foods). Sbarro's offers comfortable tables and chairs, good service, and reasonable speed; its prices, however, tend to be higher than those of its pizza-only competitors. Sbarro's wins in its chosen value area by offering higher-quality pizza and other Italian food than do its competitors.

To maintain market position, these companies must not neglect their competitive anchor or primary customer value proposition. Unless Little Caesar's wants to create a completely new image, it should not try to compete with Domino's on speed and delivery or with Sbarro's on variety or quality; it must continue to make offerings consistent with its unique low-price value proposition. On the other hand, Little Caesar's should get nervous if another national chain attempts to compete using the low-price value proposition. If this happens, the result would be a pizza price war, with each company trying to drive out the other by cutting prices. The winner would, inevitably, be the company with the lowest costs.

Leaders who have achieved a clear value proposition face the task of inculcating employees with a fundamental understanding of how this value relates to its customers. Chuck House, the former leader of Hewlett-Packard's research and development group, has described his first impressions of the HP R&D scientists of ten years ago as "completely out of touch with the needs of the engineers who buy our products." House responded by insisting that all research activities stop and that HP scientists visit the offices of its customers and attend professional conferences alongside them. HP scientists resisted, but in vain. House prevailed, and only after about three months or so of this field-work did he allow them back into the lab—this time with the explicit directive that understanding customers through continued visits and conferences was now a basic R&D requirement. The resulting in-depth understanding by HP's R&D staff of its engineer-customers has opened the way to product innovations highly attuned to those customers' needs.

Nike leaders, too, have consistently demonstrated their understanding of their customers. Nike's targeted customer is the high-performance athlete. Nike's "not" customer is everyone else, including the millions of people who regularly buy Nike clothing, shoes, and equipment because they identify with high-performance athletes. Nike does not modify its product specifications in response to the desires of its "not" customers. Nike's primary customer value proposition is innovation. Nike leaders recognize that Nike sells high-performance products, and they know that they can do that best by cultivating an equally innovative "in-your-face" image and corresponding advertising campaigns. Nike, however, maintains a distance between its products and its image and advertising innovations.

As part of its innovation platform, Nike has developed a proprietary air sole technology. Nike doesn't advertise its proprietary air sole technology, for example. It advertises an image, trying to capture the spirit or philosophy of high performance. This approach works because it knows its customer.

DEFINING VALUE PROPOSITIONS

The exercise in Figure 5-2 helps leaders assess the extent to which they understand their own value propositions and those of their competitors. To create firm equity, leaders must build both culture and firm brand in a manner consistent with the firm's value proposition. This process is encapsulated by the exercise in Figure 5-2.

The following steps and questions guide leaders to completing the worksheet in Figure 5-2 to greatest effect. Before working through the steps, evaluate the appropriateness to your firm of the five basic value propositions, and add one or two others, if required, inserting them as indicated in the left column in Figure 5-2.

Step 1: Assess your firm's current ability in terms of its primary value proposition.

To complete this section, ask different employee groups (for example, senior management, R&D, or marketing) to consider and respond to the following questions:

1. How critical is each of the five (or more) value propositions listed to our targeted customers? (Participants should do this by dividing 100 points across the listed value propositions. This score indicates what employees think targeted customers value most.)

2. How well do we currently deliver each of the value propositions? (Employees rate each value proposition using a scale on which 1 is low and 10 is high. This score reveals employees' self-assessment of their firm's ability to deliver value.)

Step 2: Invite targeted customers to assess value propositions.
Targeted customers may ascertain their value propositions and how well your firm delivers on them. The segmentation matrix in Figure 5-1 may be used to guide your choice of which customers to interview. After selecting three for this exercise, ask them the same two questions you asked your employee respondents.

1. How critical is each of the five value propositions to your buying decisions? (Ask respondents to divide 100 points across the listed value propositions. This score indicates what customers say they value.)

2. How well does this firm currently deliver each of the value propositions? (This rating reveals customers' assessments, on a scale ranging from a low of 1 to a high of 10, of your firm's ability to deliver value.)

Comparison at this point of employees' and customers' assessments of the relative importance and success in delivery of your firm's value propositions can be very revealing. If the assessments are similar, all is well; if they aren't, trouble looms. One oil service firm that used this exercise discovered that employee perceptions overlapped customer values by only 70 percent. In fact, the more senior the employees, the less congruence between what employees thought customers valued and what customers actually valued. Leaders who engage in the first two steps of this exercise may quickly discover how well they deliver what customers value. The responses to the second question help leaders to see the firm's strengths and weaknesses through a reflection in their customers' eyes.

FIGURE 5-2

DEFINING VALUE PROPOSITIONS

VALUE PROPOSITIONS	STEP 1: EMPLOYEES* How important is, and how able are we to deliver, each of the competitive anchors? (1 = low, 10 = high) RELATIVE IMPORTANCE (divide 100 points)	A	B	C	STEP 2: CUSTOMERS* How important is, and how do targeted customers rate us on, each of the competitive anchors? (1 = low, 10 = high) RELATIVE IMPORTANCE (divide 100 points)	A	B	C	STEP 3: COMPETITORS* How important is, and how do our competitors deliver, each of the competitive anchors? (1 = low, 10 = high) RELATIVE IMPORTANCE (divide 100 points)	A	B	C
Cost												
Speed												
Service												
Quality												
Innovation												
Other:___												
Other:___												
	Total 100				Total 100				Total 100			

* For purposes of this exercise, "Employees" refers to a consensus provided by key employee groups charged with anticipating or meeting customer needs (for example, senior management, sales or marketing managers, or product development teams). "Customers" should be the top three *targeted customers* in terms of sales, stimulation of new products or services, or any other criterion or combination of criteria of importance to the firm. "Competitors" included should be those presenting the greatest challenge to the firm.

Step 3: Assess competitors on value propositions.

The final step, competitor assessment, asks respondents to imagine what key value propositions the competing firms seek to offer, the relative importance they place on each, and their assessments of their competitors' strengths. To proceed with the exercise, leaders must first identify major competitors in a particular market. Different competitors may have different value propositions, depending on what they emphasize in meeting their customers' needs. Second, determine what constitutes their key value propositions. Third, solicit answers to the following questions from informed employees, customers, or both.

1. How critical is each of the five (or more) value propositions to this competitor? (Respondents should do this by dividing 100 points across the listed anchors. This score indicates what respondents think the competitors offer their customers.)

2. How well does this competitor currently deliver each of its value propositions? (This rating—scored on a scale from 1, low, to 10, high—reveals respondents' assessments of your competitors' success in delivering on its value propositions.)

Although based only on informed guesses, the results of this part of the exercise can nonetheless be useful for leaders seeking an objective view of, and new approaches for, grappling with their most successful competitors.

This complex exercise may be done in stages (for example, start with employee groups, move to targeted customers, and then to competitors). The data accumulated by doing this exercise help leaders see where they have opportunities to build firm equity. Once leaders know their targeted customers' value propositions, management actions may proceed to ensure that these propositions are thoroughly embedded in their firms' procedures. As a consequence, firm equity grows.

MEASURING CUSTOMER VALUE

Many traditional methods of evaluating a firm's connection to its customers, such as market share, may not be sufficient when focusing on firm equity. Financial measures are exclusively post hoc; they assess past performance and don't always reveal what leaders are *trying* to achieve with customers, as opposed to what they may have achieved.

Financial measures alone are therefore insufficient indicators of customer results. The value propositions, on the other hand, provide helpful new "measures that matter."

Measures of customer value rightfully begin by taking the customer's viewpoint. Leaders need to put themselves as much as possible in their target customers' place and find answers to these questions:

- What would I (target customer) define as value?

- How would I (target customer) know that one firm created more value on a given proposition than another firm?

- What will keep me (target customer) committed to using the products and services of this firm?

Creating measures from the outside in, beginning with what customers define as value, helps leaders to focus their customer results efforts on what their targeted customers most want, thereby generating firm equity. Let's take the five key value propositions one at a time.

Cost.

Traditionally, costs have been measured as unit costs; that is, the costs of a particular product or service. Focusing on targeted customers shifts this measure to cost in use, that is, the overall cost of the product. The Scott Paper company (a division of Kimberly-Clark), for example, measured its away-from-home business in cost-in-use, not unit cost, terms. Their customers purchase bathroom supplies for office buildings, hotels, airports, stadiums, and other public places. Unit cost measures the cost of the actual materials, the paper towels, toilet paper, and liquid soap; cost-in-use measures that plus the cost of hiring custodians to refill soap dispensers, change toilet paper and paper towel rolls, and other tasks related to the use of Scott products. Scott increased firm equity—and revenues—by developing proprietary dispensers that increased unit cost but decreased total cost in use. It could show its customers that, despite an initially higher outlay, cuts in usage cost meant significant cost savings overall.

Speed.

Traditionally, speed refers to cycle time, that is, how quickly a product can be produced. Customer usage, on the other hand, shifts the measure to how quickly the customer receives use of the product. A General Electric division that repaired rail cars used, as a measure of speed, how much time was spent repairing a given car. The division reengineered this process from twenty to ten days and was pleased with its efforts, thinking that it would delight customers. What it found, when it thought about speed from the customer's viewpoint, was that the key measure of speed was not how long the repairs took, but how long the cars were out of service and unavailable for use. GE found that the twenty days it had taken to repair the cars represented only half the downtime experienced by customers, who spent another ten days getting the car to the service facility and yet another ten days returning the car to full service. The ten-day reduction in repair time did not improve customer usage as much as the GE employees had anticipated. When GE refocused its perception of speed using its customers' perspectives on cycle time, it looked for—and found—ways to streamline the entire repair and return-to-service process.

Service.

Traditionally, service has referred to how quickly a firm responds to its customers' needs. As for the previous value propositions, this turns out to be a rather limited, internally focused view of service. If service is redefined from the customer's viewpoint, new measures emerge. One manufacturing company used to measure service by using a shipped-on-time index but found that its customers used a different measure: received on time. Using its customers' assessment of good service, it had to drop its service scores from about 90 percent to 60 percent. Shipped on time meant out the factory door, whereas received on time meant ready for use. The 30 percent drop in service value represented products shipped incomplete, or needing time for assembly or transit delays (for example, held up in customs), or delays stemming from procedures required to make products fully operational. To improve service in ways meaningful to its customers, the company had to address these issues.

Quality.

Traditionally, quality might include a measure of defect-free product or a record of service calls. Following the same logic as above, however, the best place to start measuring quality is by starting with the customer. In the mid-1990s, for example, the telephone companies competed on quality as measured by sound clarity. Each major carrier declared its sound to be better than that of any other carrier. This competitive battle increased tone and quality of telephone transmission to a very high level, with the result that customers could no longer differentiate one from another. The continued preaching of better quality as measured by tone meant less to customers than easy access or reliability as a basis of choice among telephone companies. Leaders striving to increase firm equity must be sensitive to their customers' perceptions—and shifts in perceptions—of what constitutes quality.

Innovation.

A company may be proud of its legacy of innovation as measured by the number of patents it holds. Again, this is an inside-out measure, not necessarily meaningful to its customers. The vitality index used by 3M, on the other hand, representing the percentage of revenue produced by products created within the preceding five years, does reveal customer values by measuring not what is produced but what is purchased and used. Among academics, promotions often depend on the number of articles or books a candidate has published; a more revealing index might assess the impact of those publications. Hewlett-Packard measures the cost of developing a new product against the time the product requires to break even in the market. After reaching the break-even point, HP can begin cannibalizing the initial product by making incremental improvements.

Myth 3: Customer Connection Comes from Collecting Customer Data

Leaders working to understand and connect with customers have come to depend on myriad market research techniques. Using data collected from focus groups, customer surveys, mystery shoppers, customer panels, customer contact information, and other sources, leaders try to better understand their customers' needs and buying patterns.

Typical data-based market research, although necessary, may mislead leaders working to know customers better for a number of reasons. First, many of the data collected on customers may be post hoc, reflecting what customers think after they have done or attempted to do business with a company, rather than anticipatory data about what the customers tried to do and why they went about it as they did. Focus groups and customer preference surveys often look backward, not forward.

Second, customers don't know what they don't know. Early market research on what later proved to be hit products can often be negative. Early customer panels for 3M's Post-it Notes and Chrysler's minivan were bemused by these innovative products and unsure what they were, how they could be used, and whether they would add value to customers' lives. Customers responding to products through focus groups naturally tend to respond based on what they know or have experienced, not on what they don't know or have not experienced.

Third, market research data often evolve too slowly to keep pace with changing customer expectations. By the time surveys are prepared and focus groups established, new products may have entered the market, following or even creating new customer expectations.

A fourth problem with surveys and similar tools is that respondents may be strong potential or target customers not using a product or service and may choose not to respond. Generally, customer data may be collected only on or from current customers. Sometimes new customer segments may be undefined or overlooked in customer typologies based only on existing customers. The "soccer mom" customer segment did not exist—for market surveyors—when minivans were first created. The minivan essentially labeled this customer segment which market research had not identified.

Spending ever-greater sums on market research thus may increase neither customer connection nor firm equity. Leaders must find ways to shift their efforts from collecting data on customers to influencing how their customers think about the firm and its products and services.

Reality 3: Customer Connection Comes from Involving Customers

Leaders need to find imaginative ways to connect with customers so that customers become completely committed and satisfied.[13] Figure 5-3 illustrates this proposition using four elements of customer relationships, each indicating increasing customer intimacy. *Sales* occur when firms take and process customer orders; *marketing,* when the firm understands customer needs so thoroughly that the meeting of those needs can be guaranteed;[14] *partnering* represents a firm's capacity to anticipate what customers need even before they know they need it; and *influencing* indicates creating customer demand for a product or service, the need for which the customer would not otherwise have felt. The higher up this intimacy chain a firm goes, the more value is created.

As indicated in Figure 5-3, firms may connect with customers in four ways. Two traditional methods—market research and technology—have both uses and limitations. Market research often collects data on what has been and what is more than what might be. Technology connects firms with customers and provides immediate and accurate information of use to both customers and the firm.[15] Procter & Gamble (P&G), for example, has a data link with Wal-Mart which gives it instantaneous information about the sales of their product throughout the chain. P&G thus knows quickly how its products perform. Many leaders rely on market research and technology to move up the customer intimacy chain.

Two newer approaches to connecting with customers—management practices and values—do even more to build firm equity. These can be pursued using a variety of techniques, the most important of which—customer interactions, recruiting, reward systems, development systems, and governance—are discussed more fully below.

CUSTOMER INTERACTIONS

Interaction with customers on a regular basis remains one of the best ways to gain insight about customers and to understand their needs and desires. As straightforward as this sounds, firms rarely develop formal or even informal customer interaction systems. Texas Instruments and Levi Strauss constitute the exceptions that prove the rule.[16]

TI's calculator division, in striving to make its products the de facto standard in high schools, works directly with mathematics teachers to study how they teach calculations. TI also simulates mathematics classroom situations to understand the interaction of students and teachers in learning mathematics and the possible roles for calculators in facilitating effective teaching and learning.

Tom Kasten, currently a vice president at Levi Strauss, first undertook direct interaction with customers when, as a merchandiser responsible for developing jeans products for teenagers, he drove to Fillmore

FIGURE 5-3

CREATING CUSTOMER CONNECTIONS

WAYS TO LINK WITH CUSTOMERS

	PRODUCT/SERVICE (market research)	TECHNOLOGY (shared systems)	MANAGEMENT PRACTICE (shared HR)	COMMON BOND (shared values)
INFLUENCING (create demand)				
PARTNERING (anticipate orders)				
MARKETING (service orders)				
SALES (process orders)				

FOCUS OF RELATIONSHIPS
(degree of customer intimacy)

Auditorium in San Francisco every Saturday to talk to kids lining up for that night's rock concert. He also observed what they were doing to customize their own jeans. Kasten also takes more than his share of turns driving his kids and their friends to high school, a duty that gives him a window into the latest in teen fashion. "The kids love to talk about where they shop, what they like, and what they hate," he says. "This is where it all begins, so this is what I do to learn, by watching consumers in their natural habitat." Customer interaction may also occur when leaders become customers. How often does a hotel executive experience, from the customer's view, making a reservation, checking in, room layout, and checkout? an automotive executive, the experience of shopping for cars versus being given a car? or an airline executive, the experience of traveling in coach class? In these and other cases, leaders don't see the world as a customer sees it, thus limiting their customer sensitivity.

RECRUITING

Several years ago, Exxon sought to benchmark several "best practice" companies it had identified, as a means of improving its customer results. Interviews with these companies examined their training systems, career development practices, approaches to compensation, and the interrelationship of these three functions. The retailer Nordstrom proved to have the answer Exxon most needed to hear. After a few moments of initial bemusement at the questions, the Nordstrom representative offered this summary: "What we do is hire people who are really friendly and have great instincts about customer service. Then we encourage them to do whatever it takes to satisfy the customer. Beyond that we don't do much formal training, career development, or anything else."

Nordstrom's approach—recruit the right people and encourage them to do what they were hired to do—remains the best open secret of customer results. Casey Stengel put the same lesson another way when he was asked, "What has made you the best baseball coach in the world?" He replied, "I don't trip my players on their way out of the dugout." Countless organizations create impediments that prevent their employees from delivering on the promise of their value proposition. Most organizations need more than a recruiting-only solution to this problem, but finding a core of dedicated, skilled people with the right attitude to get the job done certainly makes a firm's systems for developing, rewarding, communicating with, and celebrating talent run much more smoothly.

Building customer intimacy through recruiting occurs most readily when leaders include customers at all stages of the staffing process, from defining criteria to sourcing, screening, and selecting candidates. This level of customer involvement builds a connection not only between customers and newly hired employees, but between customers and the firm.

REWARD SYSTEMS

One truism holds that we get what we reward. Sadly, however, it's more often the case that we fail to reward what we want to get. Steve Kerr, chief learning officer at General Electric, described this unwanted phenomenon in his article "On the Folly of Hoping for A while Rewarding B."[17] This failure and its consequences often appear in customer relations. Successfully tying customer feedback to employee rewards involves numerous difficulties, including the one most often cited—not wanting to "bother" your customers.

But Alan Alexander, president of Savage Industries, doesn't buy the argument that asking your customers for feedback bothers them. His customers at Arco, Chevron, and other large companies regularly, willingly evaluate Savage leaders. The success of the Savage mission to provide "worry-free service" for its transportation and logistics outsourcing customers depends on full, honest customer evaluations so that leaders know what's working and what's not. These evaluations also provide the means for rewarding leaders' performance. Savage has just initiated 360-degree feedback to gather this information more formally, but customer input will continue to be factored in as appropriate.

Customers may directly participate in reward systems. Northwest, Delta, and American Airlines recently sent their most frequent flyers books of coupons to be handed to employees "caught" doing something right for customers. The coupons, redeemable by the airline employees for cash or other rewards, were planned and received as a creative way to involve customers in rewarding those who serve them. Frequent travelers now control a portion of the airlines' bonus plan, and many of these travelers relish disbursing airline money.

DEVELOPMENT SYSTEMS

So far, this chapter has discussed how companies can link recruitment and reward to the achievement of customer results. But can outstanding customer skills be taught? Can you "grow your own" customer-oriented work force?

We would argue yes—but not by using traditional classroom-based training alone. Of course, there's no shortage of one- to two-day customer service training courses available. Some are quite entertaining. Employees will feel good when they're finished, but the company's customer results won't change.

Customer results aren't achieved in the classroom. As with the development of any skill, research overwhelmingly shows that experience, not pedagogy, is the best teacher. People develop their abilities and perspective best through the daily rigors of their job assignments. The most productive path to developing customer-focused people departs from the assumption that employees will maximize their own growth and satisfaction through experiences that directly meet the organization's needs.

Exxon, for example, regularly finds ways to expose its engineers, geoscientists, marketers, and finance people to the regulatory side of the business. By using "government relations"–type jobs as training grounds, Exxon teaches its employees the intricacies of oil regulation, at the same time helping to forge strong relationships between Exxon people and the government representatives who set the regulations. This type of customer awareness simply can't be developed in a training course.

DuPont and other large corporations use job rotation programs for the same reasons, with similar results. Effective development systems like these provide people with opportunities to grow their careers, their commitment to the company, and the company's customer results—quite a hat trick.

Novations Group, Inc., a consulting firm, has conducted more than twenty years of research into how employees develop on the job. Its Four Stages model articulates the way an employee's perspective and skills develop along a continuum—from depending on others on the one end to organizational leadership on the other.[18] Many companies have used this model to behaviorally anchor competency expectations for their employees. Figure 5-4 is one example of a typical "Customer Focus" competency, described for each of the Four Stages. The developmental message of the Four Stages is clear: in-depth customer service skills (or any type of skills, for that matter) are not developed overnight. They require a long-term investment in developing people, providing the requisite experience that will cultivate both broad customer knowledge and the savvy to act profitably on that knowledge.

FIGURE 5-4

CUSTOMER FOCUS
Knows who the customers are and acts with their needs in mind.

STAGE 1: DEPENDING ON OTHERS	STAGE 2: CONTRIBUTING INDEPENDENTLY	STAGE 3: CONTRIBUTING THROUGH OTHERS	STAGE 4: ORGANIZATIONAL LEADERSHIP
Seeks to understand the company's customer groups and their needs (internal customers, end users, distributors, resellers).	Incorporates a solid understanding of the team's customers into own work; shares customer knowledge with colleagues.	Well networked with key customer groups; influences the team to translate customer needs into work products and services that add value.	Sets corporate direction for providing excellent service to existing customers and for reaching new customer groups; influences the way the business interacts with its customers.

Companies need to take a proactive development approach to ensuring customer results. Several years ago, for example, one of the largest defense contractors realized it was on the brink of a customer results crisis: 80 percent of its senior account representatives were due to retire within three years. Using the Four Stages framework, it discovered that most of these senior representatives were Stage 3 contributors: seasoned, well-networked individuals who had built solid relationships with the company's Air Force clientele. The same analysis showed its Stage 2 population was rather young and inexperienced, due to recent hiring freezes in the defense industry. The organization's challenge? Grow these Stage 2 people to be able to take over these key customer relationships—and do so within three years.

The chosen solution required a major investment. Each Stage 3 representative was assigned a promising Stage 2 protégé. They teamed up for every client interaction. Before long, the Air Force officers came to respect and have confidence in the junior members of the team, so that when the senior representatives retired, the contractors' sales revenues didn't take a serious hit. A side benefit: the organization ended up with a new crop of Stage 3 leaders. This single case is representative of the many examples we've seen of a company taking a proactive development approach to ensuring customer results.

Research clearly shows that employees develop skills and perspective best through job assignments.[19] An effective development process facilitates the fruitful intersection between meeting critical business needs and providing employees satisfaction through choice in how they develop their own interests and talents. Exxon "transfers" people into government jobs where they can learn the intricacies of oil regulation while developing relationships with the people who set those regulations. Effective development systems like these provide people with opportunities to develop in ways that further both their careers and their commitment to the firm and the firm's customer results.

Recent studies of trends in development and learning show that customers have become increasingly involved in employee development—as participants, as presenters, and as live case studies.[20] Customer participation in such development experiences clearly helps both the employees and the customers. In addition, by creating a forum where customers and employees explore and debate how the firm operates, customers increase their commitment to the firm, thus enhancing firm equity.

GOVERNANCE

Governance deals with how work gets done in organizations. This might include, for example, how teams coordinate their work or interface with customers. By including customers on task forces and other project teams, firms build customer commitment to team decisions.

Gallo Wines, a privately held company headquartered in Modesto, California, uses many approaches to involving customers in the firm's decisions and governance. For example, Joe Gallo, a co-owner of the company, continually seeks customer input about his products during his business and personal travel. During a recent visit to Notre Dame, where his son graduated, he solicited student input on the company's "Cask & Cream" products. This information from college students was immediately relayed back to Modesto to be compared with market research data. Where there were discrepancies, questions were asked, and the work to be followed up on was identified. Virtually all Gallo employees willingly get their friends to try new products and to solicit feedback, both positive and negative, regarding taste, quality, the shape of bottles, and even labeling ideas. In hundreds of large and small ways, Gallo people bring customers into the business.

Governance also involves communication and information sharing. Including targeted customers in communication activities, such as e-mails, management meetings, and company newsletters, helps them feel part of the organization.

When management practices traditionally done exclusively inside a firm are opened to customers, customer commitment increases. Customers participating in these management practices contribute to firm equity through feelings of ownership and involvement with the firm. The worksheet in Figure 5-5 offers leaders a single exercise to audit and improve customer connections. By asking employees and customers to assess the degree of customer involvement in each management activity and by brainstorming ways to involve them more, customers systematically increase their firm equity.

Pulling It All Together

At the beginning of this chapter, we discussed how Nordstrom and Kellogg are working to create firm equity beyond product brand equity. We also shared a dilemma faced by Chuey Castaneda—his company

FIGURE 5-5

INCREASING CUSTOMER CONNECTIONS

CUSTOMER CONNECTIONS	CURRENT RATING (1 = low, 10 = high)	WAYS TO IMPROVE
Customer interactions		
Recruiting		
Reward systems		
Development systems		
Governance		

needed to achieve cost savings to be profitable, so they engaged in a reengineering effort. However, the efficiencies cut both fat and muscle and left his company undistinctive in the eyes of at least one important customer. Chuey believed that he could either satisfy his customer or be profitable, but that achieving both was almost impossible.

If Chuey can face and overcome the three myths presented in this chapter, he can begin to find ways to target customers, discover what they value, and organize with customers to deliver that value. Cumulatively, he can create firm equity when customers share an identity with his firm, ultimately leading to customer results.

Investor Results: Building Shareholder Value

6

FOR LEADERS IN PUBLICLY TRADED COMPANIES, shareholder value in its simplest form means creating wealth for investors. The currently prevailing, precise definition of shareholder value has been succinctly stated as "economic return generated for shareholders, as measured by dividends plus increase in the company's share price."[1] Anyone who has ever bought stock understands the relationship between shareholder value and stock price. Firm leaders are charged with regularly, predictably, and lastingly increasing the value of their firm's stock.

Many factors affecting this value lie beyond leaders' control, including domestic market upheavals, industry trends, global economic conditions, consumer confidence, debt level, and even the weather. Within an industry and over long periods of time, however, leaders at every level make decisions that increase or decrease shareholder value. Some are short-term decisions with high immediate impact on stock price, as, for example, when AT&T announced its divestiture into AT&T, Lucent, and Global Solutions (the former NCR) and its stock rose about 20 percent. Other less visible decisions affect shareholder value only in the long term; an example might be the merger of two firms to create, over time, a single, stronger competitor or the patient development of employees to better understand target customers and increase firm equity.

This chapter offers suggestions to leaders in publicly traded firms for increasing shareholder value. Because both small and large investors make rational and informed choices about which stocks to buy or sell, and because informed investors look closely at management style and the record of its accomplishments, results-based leaders must demonstrate the ability to make decisions and act in ways that build investor confidence. Leaders in nonpublicly traded firms may also benefit from this chapter to better serve and soothe their investors, whether they are holders of phantom stock or owners without stock who nonetheless expect a return on their investment. Public agencies, too, at the local, state, or federal level, serve investors. Public agency "investors" may be defined as those who vote to support the agency, either funding agencies or, ultimately, the taxpayers who support these agencies and demand that their leaders judiciously manage the financial resources provided for their use.

The experiences of Oxford Health Plans, an HMO providing care to over 1.9 million subscribers in the northeastern states, illustrate the importance of investor results. October 27, 1997, was a bad day at Oxford. The company announced that, due to problems with its computerized billing system, it had overestimated enrollment and revenue. That same day, the stock market plunged. Oxford stock was shredded. Several lawsuits filed against the company alleged that Oxford management had given investors false and misleading financial information and had hidden the extent of Oxford's problems.

The overall market fell by 7 percent on October 27, but it climbed quickly back by about 5 percent the next day. Oxford stock, on the other hand, fell 62 percent and continued to fall as its leadership problems became increasingly apparent. The Oxford leadership was young, inexperienced, and often "winged it" when making financial decisions. Analysts now suggest that Oxford leaders made three serious mistakes that contributed to the company's calamitous loss in value.[2]

First, in 1993, Oxford's management insisted on developing proprietary IS software, even though skeptics pointed out that a technological edge in bill processing is meaningless and that parity is sufficient. The software took years to develop and was obsolete, riddled with bugs, and overwhelmed when it finally went on-line.

Second, Oxford executives believed that growth was a cure-all for their financial problems. They continually sought new customers and new products, and the company top line grew rapidly during the 1990s in product, geographic, and customer expansion. This rapid revenue growth, averaging 85 percent from 1991 to 1997, masked the underlying weaknesses that led to the crushing financial problems that began to emerge shortly before the crash.

Third, when it became clear that the billing system could not handle the entire load, Oxford leadership directed accounts receivable to concentrate on large clients first, for fear of alienating the clients who generated the most revenue. As a result, many small firms and individuals slipped away to other companies (something the large clients could not easily do), forcing Oxford to write off thirty-thousand members and $111 million in uncollectible bills. Oxford did not in any way attempt to collect from these defectors through other means (such as hiring an army of temps with typewriters)—a costly mistake, as its leaders later conceded. In addition, most of the small accounts were with the younger, healthier HMO members, who put more money into the system than they drew out; the older, costlier members tended to stay on.

Oxford compounded these three errors by not thoroughly testing its new billing system, but attempting instead to convert its entire database at one go. The system couldn't handle it, throwing the entire company into chaos. These billing problems alienated both clients and providers, and several physician groups have since filed suits against Oxford. At the same time the billing problems were developing, Oxford executives began to realize that they had also seriously underestimated the costs of paying for Oxford's Medicare program. By mid-1998, Oxford stock still had not recovered, the chief executive officer had resigned, and the investment firm KKR had pulled out of a refinancing deal. The official reason KKR gave for its bailout was "Philosophical differences which resulted in our inability to agree on some of the management related terms and conditions."[3] Rumors circulated that KKR thought the new CEO's compensation package too high.

Although this story is about Oxford, similar events could happen at any of a number of firms. A series of mistakes arising out of and combined with pride, arrogance, and greed led to loss of investor confidence, and Oxford's stock plummeted 76 percent (from 68.75 to 16.18). Looking at how Oxford leaders could have avoided this provides insights into how leaders can protect and improve investor results.

Investor results accrue from the effective management of all the other results we have talked about—employee, organization, and customer.

Shareholder value may also be derived by attending to the following three issues:

- **COSTS:** How can leaders reduce costs within a firm?

- **GROWTH:** How can leaders increase revenues?

- **MANAGEMENT EQUITY:** How can leaders increase the perceived quality of management within the firm?

Leader actions in each of these areas both directly and indirectly affect investor results and shareholder value.

Managing Costs

Although reducing costs has always been important for successful financial results, in the mid-1980s into the early 1990s, reducing costs became a paramount priority at many companies. A firm trying to reduce costs often clustered them into three types: *supplier or materials costs,* including raw goods, equipment, service, maintenance, and so on; *labor costs,* meaning the costs to an organization of its people, which show up in many places in the income statement, but are clearly recorded in the sales, general, and administration item of the corporate income statement; and *process costs,* the cost of turning supplier goods into customer products or services. Some companies tried to reduce all three costs simultaneously. Following airline deregulation, for example, when frequent fare wars raged, airlines struggled to reduce costs, looking for savings in all three areas.

APPROACHES TO REDUCING COSTS

Southwest Airlines provides a classic example of a company that has succeeded in reducing supplier costs as one step toward investor results. Southwest orders only one airplane—the Boeing 737—for all its routes and has each plane configured exactly the same way. This reduces both the direct costs of equipment purchases and servicing, and turnaround time, the indirect costs of maintenance keeping Southwest planes in the air more than those of other carriers. Sharing services and outsourcing further reduce maintenance costs while maintaining high standards. Finally, Southwest offers fewer services, such as in-flight meals, assigned seats, or use of travel agents, further reducing costs.

Among other companies aggressively seeking cost savings from suppliers, General Motors, especially under Jose Ignacio Lopez de Arriortua as head of worldwide purchasing, stands out. Lopez initiated GM's policy of sourcing globally and forced each supplier to reduce costs, regardless of prior contracts, ruthlessly pushing suppliers for cost savings in every area.

Companies looking for cost savings can reduce labor costs in a number of ways, many of which have been tried in the last two decades by beleaguered airlines. They renegotiated with unions to reduce salary and benefits. They tried two-tiered compensation systems (for example, newly hired pilots at American were paid on a scale different from that applied to veteran pilots). They tried to break the union and hire nonunion workers (as, for example, when People Express hired many former teachers and social workers). They reduced cash compensation and tied increased pay to airline profitability and stock appreciation. They changed work rules to increase productivity, attempting to have employees spend more time in the air. They tried staffing planes with fewer employees per flight, including fewer flight attendants offering less service and crews of two, not three, pilots. They had employees perform multiple tasks—for example, take tickets, check in passengers, and load baggage. These activities all increased productivity, and Southwest led the way in implementing these changes.

The spate of consolidations and mergers in the last few years has created two cost-cutting opportunities. In the immediate aftermath, redundant or duplicative employees are often laid off from the newly combined company, increasing productivity and reducing labor costs. In addition, common systems and efficiency root out unnecessary costs for delivering the same value. Airlines have consolidated to the point where six major carriers control 70 percent of the United States market and each consolidation was attended by some efficiency gains or cost savings, if not quite to the extent promised.

With the goal of reducing costs came the creation of more sophisticated cost assessment tools, such as activity based costing (ABC) and business process reengineering (BPR). An ABC analysis determines the cost and, later, the value of all work in an organization. When the cost of work exceeds its value or when it is found redundant, the work is eliminated or reduced. BPR undertakes a clean sweep of projects and processes and reinvents a business top to bottom. The BPR approach looks at organizations as work processes, rather than as people joined by politics, and reconfigures those work processes to reduce bureaucracy and cost.

By the mid-1990s, business leaders had squeezed much of the excess costs out of their businesses. But a backlash ensued. Aimed at mindless, heartless cuts, attributable to no more compelling a reason than corporate greed, the backlash was propelled by the tens of thousands of employees displaced by restructuring. Articles with titles such as "Corporate Anorexia" emphasized the retreat from indiscriminate downsizing and layoffs. Larry Bossidy, the CEO at AlliedSignal, wrote the epitaph for cost reduction: "You can't shrink your way to greatness in business."[4]

THE LEADER'S ROLE

Even leaders who have successfully trimmed the "big ticket" costs, however, cannot cease monitoring two other cost aspects. First, they must ensure that difficult-to-achieve savings are not undermined by costs that creep back in. After a company has pushed hard for a few months or even a year on a particular cost initiative, it may find that, despite initial success, when its vigilance is relaxed, the costs come back. General Electric, following its job- and cost-trimming "Workout" program, found the greater challenge was not removing the work, but making sure it did not return. Leaders maintain hard-won gains by relentlessly and constantly reminding all employees about cost; keeping the magnifying glass focused on areas where cost overruns typically occur; refusing to allow managers to rehire people after downsizing; continuing to reengineer work processes; reporting on costs with all employees; and, most importantly, instituting focused business strategies.

Second, leaders must continue to reduce costs by encouraging all employees to identify and find ways to improve efficiency. Using the rubric "Act as if you are the owner," some firms invite employees to find better and cheaper ways to get work done. When Borg-Warner went through its leveraged buyout in the 1980s, the new owner-managers required all firm managers to participate in the buyout, to invest in the firm, and then to think and act like the owners that they were. They and others who have taken this approach reason that senior leaders can identify and implement "major" cost reductions, but that each employee at any level can be expected to find ways to reduce costs within his or her own operation. Among the resulting initiatives might be efforts to travel more cheaply, to use supplies more judiciously, to hire staff more carefully, and to use second-sourcing on suppliers.

Achieving Growth

INVESTOR RESULTS THROUGH GROWTH

During the last fifteen years, most executives have worked to meet financial goals by focusing on cutting costs. Numerous initiatives— total quality, continuous improvement, downsizing, consolidation, reengineering, value-based management, transformation, mergers, and acquisitions, to name a few—focused implicitly or explicitly on reducing operating costs or improving efficiency. When successful, these programs improve productivity and efficiency, which ultimately lower operating costs.

More recently, leading firms such as AlliedSignal, General Electric, and Motorola, and leading management scholars, such as C. K. Prahalad and Gary Hamel, have begun to recognize that growth provides a viable alternative to reducing costs as a way to financial goals.[5] Growth programs focus on the "top line" of financial equations, generally measured in sales or revenues. Experts stand ready to help corporations "grow into the next century and beyond." *Fortune* magazine ran a feature in 1997 entitled "Killer Strategies" about companies that grow to create investor results. *Business Week* ran a cover article on the subject, entitled "Strategy Is Back." Although growth predominates in corporate planning sessions today, most leaders are determined not to forget the cost management lessons of the last fifteen to twenty years.

Focusing on growth to improve company performance has a number of advantages over cost-cutting measures. First, growth has no upper limit, whereas with cost reductions, companies are limited by what they actually spend. Second, growth excites and invigorates a work force. Focusing on cost may be demoralizing and discouraging to people, especially when workers are let go and processes are reengineered. Growth offers new ideas and creative approaches to old problems. Third, growth generally has a positive impact over a longer term than does cost cutting, the benefits of which tend to be short term.

Growth for investor results can take one of three forms: *geographic* expansion, widening the area in which products or services are offered and sold; *product growth,* through innovation or the creation of new products or services; and *customer growth,* accomplished by convincing existing customers to purchase more of a firm's products or services.

Geographic.

Firms often grow by selling their existing products or services in new markets. Geographic growth takes place within a country or globally, or both at once. U.S. banks, for example, many of which have been in a growth mode in recent years, have expanded from regional to national to global companies in just a few years. NationsBank (now BankAmerica), originating in Charlotte, North Carolina, grew over the last decade from a mid-Atlantic regional bank to one doing business in thirty-three states and fifteen countries. Mergers and acquisitions, including Boatman's Bank in St. Louis, Barnett's in Florida, Bank of America in California, and a Brazilian bank, were undertaken explicitly to extend the banks' geographic range.

For many firms worldwide, the need for global growth has become a given for entering new markets with old or adapted products and services through independent or aligned distribution. Selecting which markets to serve, learning to adapt products and services to those markets, managing political and cultural differences in each market, and sharing information across the globe have become not only accepted, but expected practices. Technology connects the people of the world as never before, whether through information exchanges, as on the Internet, or through shared images, such as global communications and television networks provide. Brand equity is increasingly measured in global market share, as for Visa and Nike, for example, and people are increasingly attuned to other cultures, habits, celebrities, and events, from the death of Princess Diana to the career of Michael Jordan. Executives today must position their work in global terms—or have a good reason why they aren't doing so. The one thing they cannot afford to do is to fail to think it through.

Product.

Some firms grow through leveraging core competencies and innovating new products. First Union, another bank headquartered in Charlotte, North Carolina, has grown geographically by doing business in states from New Jersey to Florida, but it has also grown dramatically by entering new markets. From the traditional bank on the corner offering consumer services, it has become a full-service financial institution offering a brokerage business, insurance products, commercial loans, and risk management services. Product growth has been propelled largely by mergers with other companies, the products and services of which complemented First Union's existing product line.

Product growth requires innovation and cycle-time reduction. In the pharmaceutical industry, for example, research and development firms that invest in finding new drugs work to shorten the cycle time from discovery to commercial use through rapid, parallel testing; involving the FDA earlier; and streamlining bureaucratic processes. In addition, Merck sought to grow by acquiring Medco Containment Services. Merck had traditionally distributed its products through physicians by prescription, whereas Medco distributes through direct mail. When Merck bought Medco, it grew by offering new distribution services.

Customer intimacy.

Financial service institutions often choose to grow by aggressively pursuing ever greater customer intimacy. Often banks target wealthy clients and attempt to induce them to use all of the bank's financial services. For example, a client may have checks automatically deposited at bank A, a retirement account in brokerage B, life insurance and annuities in insurance firm C, stock portfolio in firm D, bond funds in firm E, mutual funds in firm F, checking accounts in firm G, or home mortgage in firm H. The financial institution that collapses all these assets into one account, making it easier for the wealthy client to manage the overall financial portfolio, will grow. Financial institutions often refer to this strategy as gaining "share of wallet" of the wealthy client. And as technology builds more refined and intimate ways in some banks to deal with clients, the criteria for "wealthy" continually drop; they have already dropped from a net worth of $5 million to $1 million to $500,000 to $250,000.

Other approaches to growth through increased customer intimacy include airlines that offer frequent-flier programs to induce passengers to fly as often as possible with that airline; coffee shops that hand out "buy ten, get one free" cards, bookstores that offer club members extra discounts, or retail stores that offer a personal shopping service. Each of these activities encourages customers to spend a higher share of their purchasing power with the firm, thus growing investor results.

THE LEADER'S ROLE IN GROWTH

Although many paths lead to growth, leaders must take an active part in making it happen. The growth of the Bank of Nova Scotia, one of the smallest of Canada's "Big Five" chartered banks, illustrates the effects of such action on shareholder value. The bank, with both major international banking interests and a large branch network across Canada, has in recent years aggressively sought a larger share of both domestic and international markets by expanding globally and nationally. As a consequence, profits and share prices have increased dramatically, and net income increased 196 percent between 1988, when it stood at $2,241 million, and 1997, with a total of $6,635 million.

Scotiabank's senior management has become increasingly active in deciding what businesses Scotiabank will pursue. A major growth move, for example, was the acquisition of two large Canadian trust companies, a gain not only of an expanded customer base but of the right to enter fields previously closed to Scotiabank under Canadian banking law. In another example of its product growth strategy, Scotiabank gained a major interest in a large discount brokerage house, thus becoming a primary competitor in investment.

The bank's senior leaders actively set goals in consultation with more junior leaders, assisting them in focusing on and attaining their targets. The bank increasingly supports training for employees at all levels and encourages anyone wishing to take training, whether inside or outside the bank. The bank rewards success, using an incentive bonus system that recognizes individual contributions to the bank's ROE. These policies guide bank leaders in attending to the right issues. For example, Pat Lawton, an investment manager at one of the Alberta branches, takes advantage of courses at her local university almost every semester. Having recently passed a series of courses, she can now sell securities and provide investment advice at the bank, thus expanding the bank's array of services.

John Lawton, Pat's husband, manages another of the bank's branches in the area. Among the new leadership initiatives that have worked well for him is the program Just Between Us (JBU), in which randomly selected customers from each bank branch are asked to respond to a questionnaire soliciting customers' impressions of the quality of service delivered by their branch. Distributed to the branches, the JBU results encourage the institutions to improve on weaknesses or to build on strengths in ways consistent with customer preferences, which in turn increases customer intimacy.

Branch employees become actively involved in looking for ways to follow through on the JBU assessments. Suggestions are solicited and generated at breakfast meetings, in individual reports to branch leadership, and so on. Those who make the best suggestions at this level receive prizes. At the corporate level, leaders watch for and reward significant branch improvement. At a yearly Canada-wide meeting, the branches that have made the most significant improvements are recognized and rewarded. Scotiabank realizes that improving the talents of its employees, building organization capability, and listening to customers drive financial performance.

The Scotiabank example illustrates several techniques leaders can use to help make growth happen and to increase shareholder value. Other useful ideas are described below.

Build a growth culture.

Firms have cultures or identities. Leaders focused on growth may build a growth culture, or identity, using the following strategies:

- Emphasize the future, not the past.

- Emphasize the possibility, not the constraints.

- Reach customers outside through the employees inside.

- Encourage risk taking and discourage political protecting.

- Reward collective, not individual, successes, but maintain clear individual accountabilities and keep heroes visible.

- Look for alternatives before seeking closure.

- Ensure a high level of personal freedom and trust.

- Encourage debate before consensus.

Leaders who build growth cultures establish an environment favorable to risk taking and pushback, an environment in which employees do not feel afraid to raise alternative ideas and propose new ways of doing things. Risk taking may be calculated with the formula *Desire to win/fear of failure.* An increased desire to win develops when leaders ask for alternatives, hire people driven to succeed, and reward victory; fear of failure is reduced when punishment doesn't follow the mission of stretch goals, managers are recognized for taking bold moves, and employees are encouraged to learn from both successes *and* failures. At Gillette, for example, leaders know that only about 20 percent of new product ideas will prove commercially viable, so they make sure that many choice jobs remain open for those who attempt a new product but fail, so that the potential innovator can take the risk more securely, knowing that a significant job will be available.

Hire for growth.

Some employees are temperamentally more amenable to growth than others. Engineering and technology firms find it imperative to hire "magnet" employees, individuals so well known in the industry that they attract others to work for them. Texas Instruments leaders work not only to hire, but to retain magnet employees through a new-hire entry strategy that emphasizes the leverage points needed to connect a person to a company. In Chapter 3 we called this practice "mass-customizing the employee deal." Leverage points include working on the right projects, with the right people, with the right equipment and support, and in the right work environment. Their awareness of these leverage points for magnet employees gives TI leaders a method for ensuring that new employees are fully engaged and remain committed to the firm. Committed magnet employees attract new employees, and TI's business can grow.

McKinsey, a worldwide consulting firm, grows by hiring the best and brightest from the top schools. Most McKinsey hires know they are among the best in their class and have great potential, whether at McKinsey or elsewhere. McKinsey thus treats its new employees with great respect, giving them exciting assignments and opportunities to learn new skills. McKinsey's criteria for partnership are demanding and stringent, meaning that relatively few McKinsey associates become partners. Because McKinsey employees are highly competent, however, they usually attain superb jobs at other companies when they leave. Because McKinsey treats its employees with dignity while they are employed at McKinsey, these alumni often continue to do business with McKinsey when employed elsewhere. By hiring smart people and treating them well, McKinsey builds good relationships with future clients and grows the business.

Keep the next generation of customers in mind.

Leaders worried about growth look continually to the next generation of customers. Motorola's pager division, for example, invited high school students to examine and test its products. Somewhat to the chagrin and surprise of the engineers who designed the pagers, these students expressed concern that the pagers be fashionable and color-match with their outfits. While the engineers protested, briefly, that black pagers would work just as well as multicolored ones, this next generation of users felt they would more likely purchase colored pagers. In the end, though, the next generation prevailed: Motorola now makes colored pagers.

All firms have "lighthouse customers," to use a term coined by Chris Hart, formerly a professor at Harvard Business School. These customers precede the industry in terms of expectations and demands. They exert the demand for unique products or services that leads firms to create the new ideas that put them ahead of competitors. Very frequent fliers act as lighthouse customers for airlines because they know the meaning of service and how it can best be improved. Airlines that are looking to improve regularly survey and interview these people on ways to make their experience better. When employees understand current and future customers, why customers buy today and tomorrow, and how better to serve current and future customers, growth follows.

Organize for growth.

Sometimes growth occurs within existing divisions through innovation, as when a research and development project unfolds within traditionally demarcated gateposts and guidelines. At other times, growth occurs in the "white space" between departments, as when, for example, a customer asks for a new service or product that can be provided only by combining ideas, services, or products from two or more departments. This more flexible approach encourages innovation and growth by creating virtual organizations, where teams of interested individuals form for a specific purpose and dissolve when no longer needed.

Microsoft, for example, encourages what it calls "network mapping," the identification of thought leaders for particular projects, or information that is filed and brought into play only when needed, on an informal basis. Microsoft keeps these records in a database by project and interest areas. Anyone needing their help can access this thought-leader information and work with it, sharing ideas and finding new ways to grow products and services. This process helps Microsoft quickly shift resources to future customer needs, regardless of the specific unit in which the resource resides.

Train for growth.

Development and learning experiences, too, can foster a growth culture. Texas Instruments uses leadership training workshops to focus attention on ways to create the company's future. The workshop involves several groups: customers, technology thought leaders, representatives of the business from other countries, and participants from TI's various different businesses. Ideas pour in on new products, expanding and targeting distribution, capitalizing on upcoming technologies, and many other points. Each participant prepares a personal leadership agenda on ways to grow the business. When implemented in training efforts, these ideas may lead to growth.

Creating Management Equity

Although earnings might suggest a firm's value, the truest measure of value is how much investors are willing to pay. That might sound flippant, but it focuses on some key issues leaders have faced in creating investor results.

Leaders may measure economic value indicators and dutifully report them to their investors, but the price an investor is willing to pay for a share of stock may be affected by other factors. Investment adviser and author Peter Tanous interviewed a number of investment gurus and published the results in a book of that name. His objective was to discover how they decided to purchase, and thereby place a value on, a firm's stock. While these interviews stress mostly market buying strategies, such as value buying (investing in undervalued firms) versus growth buying (investing in firms positioned for growth), the following excerpts begin to offer insights on why EVA (economic value added) and other economic indicators of firm performance may not fully reflect stock price.

> Warren Buffett first went down to Washington and spent four hours with the chairman of GEICO before he bought his first share of GEICO. He then went on to buy the entire company. Now, I'll tell you, you have to do your homework and kick the tires. It's not the answers that make you good in this [investment] business, it's the questions you ask.[6]

We're buying a business and a business has certain attributes. We're not buying a piece of paper and we're not buying soybeans. As surrogate owners, there are certain characteristics with regard to the value of the franchise, the cash generating capabilities of the franchise, and the quality of management. So you have quantitative and qualitative measure.[7]

We look for a catalyst to bring out the value. It could be a management change, like George Fisher leaving Motorola to go over to Kodak. Or, a restructuring like Federated Department Stores management coming in and turning around Federated initially, then integrating Macy's and Broadway Stores acquisitions.

We like managers. Good management is the key. We'll buy some companies with secondary management and great asset values, but we obviously prefer having a good manager.[8]

We rarely buy a company without talking to its management. That comes from my audit experience. First, you tap into the great minds at the research firms, who have known the company for years. But by talking to the company, too, you get an undertone, How positive or negative are they?[9]

There are just so many inputs that you can't put into the computer, ranging from the extracurricular activities of the CEO to how the management treats the employees. There are so many different inputs that don't fit models. That's why you can't just put data into a computer and expect it to spit out buys and sells.[10]

What is the message behind these quotations from the gurus, all of whom make successful multimillion-dollar investments? They seem to be saying that, beyond financial rigor and analysis, making good investment decisions requires insight into the quality of a firm's management. We will call the value of a firm's stock above or below what would be expected, given the firm's accounting and economic results, "management equity." The perceived lack of management equity led KKR to withdraw its offer to finance Oxford, as described earlier. Leaders must build management equity, the perception in the investment community of the quality of management of the firm.

The importance of quality of management when making investment decisions should not be a surprise. Any potential supplier evaluating doing business with and thus taking a stake in a firm—a loan officer deciding whether to make a loan to the firm, a potential hire deciding to join the firm, a venture capitalist deciding to invest in the firm—will assess the firm's standing overall, including the perceived quality of management within the firm. The higher the perceived quality of management, the more access a firm has to debt, investment, and talented employees: This is the purpose of building a positive balance of management equity.

Research by the Ernst & Young Center for Business Innovation has discovered that for most investors, more than a third of any given allocation decision is attributable to performance information other than the financials.[11] The center surveyed portfolio managers who bought stock and examined purchase decisions. The nonfinancial factors most critical to investor decisions included what it called perceived quality of management, management credibility, quality of corporate strategy, innovativeness, and ability to attract and retain talented people. Its research validates observations by the investment gurus—that management equity impacts the market value of a firm.

COMPARING HIGH PERFORMERS

One of the more interesting ways to track the ability of leaders in a company to increase the value of their company is by comparing the market value of two firms in the same industry. A useful tool for this is the price-to-earnings ratio. We are not suggesting that the price/earnings ratio measures economic value; it does, however, indicate the price, or value of a firm times its earnings. It reveals a stock's value to investors. If two companies in the same industry have the same earnings but their stocks sell for different multiples of these earnings, the source of investors' perception of a *value* differential lies elsewhere.

Let's take a look at two of America's most enduring companies, Coca-Cola and PepsiCo. Over the last seven years, Coke has averaged a price-to-earnings ratio of approximately 41, whereas Pepsi has a price-to-earnings ratio of approximately 31. Although Pepsi has positions in many industries, including restaurants and snack foods as well as beverages, the industry has not rewarded it for this diversification. Coke's price-to-earnings ratio has remained 33 percent above Pepsi's, even after Pepsi divested its restaurant businesses. Why has Coke been able to provide more shareholder value than Pepsi, even when adjusted for earnings differences? Part of the answer lies in Coke's consistent and predictable earnings. It has regularly delivered the results it promises. Another part comes from investor perceptions of Coke's projected growth and profitability.

Leadership underlies both reasons. Coke has demonstrated over the years that it can maintain the quality leadership that the market expects, ensuring both credibility looking back and posterity looking forward. Coke has effectively transferred the responsibility for leadership throughout the company and has demonstrated its commitment to having leaders who create the results its shareholders expect and need. Leadership may not be the only factor in Coke's success, but it is key to other contributing factors, among them clarity in executive strategy, global branch expansion and access to markets, continuous innovation in distribution, and so on. Coke might be selling only a slightly different "sugar water" than Pepsi, but the market values Coke more for achieving these leadership-driven results.

Enron and Florida Power and Light provide another example of one company outperforming another in shareholder results. Both companies are in the forefront of their industry, but they create different shareholder results. Over the last ten years, Enron has averaged a price-to-earnings ratio of approximately 19 to Florida Power and Light's 14. Facing the same competitive situation and comparable future prospects, Enron has created significantly more shareholder value. Why?

Again, we suggest that Enron's leadership plays a significant role in achieving the larger multiple for the company's earning. Enron provides a prime example of a company whose leadership has created an organization that can effectively implement a strategy for meeting shareholder expectations, and thus a larger valuation from and for those shareholders. Enron's thoughtful leaders deftly balance the many necessary result levers. They provide a value proposition for their customers that yields superior results. They have created an adaptable organization that can continue to generate organizational results, and they clearly understand the value to be derived from their employees. By fulfilling these leadership imperatives, Enron successfully increases shareholder value.

INVESTING IN LEADERS

To have management equity, companies must invest in the quality of management. Investors demonstrate the positive effects of this when they respond to management actions or to changes in management. When a renowned CEO takes a new job, the market often reacts. When George Fisher joined Eastman Kodak, when Larry Bossidy joined AlliedSignal, the stocks of those companies moved in response. These short-term changes are less important, however, than the long-term value that new leaders bring to a firm.

If management equity matters (and the evidence shows that it does), when firms respected and renowned for the quality of depth of their management name new CEOs, the unchosen inside contenders often leave for opportunities elsewhere. The stock of these firms will respond positively, showing both short-term results immediately (after the announcement) and long-term results (as the new CEOs build the quality of management within their new firms). Using historical data, we suggest that leaders who have left General Electric to run other companies since Jack Welch was named CEO have created investor value for their new firms.

Almost all of them have achieved remarkable, measurable success and have positively affected their new companies' profitability, competitiveness, and in some cases, viability. The nature and extent of the challenges each faced varied, of course, from one to the next, according to the condition in which they found their new companies. Some were leaking sieves trying to remain afloat while others simply needed clear vision, a coherent strategy, and a strong structure to support that strategy.[12]

When Norman P. Blake took over USF&G, the property and casualty insurer, in 1990, for example, the company was in dreadful condition: overdiversified and bloated, with out-of-control costs, inflated dividends, and a stock in free fall (from $30.38 to $9.50 in 1989). Most observers had written the company off and were waiting for it to go into bankruptcy. Through radical surgery and strategic realignment, however, Blake not only saved USF&G, but also made it prosper, restoring and adding investor value. Within a year, the stock price began to climb, and it doubled in 1992, indicating investor confidence in Blake's leadership. Not bad for a company that Blake, upon taking command, had described as "not only bankrupt financially, but also bankrupt in terms of talent, leadership, skills, and systems—all the resources you need to play the game."[13]

A similar turnaround took place under former GE executive Glen Hiner, who took over as CEO and chairman of Owens Corning in 1992. The announcement alone had a decided and dramatic impact on stock price. The company, suffering from heavy debts, lack of talent, poor morale, and weak R&D, obviously needed help, and its stock price reflected this stagnation. Within one month of Hiner's stewardship, however, the stock jumped from $26.25 to $37.63, an increase of 43 percent. This growth continued for several years, as investors rewarded Owens-Corning for Hiner's realignment of the company and focus on product development.

An even more immediate impact from leadership change followed the appointment in 1997 of ex-GE leader John M. Trani as CEO and chairman of The Stanley Works. The company, in fair shape financially, was reeling from the previous CEO's structuring efforts, and its incoherent strategy could not arrest its declining market share. The perceived need for strong, effective leadership was made manifest by the dramatic jump in stock price on the day that Trani's appointment was announced: from $29.38 to $32.28, an increase of 10 percent. The stock price continued to increase, hitting $38 by the end of the month, for a one-month gain of almost 30 percent. Stanley stock has continued to thrive under Trani's leadership, outpacing the S&P 500 by almost 2 to 1.

Another former GE leader, Harry C. Stonecipher, inherited a tricky situation when he took over as CEO and chairman of McDonnell Douglas in 1994, but he was able to turn the situation to the shareholders' advantage through solid and inspired leadership. McDonnell Douglas had been whipped into fair financial shape by the previous CEO, but it suffered from malaise. Due to cost overruns, outdated products, and shrinking market share, its future looked uncertain. Following Jack Welch's dictum, "No. 1, No. 2, or fix, close, or sell," Stonecipher sold the entire company to Boeing. Stockholders manifested their confidence in Stonecipher throughout the entire process. In the first month of his tenure, the stock price jumped from $19.25 to $23.50, a 22 percent gain. The stock price continued to climb steadily, and by July 1997, when the Boeing deal became final, the stock hit $76.69, for a three-year increase of 298 percent.

Stanley Gault, originally with GE, moved first to Rubbermaid, exhibiting tremendous leadership skills there, before taking over as CEO and chairman of Goodyear Tire and Rubber in 1991. Goodyear was overdiversified and burdened with heavy debt, low margins, high costs, and noncompetitive products, but the effect of Gault's reputation for skilled leadership was such that, on the day his appointment was announced, Goodyear's stock price jumped from $13.50 to $15.09, an increase of almost 12 percent. Gault refocused Goodyear, cut costs, streamlined supply, and pushed the development of the high-end AquaTread radial tire. Goodyear's improved financial performance pushed the stock up to $34.13 within one year and up to $68.50 in June 1996, when Gault retired. During his five-year tenure, Goodyear stock had outpaced the S&P by almost 2 to 1.

Lawrence A. Bossidy, to take one further example of champions from the GE stable, took over as CEO and chairman of AlliedSignal in 1991. At the time, the company was stagnant, with flat earnings, a sluggish bureaucracy, and high costs. "We had 52 fiefdoms masquerading as separate businesses," Bossidy has remarked, recalling the situation when he took over.[14] He streamlined the company, shed unnecessary businesses, and consolidated suppliers. Within a short time, he had begun to produce remarkable shareholder results, which pushed up the stock price. By 1996, operating margins had increased from 4.7 percent to 9.1 percent, and productivity had increased to an average annual rate of 5.7 percent. For the five years ending 31 December 1995, total return to investors was 297 percent, outpacing both the Dow Jones Industrials at 125 percent and the S&P 500 at 115 percent. AlliedSignal's stock price also grew impressively, from $9.72 to $13.88 in the first year (an increase of 43 percent to $41.50 by March 1998).

The impact of quality management brought to firms by new leaders manifests itself through various approaches and actions. New leaders might speed up change by making the hard decisions that previous managers, perhaps because they "grew up" with the firm, could not make—or, having made originally, could not unmake. There is strength in weak ties. Not being locked into and committed to a course of action they created, new leaders bring a capacity for change. Enron provides an excellent example of this, where a new management team under Ken Lay completely redefined both the company and industry. New leaders might focus a firm's products and services by divesting businesses not central to a firm's direction. New leaders might bring discipline and accountability to the firm's operations, or new ideas and innovations that the previous management team lacked the motivation to produce (or the courage to implement). New leaders might establish fresher, more intimate relationships with suppliers, customers, and investors. They might also bring with them a new management team and invite other new hires to come into the firm at all levels. Last, but by no means least, new leaders might bring a new vision and energy to a firm. New leaders thus have the opportunities to increase all the results we have talked about: employee results (bringing in new employee capabilities and commitments), organization results (the organization's ability to change, learn, be accountable, and remove boundaries), and customer results (building a new firm equity in the minds of targeted customers).

MEASURING MANAGEMENT EQUITY

Investors continually make investments in management equity. Most of these investments are intuitive, however, based on the "gut feel" of the investor. Although research has not yet confirmed which specific factors determine the management equity of a firm, the questions and practices listed in Figure 6-1 may be helpful when attempting to influence it.

The concepts, questions, and practices in Figure 6-1 apply to all leaders in a firm, not just the top leader, because management equity should be embedded in the leadership team, not just the top person. The obligation of every leader at every level is to create and improve management equity and increase shareholder value. This checklist may also serve investors trying to determine the extent and nature of a firm's management equity.

IMPROVING MANAGEMENT EQUITY IS EVERY LEADER'S JOB

Most conversations about improving shareholder value make it seem as if the "real" results are achieved because of the way the CEO and CFO manage Wall Street, not the firm. Achieving superior shareholder value, however, would be impossible without the commitment of leaders at every level. The "miracle" of investor results follows from the hard work of executing the wealth of ideas contained in all of the previous chapters. Each leader throughout an organization may make a tremendous difference in his or her firm's ability to deliver investor results. Six key areas can stand out and apply across all organization levels.

Understand your industry.

Effective leaders understand their industry and their company's position in it. With this understanding, they may interpret changing conditions and translate changes into useful actions for their people. Leaders make sense of the world outside the firm and set a direction for their firm within the industry context.

Several years ago, Taco Bell introduced "value pricing" and shook up the industry. As their next step in the quest for dominance of the fast-food market, Taco Bell and Pizza Hut began to hire a new kind of leader at the restaurant level. Rather than hiring the traditional restaurant

FIGURE 6-1

ASSESSING QUALITY OF MANAGEMENT

CONCEPT AND QUESTION	ASSESS (1 = low, 10 = high)	INDICATIVE PRACTICES *Managers in this firm . . .*
Employee Capability To what extent do investors perceive that this firm's managers are demonstrating capability and are able to attract industry thought leaders to work in the firm?		• Regularly hire individuals who are seen as the best. • Are not threatened by highly qualified subordinates. • Have a reputation for hiring talented employees who are sought after by others in the industry. • Have personal and intimate industry knowledge.
Employee Commitment To what extent do investors perceive that managers inspire, motivate, and engage others in their agenda?		• Have the confidence of employees throughout the organization. • Retain the best and brightest talent in the industry. • Consistently measure and work to improve employee commitment.
Discipline and Accountability To what extent do investors have confidence in the ability of this firm's managers to deliver what they promise and to make tough decisions?		• Continually meet stated goals (for example, quarterly financial results). • Make difficult decisions about products (divesting bad businesses and investing in good ones), customers (segmenting targeted customers), and people (letting go of employees who don't perform). • Assign accountability to subordinates and let them do their job.

Concept and Question	Assess (1 = low, 10 = high)	Indicative Practices *Managers in this firm . . .*
Learning To what extent do investors perceive that this firm's managers have the capacity to learn?		• Are willing to learn and experiment. • Are open to new ideas and innovation. • Humbly acknowledge that they don't have all the answers. • Let go of pet projects and previous investments when circumstances dictate.
Change To what extent do investors perceive that this firm's managers have the capacity to change, adapt, and work flexibly?		• Make things happen. • Demonstrate a history of success in meeting project plans. • Implement new ideas quickly. • Have a disciplined methodology for making change happen.
Connections and Relationships To what extent do investors perceive that this firm's managers have sound relationships with critical stakeholders (including suppliers, customers, and investors)?		• Have personal relationships with key external stakeholders, including investors, customers, and suppliers. • Have the confidence of key external stakeholders. • Spend time with key stakeholders.

FIGURE 6-1

ASSESSING QUALITY OF MANAGEMENT *(continued)*

CONCEPT AND QUESTION	ASSESS (1 = low, 10 = high)	INDICATIVE PRACTICES *Managers in this firm . . .*
Focus To what extent do investors perceive that this firm's managers are able to focus through clear vision?		• Focus on a few priorities, even in the midst of performing many activities. • Build employee awareness of and commitment to the firm's vision. • Articulate a clear business strategy.
Personal Ownership To what extent do current managers have their personal net worth in the firm through stock ownership?		• Have a high personal net worth (not counting home value) in the firm's assets. • Assure stock ownership among a wide range of employees.
Experience and Industry Knowledge To what extent do current managers have industry experience and knowledge?		• Are able to understand and explain how the industry works. • Articulate the unique business requirements within the industry.
Customer Equity To what extent do current managers understand and build firm equity in targeted customers?		• Differentiate between targeted and other customers. • Understand the buying criteria of targeted customers. • Work to build personal relationships of trust with targeted customers.

manager, they hired well-educated, entrepreneurial leaders and gave them widespread responsibility and accountability for their geographic territories. Their job was to understand the competitors and customers within their territory and to expand their distribution points to increase customers' ease of access. Taco Bell and Pizza Hut soon appeared at bus stations, in high school cafeterias, at airports, and anywhere else potential customers congregate and might want to eat. This approach clearly did not involve centralized planning for market penetration. What it did accomplish was to find and develop local leaders charged with building their own business within the local context of an industry.

Live within budgets.

Two fundamental rules apply when aiming for stock price increase: (1) never surprise Wall Street, and (2) maintain consistent growth and earnings. The ability to meet both of these rules derives from and adds up to good leadership throughout a company. Every year, virtually every business sets growth targets and determines budgets. Most leaders participate peripherally in the first, but every leader participates fully in the second. The budgets established at all levels of a company must be adhered to rigorously. Exceptions may, of course, arise, making budget changes necessary. Leaders must feel personally accountable for meeting growth and cost targets.

Build performance management systems to support shareholder value.

Performance management systems have three steps: setting standards, distributing rewards, and providing feedback. All three may enhance shareholder value. Standards set for and by leaders should reflect shareholder value. Standards may be set around behaviors (what leaders do) and results (what they deliver). Rewards include financial short term (bonuses, cash awards), financial long term (stock grants, stock options, long term incentives), and nonfinancials (recognition, the work itself). Feedback implies that managers know the score and track their results by continually monitoring their performance against plan. Collectively, standards, rewards, and feedback work together to establish a performance management system to drive shareholder value.

The experience some years ago of senior officials in the Saskatchewan Public Service illustrated the importance of performance management systems. The province needed to improve employee performance.

The public, shareholders of the civil service, made too many negative comments about the quality of employee attitudes, lack of employee dedication, and poor service. The proposed solution was an incentive plan based on management by objectives (MBO). Much planning and effort went into launching the program and getting employees behind it. A minibureaucracy formed to guide and monitor the system, and teams responsive for training sessions traveled throughout the province.

Even though the paperwork, staff planning, and other efforts involved quickly mounted to gargantuan levels, a major flaw was built into the plan. As with the MBO systems generally, the Saskatchewan version required managers at all levels to meet with subordinates to agree on corporate goals and objectives for each individual, with the assumption that the cumulative effect of these goal-driven individuals would be a great surge in performance. At the end of a reporting period, leaders would meet with their subordinates and grade them on a scale ranging from "greatly exceeded requirements" to "met requirements" to "did not meet requirements." Successful leaders were to receive bonuses commensurate with their performance.

The flaw, seen by most employees as a deliberate plan to save money, lay in the predetermination of the number of employees to be cited as performing at each level. Only so many in each period—say, 5 percent, for example—could get the bonus allotted to employees who greatly exceeded requirements. Managers all over the province found frustrating these constraints on how they could rate their staff's performance. It meant, inevitably, that some who deserved significant bonuses were denied them because of percentage ceilings or because other raters had better writing abilities. Morale suffered among underrated and undercompensated managers who had expected more from the program, based on the publicity it was given at launch. The plan failed, with much effort expended for little result.

Lead by example.

Leaders at each level set examples that employees follow. To build shareholder value, leaders need to model ownership and commitment to the firm. Successful shareholder value leaders act as if they own the organization by taking personal accountability for decisions, saving money on work activities (for example, flying coach, using regular dining room), and doing things that they ask employees to do.

A story told about Bill Hewlett, then company president of Hewlett-Packard, illustrates the point and defect of the precept "lead by example." Hewlett, wearing a white lab coat and doing some photocopying after hours, was stopped by a new secretary who saw him and asked accusingly, "Were you the one who left on the lights and copy machine last night?" "Uh, well, I guess I did," he replied. "Don't you know that we have an energy-saving program in the company and that Bill [Hewlett] and Dave [Packard] have asked us to be particularly careful about turning off lights and equipment?" she asked. "I am very sorry. It won't happen again," replied Bill. Two days later, the secretary again saw Hewlett, now wearing a suit and name tag, and thought, "Oh, no. I chewed out the company president."[15]

Hewlett, of course, was unperturbed by the incident, simply accepting the justified correction: he had not followed his own energy-saving policy. But neither did he pull rank on the secretary. He felt as bound by the rules he had set as he hoped others would feel, and he believed and acted on another HP idea in demonstrating it: "We are family here; we treat people with respect and as equals."

Communicate with investors.

Investors do not like surprises. Leaders communicate with investors by keeping them informed about strategy, goals, performance against goals, and unforeseen activities. When Harry Kraemer became chief financial officer at Baxter Healthcare, he developed relationships with the investment community. He began a weekly letter to investors about Baxter's performance and recent events. He held frequent conference calls with major shareholders to let them know how the firm performed against goals. He invited investors to contact him frequently and often with their questions. Harry's efforts succeeded. Investors came to appreciate his management style and candor. When he was announced as president, then chief executive officer, he received universal acclaim and support from the investment community.

Positive investor relations occur when firms know and continually work with major shareholders so that each shareholder understands the rationale behind decisions. When a medical devices firm attempted to significantly increase employee ownership, it required shareholder approval. Many large investors opposed the plan, fearing it would erode the long-term value of the firm. The CEO personally visited each major investor and spent hours going over the details of this plan, the logic behind it, and the expected impact on employee productivity. While these visits took a great deal of his time, he felt that the investors needed to fully appreciate the firm's strategy.

Channels of communication with investors may include personal visits of key leaders, visits by investors to sites throughout the firm, conferences on special events and changes, and frequent and consistent communications. These efforts help investors come to know how the firm operates and how leaders within the firm think and act. Such insights increase investor confidence and shareholder value.

Create a values mind-set, then align employee behavior to that mind-set.

A mind-set represents the implicit assumptions that shape behavior. For example, Intel has created a mind-set in which employees challenge ideas and push back on leaders; Ritz-Carlton has instilled a mind-set of guest service; and McDonald's has shaped a mind-set of speed. The mind-sets in these firms determine how employees behave. Leaders who instill a shareholder value mind-set focus employee attention and behavior on meeting financial obligations. This occurs when leaders translate revenue growth and cost reduction goals into employee behavior.

In one firm, each leader facilitated a workshop with direct reports. In this workshop, the leader shared the firm's financial standing. This firm had recently made acquisitions and promised Wall Street improved margins from these acquisitions. These margins failed to materialize, and the firm risked missing stated earning and profit goals. Leaders presented this information to direct reports with simple charts that showed promised versus delivered results. Leaders then asked their employees to brainstorm answers to three questions:

1. What are some "silly" ways we could make our margin goals? This question let employees voice what they felt would be ill-informed ways to reach goals. For example, lists often included such things as cutting advertising, reducing headcount 10 percent across all units, stopping all travel, and so forth. This question and subsequent discussion allowed employees to express concerns about cost reductions and to made sure that employees set parameters on what would subsequently occur.

2. What are some "bold" moves we could make to meet margin goals? This question allowed employees to brainstorm more dramatic ways to reduce costs and grow the business. They identified such innovative and out-of-the-box ideas as closing a plant or site, reducing product lines, or ending service to some customers. These more drastic ways to reduce costs require bold and aggressive decisions by senior management. Allowing employees to generate this list helps soften the blow if these solutions follow.

3. What are some "incremental" moves we could make to meet margin goals? This question and subsequent dialogue allowed employees to take personal responsibility for cost reduction. Employees make dozens of daily decisions, the aggregation of which affect margins. As leaders direct their teams through decisions about workflow, inventory, use of supplies, and other productivity actions, each employee sees how daily personal actions impact overall business results.

Collectively these actions helped create a shareholder value mindset for the firm which translated to employee behavior.

Leaders' Role in Shareholder Value

Leaders' actions throughout a company help grow a business, reduce costs, and increase shareholder value. Collectively, the actions described in this chapter will increase investor results as measured in financial terms. Acquiring the knowledge and mastering the tools for financial discipline increases as leaders collaborate with financial staff within the company. Our final caveat is to ensure that leaders do not assume that financial results are the only result. As suggested in Figure 6-1, many management actions create financial results, and positive financial results allow for investments in employee, organization, and customer results.

Becoming a Results-Based Leader

7

THIS CHAPTER ADDRESSES how any person currently in a leadership position can modify his or her leadership behavior to better focus on results and take charge of his or her own leadership development to become a more effective results-based leader.

Most leaders receive countless invitations to attend leadership development seminars and conferences sponsored by universities and by professional and commercial organizations. The prospectuses describe appealing content, absolutely essential to every leader's career survival and success, taught by academics and others of impeccable credentials to groups of powerful, like-minded executives. These programs may be tempting, but although they may have been developed with the best intentions, they very often fail to produce measurable returns.[1] The theories may be interesting and the proposed attributes and behaviors compelling, but participants do not improve their performance.

The following suggestions, on the other hand, which may be implemented right now by any leader occupying any position, will modify behavior and improve performance—all without a month-long absence from work or expenditures of large sums of money.

1. Begin with an absolute focus on results.

2. Take complete and personal responsibility for your group's results.

3. Clearly and specifically communicate expectations and targets to the people in your group.

4. Determine what you need to do personally to improve your results.

5. Use results as the litmus test for continuing or implementing leadership practice.

6. Engage in developmental activities and opportunities that will help you produce better results.

7. Know and use every group member's capabilities to the fullest and provide everyone with appropriate developmental opportunities.

8. Experiment and innovate in every realm under your influence, looking constantly for new ways to improve performance.

9. Measure the right standards and increase the rigor with which you measure them.

10. Constantly take action; results won't improve without it.

11. Increase the pace or tempo of your group.

12. Seek feedback from others in the organization about ways you and your group can improve your outcomes.

13. Ensure that your subordinates and colleagues perceive that your motivation for being a leader is the achievement of positive results, not personal or political gain.

14. Model the methods and strive for the results you want your group to use and attain.

The following is the reasoning behind each of these proposed actions, plus some ideas about their implementation:

1. *Begin with an absolute focus on results.*

This step is both the first and the most important. By starting with results, leaders find the one log in the logjam that prevents the hundreds of others from moving downstream. To find that log, ask and answer this question: What are the results that my organization needs and expects from my group?

The required question emphatically is not: What kind of a person must I be? Results must be clear before attributes can be brought into play. Ways of achieving balanced, strategically aligned, lasting, and self-less results in each of the four key results areas—employee results, organization results, customer results, and investor results—are described fully in the preceding chapters. When leaders get a clear picture of desired results, everything else can connect.

After clearly defining results, leaders can identify any results gap by asking the question: What results am I getting now? Some of the best results-based leaders, such as Jack Welch of GE and Andy Grove of Intel, have adopted the mantra "See the world as it is, not as we would like it to be." The requisite ruthless, rigorous, and relentless examination of "what is" can be accomplished using various data-collecting techniques and extensive interviews with current and former employees, industry experts, academicians, present and past customers, shareholders, investment bankers, market researchers, and technology leaders. Careful analysis should be made of all available performance indicators, which should, in turn, be objectively compared with those of the company's best competitors. But the key to getting a useful answer to the question is brutal honesty. Wash away all the sugar coating and home team prejudice. Comparison of what is desired with what is expected should take place only after the leader has a thorough understanding of the reality the organization or group faces. Only then will it begin to be clear what needs to be improved or changed.

One aspect of an absolute focus on results is giving results priority over everything else, except adherence to the organization's ethical standards and values. To attain positive results, leaders must be willing to work long hours, often at significant personal sacrifice, and must be willing to make tough, sometimes unpleasant decisions that may impact others negatively. Leaders who, as people, need to be liked more than they need to achieve high-level outcomes have made bad career decisions in becoming leaders.

2. *Take complete and personal responsibility for your group's results.*

Leaders can easily pass blame for the poor performance of a work group, or even an entire corporation, to others. Frequently leaders blame their predecessors, the economy, government regulation, foreign competition, domestic competition, incompetent subordinates, internal sabotage, or just bad luck for their poor performance. Leaders who detach themselves from the results of their group act as if they were blameless strangers who just stumbled onto the scene of an accident. This impulse must be countered.

Such buck-passing not only undermines morale, it undercuts the possibility of change and improvement. For example, at one large corporation that had fallen to the bottom of its lagging industry, executives at monthly operating committee meetings announced their group's performance figures as if they were TV news anchors giving the day's business report. These executives, surrealistically detached from the emotions that would normally accompany the realization of such terrible performance, were equally estranged from the kind of personal commitment to organization results that would help them overcome their problems.

Effective leaders don't place blame on anyone else or anywhere else. This must be true *especially* when things go poorly. In this situation, the best leaders accept complete responsibility for any shortfall in performance and any mistakes that have been made. And the best leaders, because they accept complete responsibility for their group's performance, are far from dispassionate observers. Effective leaders should step out of the "responsibility box" only when things go extremely well. When this happens, they praise their subordinates and pass on to them the credit for the group's excellent performance and outstanding results.

Unfortunately, many weak and insecure leaders (and anyone who has spent any time in the business world can no doubt think of an example) do just the opposite, blaming subordinates for every failure and taking credit for every success. These leaders will never achieve the highest level of results because they inevitably alienate coworkers and subordinates and create discord and mistrust where they should strive for cooperation and communication.

Results-based leaders support the efforts of their group members, but at the same time, they must be willing to make tough decisions regarding people who do not perform to an acceptable level. Leaders who care about results address poor performance first with coaching. Should that fail, they proceed to transfer or terminate the underperforming employee. If leaders fail to act in these circumstances, they send the clear signal that they value avoiding the personal discomfort of taking painful measures above the performance of the group. Such a position would not be appropriate for a results-based leader.

3. Clearly and specifically communicate expectations and targets to the people in your group.

A common complaint about leaders from the people who report to them is that that they don't know what is expected of them, that they have been left to guess about what is important. And even when general agreement does exist about the things that need to be done, significant disagreement may remain over priorities. When leaders do not take a results focus, these ambiguities persist. The results focus clarifies for everyone what targets should be sought. When the results are clear, priorities fall into place more readily, and the creative energies of group members can be productively applied to finding ways of achieving the desired results.

Goals that have this kind of power tend to be lofty, challenging, and noble, or what one popular text rather incongruously terms BHAG, "bold, hairy, audacious goals."[2] Leaders determining what targets to pursue should always aim high rather than low. Worthwhile causes challenge people to stretch; they energize and motivate people. But aspirations, however noble, must also translate to specific, measurable results; without that, goals remain elusive dreams and ethereal wishes rather than results. Chapters 3 through 6 provide a number of ways to measure employee, organization, customer, and investor results in ways that stretch thinking, while focusing action.

Leaders should not decide alone on these outcomes, causes, objectives, or goals. The more input they solicit, the better the quality of goals formulated and the wider and deeper their acceptance. Because leaders are frequently asked to express a vision, to let people in their group know "where we are going," they often assume that they must derive that vision on their own. Nothing could be worse for a group than to isolate this obligation. One of the paradoxes of leadership resides in this very dilemma: the word *leadership* seems to imply an individual activity, but those who succeed best at it do so because they involve and energize others. They rely heavily on the people around them: they build leadership *teams.*

After collecting dozens of ideas, and after ample discussion, someone does need to pull these ideas together and select the road the organization will follow for the coming six to eighteen months. Equally as important, the decision needs to be made regarding what the group *won't* do. Often harder to determine than a course of action, knowing what activities to avoid or renounce may provide a great deal of clarity to subordinates and others in an organization.

By focusing on results, leaders are more likely to address the truly important and most challenging issues before the group. However long these may have been skirted, the results-based leader will inevitably be drawn into them, if they stand in the way of getting good results.

The following example illustrates the opportunities for change open to leaders who focus on results.

Employees of a pharmaceutical company facing a significant sales shortfall attributed the problem to an almost total lack of coordination among product development, marketing, and sales. Not uncommonly, the company's product development team spent years on products the sales force didn't think it could sell and consequently *didn't* sell. Marketing strategy, too, was developed in complete isolation from sales. Few in the company dared talk openly about the problem, even though nearly everyone recognized its seriousness. But this lack of coordination among three major functions was something few dared talk about, and those who did were convinced nothing would happen.

When a new general manager was appointed, he set as a goal and priority increasing sales. When he investigated the causes for the continued sales shortfall, people cautiously pointed out the conflict among the three groups. In contrast to previous leaders, he chose to ignore the politics and the past. In operating committee meetings, he pressed subordinates on the problem of poor sales performance until they finally began to address, on their own, the lack of coordination—because it stood in the way of getting crucial results. (Although the leader did get results, the exercise on boundarylessness in Chapter 4 would have helped him do so more directly.)

In an example from the public sector, a senior executive directed one region of the Social Security Administration to streamline its operation and improve overall efficiency by increasing, by a specific date, the number of subordinates under the management of one supervisor from seven to fifteen. Much grumbling and many cries of "Impossible!" followed the directive. But the goal and time frame were set and clearly understood. Managers were given discretion on execution, and some quickly saw the benefits and how most efficiently to achieve them. Without its specificity, the directive very likely would have languished as vague good intentions. The results might have been even better had the agency executives started, not with structure, but with capabilities, as described in Chapter 4—a surer route to lasting change.

Leaders need to ensure that everyone in their organization understands thoroughly what strategy is to be pursued; that is, that they have a clear operating definition of what their organization will and won't do. When everyone understands the mechanism by which an organization links with its customers (as illustrated by the value propositions in Figure 5-2), alignment of means and goals is enhanced.

A basic target for every organization is to better serve its target customers, and nearly every leader needs to find ways to involve subordinates in improving customer connections, whether they lead accounting, manufacturing, human resources, sales, customer service, or an entire corporation. Basic techniques, described in Chapter 5, illustrate several ways leaders could build customer connections through management practices, including recruiting customer-oriented people, involving people in development activities that enhance their customer orientation, celebrating customer successes, and having good feedback systems that keep everyone apprised of how well the organization is serving customers.

4. Determine what you personally need to do to improve your results.

Many activities can and should be delegated. Indeed, delegation is one of those rare occasions when both parties win. Leaders win the time to do the things only they can do, and subordinates win new assignments through which they can grow. However, if organizations are to attain peak results, only leaders should perform certain key tasks. It is the leader's job as well, especially the results-based leader, to define those tasks that only they can do and then to make certain they do them well and on time.

Obviously, *what* the leader must personally do is not fixed. In some cases, a leader may be needed to repair relations with a key customer; in others, to change a repressive culture to be more adaptive and responsive. Other situations may call for technology improvements; the streamlining of internal work processes; or the definition, communication, and execution of a new or existing strategy.

What determines those tasks the leader alone must perform? Perhaps no one else is available. Perhaps the activity requires an executor with a certain level of title, role, or power. Such considerations often prevail, for example, in relations with key suppliers or major customers. The fundamental nature of the task, too, may demand a leader's participation. Clarifying a group or organization's vision and mission, dealing with poorly performing individuals, setting pay, or changing organization structure requires broad-based involvement and authority. Difficult decisions impacting conditions of employment, such as relocation activities or moving from an inside to an outside supplier, always involve the leader. The success achieved by results-based leaders hinges on doing those things only they can do and not holding back their organization by being unwilling to accept those difficult assignments.

When Kay Whitmore was CEO of Kodak, most analysts thought a major slimming was needed to keep Kodak competitive and reduce its cost structure. But Rochester, New York, was a "company town." The people who would have lost their jobs were friends, neighbors, and longtime work colleagues and associates. An insider just could not take the harsh steps needed for a major cutback. Whitmore was removed by the board, and the difficult task fell to his successor, George Fisher. As an outsider, Fisher could more easily make the needed changes.

Canceling projects, shutting an unproductive sales office, stopping a line of research, and implementing new work processes that relocate people constitute leadership responsibilities that are easier to let go of than to execute. But failing to step in when issues press on a company's results undermines leaders and leadership; the executive becomes a mere time server or seat warmer and loses the opportunity to be a strong, results-based leader.

Some leaders expect others to produce effective results without recognizing that their own personal productivity may be the key to the organization's overall success. Results-based leaders never form a bottleneck to decisions. If work gets delayed or jammed up because of the leader's indecision, he or she is blocking the system and failing to lead. Even when the leader finally does decide, the organization will face a struggle to catch up and will have incurred a high cost in loss of effectiveness, timeliness, and coordination.

5. *Use results as the litmus test for continuing or implementing leadership practice.*

Having and using a results litmus test to judge any leadership practice will, in the long run, greatly improve anyone's leadership style. This can be seen in the demise, slow but now sure, of "command and control" management. The history of the shift to management practices favoring "communication and commitment," which correspond to greater employee participation, is telling. Such systems achieved dramatically better results in quality, innovation, and productivity, as companies in Japan and Scandinavia demonstrated. U.S. industries, competing globally, such as the automobile industry, simply could not keep up without changing their management approach. Leadership practices didn't change because executives and managers tired of autocratic decision making; for centuries leaders have thoroughly enjoyed "command and control." Only lagging results obtained from such behavior could have caused its fall from favor.

Similarly, we have known since the 1950s that flatter and less hierarchical organizations attract more entrepreneurial people and attain higher performance levels than do highly bureaucratic organizations. But organizations didn't pursue delayering and downsizing until the 1980s. Why? Because, until then, we could live with the mediocre results. When this was no longer tolerable, organizations began to change. Again, the reason was not a change in philosophy or abandonment of the practice of judging leaders' worth by the number of people reporting to them. No. The reason was that results took center stage and could no longer be overlooked.

Any leader making results a starting place for change will find style considerations easy to resolve. Current practices can and will change. Any management practice or policy should be examined using the question: What kind of results does it produce? Leaders can no longer rely on questions such as "What practices do I personally prefer?" or "What leadership practices make me most comfortable?"

Chapters 2 through 6 offered a number of specific ideas for managers trying to deliver employee, organization, customer, and investor results to their organizations. Among them were the following key points:

- Intensifying focus.

- Streamlining work processes.

- Changing organization structure.

- Revising the compensation systems.

- Outsourcing certain activities now performed internally.

- Sponsoring organizational culture change interventions, such as GE's "Workout."

- Encouraging employee development activities.

- Instituting performance management systems.

- Clarifying vision, values, and mission.

- Improving measurement systems.

How should leaders decide which ideas, or combination of ideas, to pursue? All too readily, leaders fall into the trap of following current trends, mimicking what others do, or of succumbing to pressures from board members or to suggestions from outside consultants. The test that leaders should apply ought to be, simply: Which ideas will have the biggest impact on our results?

Some cynics argue that the total quality movement lies dead or dying. It had its decade of popularity and produced spectacular results. And like any popular movement, however, the crowds tire of it and move on to the next "program du jour." But consider the announcement by Jack Welch that GE would embark on a "Six Sigma" total quality program, patterned after one at Motorola, with a goal of only 3.4 defects per million on products and service. Some observers expressed shock that Welch would undertake such an outdated program. But Welch focused only on the results the program would produce for GE, not on whether it was a politically correct or popular initiative.

6. *Engage in personal development activities and opportunities that will help you produce better results.*

Leaders today engage in many activities that they claim will make them more effective. They seek outsiders' insights by attending lectures given by academics and management gurus; by reading the latest management books and articles; by participating in business simulations; by taking part in laboratory learning activities to examine their interpersonal behavior through small, facilitated group activities; by joining teams engaged in action learning projects in which leaders work together to solve real problems their organizations face; and by discussing business case studies.

They also look to themselves or to others within their organizations for insights to help strengthen their skills. They take batteries of psychometric tests to measure personality or social skills; do in-basket activities to simulate paperwork handling; rehearse presentations in front of video cameras and get feedback on how to improve their face-to-face communication; send out 360-degree feedback instruments to solicit comments from bosses, clients, and subordinates; and engage in physically challenging group activities, such as kayaking, rope or rock climbing, and mountain climbing, to build teamwork and confidence.

Each of these activities may have value, but what and how much depends on the worthiness of the source, the receptivity of the learner, and the immediacy of application of the skill, information, or insight. When any developmental activity is widely separated from the time when it will be used, there is an enormous falloff in the likelihood that it will be implemented. One of the prime measures of the value of any developmental activity should be: Can this be applied immediately?

A results-based orientation, as suggested in Chapter 2, would guide the leader into formulating, for any proposed developmental activity, the statement "I will do _____ so that _____ will happen." If studying a business case, listening to a speaker, taking a psychological test, doing in-basket exercises, or any one of the many other popular leadership development activities doesn't produce some measurable result, then why do it? Does it relate to the leader's job? Will it be rewarded? Will it last?

Leaders must seek developmental activities that address areas in which they would benefit from personal growth. Tailored activities are clearly best for this. Herding large numbers of executives into a classroom and giving them all exactly the same information or engaging them all in exactly the same activity does little to respond to their very different learning styles and needs. It's a bit like giving Prozac to all of the patients in a hospital, or removing everyone's appendixes, no matter what their symptoms or diagnosis. Everyone would say, "How foolish!" But large groups of leaders attending development programs experience exactly the same treatment.

Leaders need to invest in development with impact by looking to make the most of the time they devote to developmental activities and by keeping in mind the following principles:[3]

- Choose concrete, practical content that was well researched and has been proven to be conceptually sound. Avoid totally academic, purely theoretical, or merely storytelling sessions.

- Choose job-related activities, such as action learning projects with teams of leaders working on and learning from real problems.

- Choose personalized, tailored leadership development activities. This includes soliciting feedback from peers and colleagues, and personalized coaching. Leaders should make a clear-eyed assessment of their flat sides and select development activities that will round them out.

- Choose active rather than passive processes. People learn more when they are intensely engaged, and the learning sticks with them longer. An active problem-solving discussion will have far more impact than listening to even the most engaging and persuasive lecturer.

- Choose ongoing activities or activities with a number of sessions over time rather than single events. More learning will be gained, retained, and more likely applied on the job.

- Select development activities with immediate application. Most training has a definite "half-life," and if it is not used rather quickly, it will be lost.

- Select measurable activities that allow participants to see how well they are learning and applying the lessons received.

- Make sure every development activity connects to a clearly defined result.

Increasingly, large organizations, both in the public and the private sector, consider their employees' development the employees' own affair. The organization no longer guides careers, but favors self-reliance, providing feedback at times on what development is needed, and, even more occasionally, making it available. Leaders today must take responsibility for their own development, both in content and in timing. Each leader must be sure that his or her development happens and continues to happen.

7. Know and use every group member's capabilities to the fullest and provide everyone with appropriate developmental opportunities.

Both to enhance group capabilities and to be sure that they mesh with the organization's capabilities and goals, leaders must know the strengths and weaknesses of each individual within their group, so that the former can be played on and the latter shored up or eliminated. To start with, leaders should have or obtain an up-to-date assessment of the capabilities of the individuals for whom they are responsible. (One possible form for such assessment appears in Figure 3-1.) After then analyzing their organization's overall intellectual capital (an exercise for this also appears in Chapter 3), they should determine which of the six "B" steps for enhancing employee capability—build, buy, benchmark, borrow, bounce, or bind—the organization is using, and how well it is being executed. Next, leaders should look at group members' level of commitment (also using tools found in Chapter 3), as revealed in productivity, climate, surveys, and retention figures. Finally, they should use the checklists in Chapter 3 to customize the employee deal and increase employee commitment.

Development designed to enhance a subordinate's attributes is appropriate; it can even be desirable or necessary when some dimension of a subordinate's attributes gets in the way of his or her success. But a test should be applied before a decision is made. The leader and the employee should be able to find a compelling way to complete this sentence: "This person exhibits behavior that is having _____ effect, and we want to change it so that _____." If the behavior has no clear negative results or if the change resulting from the development opportunity has no clear benefit, then it may be an unnecessary development exercise. Effective results-based leaders emphasize development that produces important near-term results.

8. *Experiment and innovate in every realm under your influence, looking constantly for new ways to improve performance.*

Results-based leaders avoid getting locked into once-useful approaches or points of view that once worked but have now outlived their usefulness. Some hold decentralization, for example, as a sacred organizational principle, to be chiseled in stone on every home office building. But in recent years, many organizations have found that some activities can be handled more economically through shared services, including many high-volume, low-dollar-value transactions, such as travel reimbursement. A number of Fortune 500 companies looking into payroll costs found that, although the average payroll check costs between $5 and $6, one company—which had centralized the function—was processing payroll checks for only 72 cents each. Accounts payable, accounts receivable, and employee benefits claims processing, too, are often more economically handled through shared services.

For decades, common wisdom held that managers could supervise no more than seven to twelve people, a widely accepted management axiom. Then came new forms of organization, including self-managing teams: one manager might now be responsible for sixty to seventy people. Productivity increased. Quality improved. Morale rose. When tested, the old span-of-control ratio gave way. Better results could be obtained in a different fashion. But making that discovery required innovation and experimentation.

Some leaders react instinctively to any reasonable suggestion with "Yes, let's try it." Others, similarly challenged, give a knee-jerk, flat "No." These types of leaders develop groups with markedly different cultures. Organizations that tend to be stodgy, traditional, and locked in the past got that way by listening to a preponderance of nay-saying leaders. The highly adaptive, change-friendly organization, on the other hand, has a history of leaders eager to listen to everyone's suggestions, who encourage people to try whatever makes sense to them.

Many people view suggestion boxes as a throwback, but some organizations today make them work. Any system that encourages a mentality favoring innovation and experimentation will prove valuable to the organization. Leaders both set a tone of open-mindedness and acceptance and create a culture that generates continual improvement and innovation.

Chapter 4 includes a number of specific strategies that leaders can use to build organizational capability. The most important points are listed below:

- Make sure the right organization is in place, based on capabilities, not structure.

- Develop efficient systems and work processes to streamline work.

- Embed and monitor fundamental critical capabilities in the organization.

- Foster the organization's ability to learn (see Figure 4-5).

- Control the pace at which the organization works, assessing such qualities as speed, agility, flexibility, and responsiveness.

- Strive for a boundaryless mentality to allow people and ideas to freely move across organizational units and to act as a virtual organization when necessary (see Figure 4-7).

- Maintain an ethos of accountability, holding people's feet to the fire about getting work done, meeting deadlines, and ensuring work with high quality and with the customer's interests always in mind (see Figure 4-8).

9. *Measure the right standards and increase the rigor with which you measure them.*

If this book leaves leaders with only one message, it should be that results matter and that results must be measured. Results-based leaders must feel comfortable with metrics. They must create a unique dashboard of gauges to monitor organizational performance. No two dashboards will (or should) be alike. The important point is to select the handful of significant measures that reveals to the leader and everyone else how well the organization performs.

Leaders should periodically get personally involved in calculating some of the numbers shown on the dashboard. Such calculations can, for the most part, be done by computer, but there is no substitute for taking paper and pencil and working the figures through. Compute the gross margins on your business's major products; calculate the revenues per salesperson. Pushing the pencil somehow brings numbers alive; they mean more. Leaders cannot, of course, spend hours doing what their bookkeepers or computers should do, but they will benefit from doing however much will make the numbers really sink in and have meaning for them.

The results of the chosen measures should be presented in as simple and graphic a way as possible, and posted in a public place (or places). Tables with rows and columns of numbers won't generate much excitement. Bar charts, pie charts, simple diagrams, and graphs do a far better job of catching the eye and communicating information. Charles Schwab, the industrialist (not the stockbroker), while one day visiting one of his steel mills as the day shift was leaving, took a piece of chalk and wrote on the floor the number of steel ingots that shift had produced. The night shift, seeing the number, took it as a challenge and proceeded to produce more ingots than the day shift and wrote the number in chalk on the floor. As days went by, productivity escalated shift by shift—simply because Schwab had written a number in chalk on the plant floor.

Leaders benefit as well from documenting what they learn from their experience—especially results obtained from specific decisions. Make it a practice to write down what you anticipated would happen when you made a decision, and then write down and compare your expectations to what really did happen. Every group member should also be encouraged to keep a log of decisions he or she makes, their intended outcomes, and their actual results. This provides a mechanism for reflecting on what brought success and what brought failure. Leaders can ask themselves and others about how problems might have been foreseen and about the underlying causes of both huge successes and painful failures. Such memoranda aid in the search for recurring factors that proved to be important but had not been taken into account.

10. Constantly take action; results won't improve without it.

Leaders must act to produce results. This doesn't mean firing without aim or leaping without looking. But if leadership means getting results, then leaders must constantly push tendencies into results. The necessity to take action extends into every dimension of the work leaders undertake.

When *staffing,* leaders must ensure that their organizations recruit top-flight people with proven track records of achievement and results. Leaders themselves often exhibit some personality or character flaw. These don't matter if the leaders get the job done—with one strong caveat: leaders cannot willfully and deliberately violate the values of the organization or act dishonestly and unethically in their business dealings. To do so is to fail the organization.

Leaders must *organize* to get things done. Task forces or teams should be given clear charters to accomplish their goals within sixty days or some other specific, reasonable time frame. Committees should not be appointed to study a problem but should be given responsibility for understanding an issue, proposing a solution, and implementing that solution once it has been approved. Every organizational decision should be driven by a specific result to be achieved.

Leaders must *communicate.* They convey their enthusiasm for the end result to be accomplished. Nothing helps to move a project along faster and further than having a leader who is clear about the end objective, excited and positive about the process, and capable of and willing to run interference with the larger organization when necessary.

Leaders *focus* on opportunities for results. By focusing on what people can do rather than on what they can't do, leaders encourage results and avoid paralysis. So many of the guidelines published in large organizations deal with what is forbidden. How much more productive it would be to focus attention on the horizons and wide latitude for action open to employees. Encourage people with good ideas to go ahead and implement them, if they can provide reasonable assurance that the change won't negatively affect others.

11. Increase the pace or tempo of your group.

One surefire way to improve most groups' results is to pick up their tempo. Emphasize speed. Get things done more rapidly.

The point here is not to ask people to perform like Charlie Chaplin in the classic silent movie *Modern Times,* in which the Little Tramp must race desperately against the ever-increasing pace of a conveyor belt until it finally drags him into the machinery's massive gears. Unsustainable, frenetic work should be avoided, not sought.

But organizations develop a pace and rhythm for their activities, a pace that can easily become unnecessarily lethargic. One of the most powerful challenges any leader can put to a group is to cut the time it takes to produce a given output by one-third or one-half. This requirement forces a new mentality on everyone. People begin to ask new questions, not "How can I do that a little better?" but "Why do we do that? Is that necessary?" For many if not most activities, truly accelerating their pace requires eliminating one or more constituent tasks.

The beauty of this simple recommendation is that every department can do it. Human resources can cut in half the time required to design a new compensation system. Customer service can cut in half the time needed to respond to a customer inquiry. Order fulfillment can improve response time as well.

Increasing speed has the paradoxical consequence of cutting cost. Many would intuitively assume that doing tasks more rapidly costs more. But just the opposite seems usually to be the case. Cutting the time allotted to any task eliminates extraneous activities. Barnacles don't collect on the hull of a ship speeding through the water—they don't need to be scraped off.

The leader can do a great deal by personal example to pick up the work pace. The leader's pace usually sets the pace of the entire group.

The leader's dedication to doing whatever it takes to make a deadline or fulfill an assignment stimulates similar dedication on the part of the group.

12. Seek feedback from others in the organization about ways you and your group can improve your outcomes.

Other people have valuable perspectives on how well leaders and their groups function and what good they produce for the overall organization. Even in large organizations with a thousand senior managers, studies have found that, on average, any one leader had strong opinions about the leadership practices of two-thirds of his or her colleagues.

Approach colleagues directly and ask for their feedback, offering in return an analysis of their group's strengths and weaknesses. The following questions will generally elicit useful comments, particularly from internal or external customers of the group:

- Are we producing the right outcomes for you?

- If not, what would you like to be receiving that you're not?

- Are we performing in a timely way for you?

- Are we performing at the right level of quality?

- Do you see ways for us to improve our efficiency or productivity?

- What suggestions do you have for better ways for us to supply what you need?

- What should we start doing that we're not doing now?

Most of the important work of an organization doesn't get done in the traditional hierarchical silo, but in the horizontal channels that connect the functional activities. To improve results, leaders must know what is flowing through those channels, that it is exactly what is needed, and that it is timely, high quality, and produced using the best possible methods.

13. Make sure that your subordinates and colleagues perceive that your motivation as a leader is the achievement of positive results and not personal or political gain.

Every organization has a large number of people who aspire to leadership for the wrong reasons. Like moths flying toward candle flames, attracted by the light, they are singed or killed by the heat. The moths get something entirely different from what they were expecting.

For leadership, too, some perceive the lures and trappings which unfortunately destroy many people. Some expect that occupying a leadership position gives them power over others, that it is their position and not their ideas and commitment that count. They see the ceremonial public role of the leader as glamorous and the routine connected with leadership—chairing a task force, conducting staff meetings, or divvying up assignments—as sources of prestige. Some people value the leader's high salary, lofty title, opulent office, prime parking space, liberal expense account, or ample support staff, or the leader's opportunities to look good handling exciting crisis and emergencies. Finally, many aspiring leaders mistakenly believe the job involves not a lot of dedication and hard work, but merely keeping tabs on others in the organization.

Leaders do, of course, experience or perform all of the above. What these superficial, limited perceptions of leadership overlook, however, is the substance of the job—the goals, the efforts, the results. And these shallow aspirants overlook something else, too: the "heat" that every leader contends with, the uncomfortable things that every leader must do to produce peak results.

One organization involved hundreds of talented professionals in week-long career development workshops to give them a taste of being a manager. More than a third of the participants concluded at the end of the experience that dealing with all of the thorny people decisions, the paperwork, the meetings, and the responsibility for others' performance was not what they wanted to do. They were much happier, they concluded, and better suited to their careers as individual contributors, and they realized that leadership was simply one career alternative among many, not the only valid and challenging future path. Initially enticed by the trappings of leadership roles, they quickly realized that the basic responsibilities and activities leaders must fulfill and perform were not at all attractive to them.

Results-based leaders can't afford to have either subordinates or colleagues attribute shallow, selfish, or political motives to them.

The right motivation for wanting to be a leader is the desire to see worthwhile things accomplished. Leaders with that motivation are driven to achieve positive results and are willing to accept personal responsibility for seeing that positive results happen. Another key motivation of good leaders is the desire to multiply their results through high-level group performance, thus creating greater results than any one person could achieve.

For leaders contemplating the future, one burning question should be: What will be my legacy to this organization? The days of the whiz-kid MBA coming into a managerial job and leaving after nine months are gone. Most organizations want people to learn from the consequences of their actions. Some leaders leave an organization weakened or flabby, whereas others leave it much stronger than it was when they arrived.

14. *Model the methods and strive for the results you want your group to use and attain.*

Leaders lead, and good leaders are worthy of being followed. Indeed, most leaders are chosen because they best represent the group's values.

The biggest, toughest boy becomes the leader of the street gang; the most athletic girl leads the soccer team. When the College of Cardinals meets to select a pope, its choice falls on whomever best represents the values of the Roman Catholic Church. His behavior is an example of what they would hope that all priests and Catholics are expected to emulate. When any organization selects a leader, one of the implicit criteria is the degree to which this individual personifies the values the organization represents. When leaders are appointed, their behavior must constitute a role model for everyone in the organization.

Leaders who make public pronouncements about the importance of technology to their organizations garner snickers, not compliance (let alone enthusiasm), if their people know they can't send or retrieve an e-mail message and don't care to learn. A sales manager answering questions from a group of new salespeople about handling telephone expenses, accounting for personal use of a company automobile, and filing expense vouchers for entertaining clients should be able to say to them, "Look, do anything you see me doing."

Leaders who observe a lack of urgency in their organization pick up the pace. A sense of urgency is conveyed by what the leader says, how quickly the leader makes decisions, what the leader rewards. Leaders concerned about a flagging work ethic set a positive example by working long hours, cutting lunch short, and maintaining high personal productivity. Leaders often focus on the productivity of their work force without taking note of their own. Yet their productivity is highly visible to those around them, and its level sets a tone the group will follow.

Leadership Development Is Self-Development

Ultimately, all leadership development is self-development, and the most powerful self-development takes place on the job. Any leader can take steps in his or her current position that will accelerate the attainment of results. This might include participation in high-quality leadership development programs, but for those unable to attend them, this chapter offers numerous methods and suggestions for honing leadership skills in the workplace. Producing ever-improving results provides, like little else, constant motivation and reinforcement of development efforts and intensifies the desire to produce even more.

Clearly, leaders who can get other people to change their behavior can have profound impact, not only on their contributions to the organization, but ultimately on their attitude and character as well. Such transactions work far more effectively than does trying to inject new information or change attitudes or improve another's persona in the *hope* that these measures will translate into more effective leadership behavior.

Leaders Building Leaders

8

RESULTS-BASED LEADERS have the responsibility to help other leaders achieve results, to establish a leadership "bench." Unless leaders build leaders, results will end when the leader who first achieved them moves on. Ultimately, the results-based leader succeeds because the next generation of leaders exceeds the results of the current generation.

The paramount responsibility for leaders building leaders rests with the top executive in an organization. This person must ensure that the next generation's leaders exceed the current generation's results. However, this responsibility is often shared with each leader throughout the organization and with the chief learning officers (or other HR professionals) who are tasked with crafting leadership development experiences.

This chapter provides all leaders with a road map for building a deep leadership bench and suggests innovative ways to invest development dollars most effectively to upgrade the quality of leadership. To use these tools, leaders must understand the relationship between attributes and results, and see how both fit into leadership development.

The Virtuous Cycle of Attributes and Results

Effective leadership requires connecting leadership attributes (who leaders are and what they know and do) and results. Both attributes and results must exist for leaders to be effective. Much of the recent work on effective leadership has neglected results for attributes. The material here, however, helps leaders find the right balance of these two factors by focusing on employee, organization, customer, and investor results.

When leaders understand both what they need to do to be successful (results) and what they need to know and do to be successful (attributes), they fulfill the virtuous cycle in Figure 8-1. These leaders see connections between what happens and how it happens. These leaders understand why particular attributes impact results and how results derive from attributes. This virtuous cycle replaces a vicious cycle that focuses too much attention on either attributes or results.[1] Neither can stand alone. Attributes without results produce leaders with talent and good character who can't or don't meet their goals. Results without attributes produce only short-term, unsustainable results.

Some line managers, human resource managers, organizations, and leaders themselves have a propensity toward either attributes or results. In Figure 8-1, this bias may be plotted as leaning toward attributes (score of 1, 2, 3, or 4) or results (score of A, B, C, D). When line managers emphasize results (score of C or D) and human resource

FIGURE 8-1

VIRTUOUS CYCLE OF ATTRIBUTES AND RESULTS

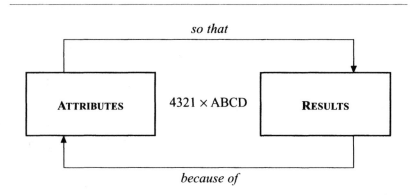

managers stress attributes (score of 3 or 4), the two groups, despite the common goals of building leadership, end up in a vicious circle, each arguing his or her position without connecting them. As a consequence, they end up debating what makes a successful leader rather than working together to create better leadership.

Organization tendencies toward either attributes or results may also be plotted on Figure 8-1. In one company, each member of a senior leadership group identified where they perceived their firm focused leadership attention (attributes versus results). Each member of this senior team scored the company either C or D (a strong results focus). This shared bias helped them understand the gap in their leadership development efforts; they had been so consumed by results and pressure to achieve that they were not building a long-term leadership bench.

Leaders themselves likely have a predisposition toward either attributes or results. Knowing this tendency, a leader may then explore the alternative to ensure a virtuous cycle of leadership. Leaders more comfortable with results may examine the personal attributes to sustain results; those more oriented toward attributes may define more rigorously the results they must achieve.

Consider the events at one company that held leadership development as a priority and charged the human resource department with creating its leadership model. The attribute model HR produced, after much work, included ten effective leadership competencies specific to the organization. Each competency was anchored behaviorally and formed into a 360-degree feedback instrument. HR created the model without the participation of senior managers, however, except for some discovery interviews. These managers approved the model presented to them, but felt little ownership in it. They did not use it for leadership assessments or for compensation or promotion decisions, and ended up bypassing the results of the 360 for critical leadership assessments. Within a short time, the model soon ceased to concern the executives, and although HR pushed for its use, it became less visible and less useful for building leadership depth. When asked about it, the line managers responded that, although the model was OK, it had little to do with running the business; they saw it as an extraneous, unproductive activity. The line managers focused on results; the HR managers, on attributes. As a result, neither attributes nor results were fully delivered.

Such vicious circles can be broken when attributes link explicitly to results and when results link explicitly to attributes. For the individual leader, this connection increases not only personal success, but also the ability to produce future leaders who can attain both attributes and results. For those given the task of building a leadership bench, this connection ensures wise allocation of leadership development resources.

STARTING WITH ATTRIBUTES:
LINKING ATTRIBUTES TO RESULTS (*SO THAT* . . .)

We were recently involved in a one-week leadership training program in which the program began on Monday with an introduction by the senior executive of the business. She extolled the importance of leadership, responsibility, and accountability for making things happen to the excited participants. Monday afternoon, each participant received his or her personal 360-degree feedback, in which each learned how he or she was perceived by supervisor, peers, clients, and subordinates on a series of leadership attributes. These 360 data became the basis for the week of training, with subsequent content modules tied to the dimensions of the 360: setting a vision, managing teams, dealing with conflict, making change happen, getting to know customers, and thinking globally. At the end of the program on Friday, one of us spoke to the group about our thinking on leadership. When we went through the importance of shifting from attributes to results, many of the line manager participants understood our message. However, the human resources executive who designed the program stood up and said, "You have just undermined our entire week." She was quite upset and discouraged about our saying that "attributes are not enough."

Leadership development that starts with attributes needs to get to results. One method is to use the "so that" test, first introduced in Chapter 2: "Attribute X is important *so that* I can achieve result Y." This is done in three steps:

Step 1: Derive the attributes needed to accomplish strategy.
Various methods can be used to figure out which attributes are most critical for a company's leaders. An effective attribute model provides the theoretical foundation for a firm's leadership. It represents who leaders need to be and what leaders need to know and do. Effective

attribute models need to be behavioral, future oriented, tied to management practices (such as staffing, training, and compensation), accepted and used by line managers, aligned with specific business strategies, and applied to leaders at multiple levels of the organization. Responsibility for deriving a leadership attributes model falls to line managers, HR professionals, or outside consultants individually or collectively.

Tools for developing tailored, strategic, and future oriented leadership models have become popular. The Career Architect set of tools, for example, includes sixty-seven possible core leadership competencies a leader might possess. Using a sorting methodology, line managers or HR professionals may create a subset of attributes needed by any target leader population.[2]

Chapter 1 summarized many of these attribute models, dividing them into four categories (set direction, mobilize individual commitment, engender organizational capability, and demonstrate personal character), and then identified a number of dimensions and behaviors within each category. Leaders may use Figure 1-2 to derive the attributes and behaviors necessary for successful leaders.

Step 2: For each derived attribute, ask the leader to identify the results that can or should occur by completing the statement "Attribute . . . so that . . ."

The linking of attributes to results creates more complete and robust leadership effectiveness models. As suggested above, the four necessary results areas are employee results, or measurable human capital (employee capability and commitment); organization results, or measurable organization capability (learning, speed, boundarylessness, and accountability); customer results, or measurable firm equity (target customers, value propositions, and customer intimacy); and investor results, or measurable shareholder value (reduced costs, increased growth, increased management equity).

For each attribute in each category, complete the "so that" statement. Figure 8-2 illustrates how to do this. Each desirable attribute listed on the left may be examined according to the results categories across the top of the figure. The attribute is thus fully defined only in terms of a result, and the appropriate connection of attributes across the four results can easily be verified. Examples of the completed statements include the following:

FIGURE 8-2

TURNING ATTRIBUTES INTO RESULTS
(So That . . .)

ILLUSTRATIVE ATTRIBUTES (from Chapter 1)	EMPLOYEE	BALANCED RESULTS		
		ORGANIZATION	CUSTOMER	INVESTOR
Understand external events				
Focus on the future				
Turn vision into operational outcomes				
Build collaborative relationships				
Share power and authority				
Build organizational infrastructure				
Deploy teams				
Make change happen				
Have and create a positive self-image				
Possess cognitive ability and personal charm				

- "Understand external events *so that* they identify target customers and create unique value propositions for each target customer better than competitors."

- "Turn vision into operational outcomes *so that* the organization can respond more quickly than competitors."

- "Build collaborative relationship *so that* employees feel more committed to their work team."

- "Possess cognitive ability and personal charm *so that* investors experience credibility with the management team."

Our point of view is that when attributes explicitly link to results, leaders can be clearer about both what they should accomplish and how they should accomplish it.

The "so that" framework allows a generic leadership model to be tailored to the needs of specific leaders within an organization. The same attributes may evoke different "so that" responses depending on the leader's title, level, and needs. For example, the attribute "Deploy teams," may link to different results for a senior officer ("Deploy teams *so that* boundaries are removed across organizational divisions, product lines, and geographies") than for a first line supervisor ("Deploy teams *so that* individuals within the work unit learn different skills and build team unity.")

Because each leader may have unique answers to the "so that" query, the exercise is best done by the leader working with his or her supervisor. This results in both a common definition of leadership within an organization (the attributes for effective leaders) and the tailored results needed by the individual employing attributes.

Even where company leaders feel secure that they have chosen the attributes to emphasize because these leadership behaviors or actions are tied to results, the "so that" test can be revealing. Attributes should align with strategy and differentiate results. But many leaders who examine the 360 instrument they use for leadership assessment and development, and then ask what percentage of the items have a "so that" aspect, find that only 15 to 20 percent explicitly link to results. So, even with the good intent of linking attributes to results, without the discipline of the "so that" query, the connection may not occur.

Step 3: Evaluate the attribute-result statements for balance of attention and energy across the four results areas. To do so, check down the four columns of Figure 8-2 to test the balance of the four in terms of attention and energy.

After answering the "so that" query for each attribute, it is important to review the overall responses by result (by column in Figure 8-2). Some firms create a large majority of "so that" statements that pertain to employee and organization results, but neglect customer and investor results. They emphasize leadership behaviors resulting in more capable and committed employees and more agile, learning, boundaryless, and accountable organizations, but their overall results will be unbalanced.

Not all leaders, of course, should be expected to have the *same* mix of employee, organization, customer, and investor results. The appropriate results for a given organization will depend on strategy and on the organization's prevailing criteria for lasting, selfless results. Leaders, however, do need to balance results across the four areas to some extent to achieve this. Leaders whose organizations have invested in attribute models, or who have personally studied the qualities of successful leaders may effectively shift these attributes into results by formulating "so that" statements for each and then verifying that the mix of responses aligns with expected corporate results or personal goals.

STARTING WITH RESULTS:
LINKING RESULTS TO ATTRIBUTES (BECAUSE OF . . .)

At times, leaders may create a virtuous cycle of attributes and results by starting with attributes; at other times, leaders may start with results, which in turn lead to attributes. Leaders starting with results need to discover *why* the desirable results occurred, so that those results can be appropriately replicated. This is true even when the results derive from serendipitous conditions outside the leader's control, as when, for example, a booming economy leads to financial success, or an outstanding new product increases customer loyalty, or a good work location provides a business with highly qualified and committed employees. Leaders who achieve and take credit for results, without fully understanding how the results came about, risk never being able to attain them again. Gaining insight into why a result occurred may be more valuable—and, especially, of more lasting value—than the result itself.

Often, leaders who succeed once fail to succeed again in a changed setting or changed circumstances. Some leaders may be especially attuned to a particular type of results challenge—the turnaround situation, say, in which they can quickly find ways to stop a flood of losses and restore profitability, or the situation in which customer trust has been lost and they are able, through their personal talent in that area, to reestablish customer intimacy. When leaders whose talents lie exclusively in one results area are called on to cope with situations in which other results are needed, however, they often fail to live up to expectations.

These leaders move beyond producing results as isolated events by examining the attributes they demonstrated to obtain them, then by identifying those attributes they might require for other desirable results and acquiring these attributes. The logic for moving from results to attributes comes from the "because of" query as shown in Figure 8-3 and follows the same steps as "so that" in Figure 8-2, but it starts with results, not attributes.

Step 1: Operationalize the results required to make strategy happen.

Leaders, as discussed in Chapter 2, need to focus on four result areas: employee, organization, customer, and investor. Chapters 3 through 6 offered guidelines on how to produce results in each area that could be measured, actionable, and integrated into any business strategy or corporate culture. Leaders starting with a results focus fulfill expectations and accomplish goals with these characteristics by starting with these four questions:

- What is the strategy of my organization unit? (What are we trying to accomplish?)

- For what results will I be most accountable to help make this strategy happen, in each of the key results areas: employee, organization, customers, and investors?

- How should the four results be balanced in terms of importance? (This can be demonstrated by dividing 100 points across the four results areas, awarding no one result more than 60 or fewer than 10 points.)

- How will my performance be measured in each of the four results areas?

FIGURE 8-3

TURNING RESULTS INTO ATTRIBUTES

(Because of . . .)

ATTRIBUTE CATEGORIES (from Chapter 1)	BALANCED RESULTS			
	EMPLOYEE	ORGANIZATION	CUSTOMER	INVESTOR
Set direction				
Mobilize individual commitment				
Engender organizational capability				
Demonstrate personal character				

By answering these four questions, leaders gain clarity about what is expected of them.

Step 2: Define the attributes required to make each happen.

Having clarified the results expected, leaders must complete a "because of" statement, a parallel version of the "so that" proposition mentioned above. Expressed generically, such a statement would run something like this: "It would only be possible for me to achieve result Y *because of* my attainment of attribute X." Leaders can turn results into attributes when they can answer the "because of" query. Leaders who do so demonstrate that they can identify the behaviors they need to make results happen, the first step in achieving both the behaviors and, ultimately, the results. Figure 8-3 illustrates one way leaders isolate and appropriately emphasize strategically consistent, appropriately weighted, fully desirable results. Examples of "because of" statements that might fill the figure's cells include the following:

- "Achieve higher employee commitment and lower turnover *because of* the deployment of high performing teams and building a culture of trust."

- "Create a learning organization *because of* the ability to share knowledge from one unit to another."

- "Build long-term customer partnerships with target customers *because of* the ability to create a customer-focused culture."

- "Increase revenue *because of* the capability of encouraging change and innovation."

The phrases following "because of" in each example constitute the attributes leaders must demonstrate to achieve results. These items can be drawn from the list provided in Figure 1-2. These attributes represent specific ways for leaders to invest their time and attention.

Step 3: Assess the attributes most difficult for the individual leader.

Leaders moving from results to attributes should make a clear-eyed assessment of what attributes they find most difficult to acquire and then make a special effort to acquire them.

Leaders achieving only a limited range of results may be doing so because they possess only a limited range of attributes. As leaders think seriously about their formulations of the "because of" statement, they may even find that some of their attribute predispositions *hinder* their ability to produce the results required by their unit or corporate strategy. Generally, although not always, when leaders understand what attributes they need to obtain desired results, and when those leaders face, with brutal honesty if need be, their present incapacity to demonstrate the competence, they almost always find ways to learn or acquire the attributes required. Often failure to acquire new attributes—and, therefore, failure to produce new results—dogs leaders who either can't see clearly the attributes they require or who refuse to acknowledge their lack of required attributes.

SUMMARY: A VIRTUOUS CYCLE FOR LEADERSHIP

When leaders understand both what they need to do to be successful (results) and how to behave to be successful (attributes), they fulfill the virtuous cycle in Figure 8-1. These leaders see connections between what happens and how it happens. These leaders understand why attributes affect results and why results come from attributes. When leaders master these "why's" they create patterns of success. Leadership is neither a random act nor a single event repeated over and over. By answering the "so that" and "because of" queries, attributes and results become connected and leveraged.

Learning Results-Based Leadership

To improve the quality of leadership by imparting a results focus necessitates a new approach to both leadership training and development activities.

LEADERSHIP TRAINING WITH RESULTS IN MIND

Most traditional, one-week leadership training programs use an implicit or explicit attribute model, with each day or module in the program linked to a specific set of behaviors for the participant to "take home" (for example, setting a vision, managing teams, or relishing change). Such programs, however, even when they produce the intended effect of discharging leaders with more or improved attributes, may not be helping those leaders learn how to get results. The information and tools may have been transferred for making the participants better people, but not for helping them achieve better performance.

Training for results-based leadership differs in that it focuses first on results and second on how to achieve the results. Participants in such training would learn how to determine the results required by a firm's strategy and goals and then how to identify and pursue the attributes needed to ensure that desired results continue. Possible modules for such a training program might include the following categories of activities:

Results diagnosis.

The strategy frameworks in Chapter 2 can help leaders in training to define the results they need to produce. A results diagnosis module could help specify the relative importance of each of the key areas of employee, organization, customer, and investor results.

Employee results.

Employee results increase human capital. Training leaders to assess and improve employee capability and commitment may include collecting data on employee abilities prior to a workshop, clearly defining expectations for employees, evaluating employee skills, and providing employees with opportunities to enhance intellectual capital. These skills can often be transferred through cases, action projects, and personal learning contracts between participants and their employees. (See Chapter 3 for more specific information.)

Organization results.

Organization results instill capabilities of learning, agility, boundarylessness, and accountability. Training leaders to diagnose current capabilities and define desired capabilities needed to win could come from examining how successful and unsuccessful firms build capabilities, using action learning projects and case studies, and having participants use their units as living cases. (See also the ideas presented in Chapter 4.)

Customer results.

Customer results build firm equity through identifying target customers, defining the value proposition for those customers, and building increasingly intimate ways to connect with those customers. Training leaders to create firm equity may be done by assessing and anticipating customer needs, partnering with customers, and sharing management practices with customers. The best customer results training occurs when customers actually participate in the training experience, creating real time solutions to customer intimacy concerns. (See Chapter 5 for more ideas.)

Investor results.

Investor results improve shareholder value through cost, growth, or management equity. Training leaders to assure continuous financial performance may include training on basic economic liberty before moving on to more focused training on reducing costs, creating growth, and sustaining management equity. These skills can best be conveyed in workshops with investors who make significant financial commitments to the firm so that prospective leaders can understand their perspective and expectations. (See also the specific tools identified in Chapter 6.)

"So that" and "because of."

Training results-based leaders requires that they complete the virtuous cycle shown in Figure 8-1. This means that during a workshop, leaders should be able to identify the specific attributes required for success and connect these to results expected of them. As discussed above, this connection can be made beginning with either attributes or results, as long as in the end they appear as fully formulated statements joined by "so that" and "because of."

Training programs incorporating these ideas can move from attributes to results by asking participants to answer the question: What does it take to be a good leader in this company? Using the material in Chapter 1, participants can derive a list of attributes for use in the attribute-result cycle illustrated in Figure 8-1. The participants then examine their list of links to results, which all too often are lacking. Participants should then consider the concept of balanced results, defining the specific results they need to satisfy their strategy in each of the four results areas. Finally, by taking their original lists of attributes and formulating "so that" statements for each, they forge links with the results they must attain.

Training programs taking the opposite tack—starting with results—can be equally successful learning opportunities. Participants first consider the balanced results framework and the four criteria for successful results (covered in Chapter 2), dividing 100 points across the four results to define their individual balance and recording in each quadrant of Figure 2-3 the specific results they must achieve. After expressing these results clearly, specifically, and concretely, they can derive the list of attributes needed to bring them about. (Some aspiring leaders use the list in Figure 1-2 as a source of ideas for attributes.) Finally, leaders build a ninety-day plan that will guide them in gaining knowledge and taking action to make progress on achieving the results. To devise a ninety-day plan, leaders in training should answer the following questions:

- Where should I spend my time?

- With whom should I meet?

- What questions should I ask?

- What information should I collect, seek, or track?

- What projects or initiatives should I support or sponsor?

Training leaders is a large and complex industry. A focus on results may shift some of that training so that participants in forums, workshops, and seminars leave with a clear sense of the results they should produce and the mechanisms whereby they might produce them.

LEADERSHIP DEVELOPMENT WITH RESULTS IN MIND

Workshops, courses, and structured activities have their place in the process of building leaders, but most would-be leaders who become leaders in fact, capable of achieving long-term success, often gain most of their skills through experience.[3] Experience creates more lasting impact; it often constitutes an emotional event or series of events for the learner, and although it leads to change, it does so at a variable pace that can accommodate personal needs and preferences. Direct experience can be obtained in a number of ways.

Job assignments.

Figuring out which job assignments to provide aspiring leaders might vary if the goal is to ensure results. It is not uncommon to have leaders who are talented at accomplishing a particular result, for example, commonly receive job assignments requiring exercise of their unique skill. For example, a leader gifted at creating customer intimacy moves continually to new jobs in divisions, groups, or locations with customer aversion problems. Although such moves may make sense in the short term, they may not allow the aspiring leader to produce a balanced array of results in the long term. Job assignments for results create experiences fashioned so that leaders encounter and master the pressures related to all four results. This means considering what impact different job assignments will have on leaders' abilities to deliver results. A strong customer leader may be moved to an organization that requires high employee commitment as a way to develop a leader's ability to define and deliver this result.

Coaching.

Often leaders coaching leaders focus on attributes, and the coach helps the aspiring leader recognize how to secure future attributes for success. Results-based coaching should begin with dialogues focused on results and on helping the aspiring leaders become clear about turning strategy into results, using the tools in Chapters 3 through 6. Most importantly, however, coaches should make sure that their protégés understand and participate in the virtuous cycle approach, illustrated in Figure 8-1, in which the aspiring leader maintains the constant interplay between attributes and results by answering, at the insistence and with the help of the coach, "so that" and "because of" queries.

Mentoring.

Aspiring leaders look to mentors for insight and direction. Mentors often approach their task by sharing experiences. Mentoring for results would depart somewhat from this tradition in that aspiring leaders would seek mentors known for delivering results and would then observe how their mentors defined and achieved those results. Mentoring for results would also encourage the mentors to continually focus dialogue and tutelage on what results are required, how to achieve the results, and what to do to connect results and attributes.

Succession planning.

As restructuring continues to contribute to a decline in leadership depth at many firms, succession planning becomes ever more critical. Succession planning for results focuses not only on the attributes of the aspiring leader, but also on the results the candidate has attained and will need to attain in the future. Such succession planning can be undertaken effectively by putting requirements in these terms: what results may be needed in the future, and how able is the aspiring leader to deliver those results? The succession-planning dialogue should thus start with results, including all of employee, organization, customer, and investor results. It should continue by evaluating aspiring leaders in terms of their capacity to deliver those results.

Action learning.

In recent years, action learning has become a major trend in the development of leaders.[4] Action-learning participants working in teams apply specific ideas and tools to a real business problem or issue. In one company, leaders on an action-learning team were asked to identify projects or initiatives likely to either increase revenue or decrease costs by $250,000. Teams were then selected to attend a development experience where they would learn and apply concepts to deliver the $250,000. Such action-learning projects succeed because participants immediately transfer learning to ongoing real-time work projects.

A results focus on action learning means that each team's project is driven by a clear set of results. The typical action-learning workshop, however, relies for focus on investor or financial results. However, great benefits could also derive from an expanded results basis that includes employee results (attracting or retaining more competent and committed employees); organization results (building speed, learning, accountability, or teamwork into the organization); and customer results (creating firm equity with target customers). With more clarity about the results from the action learning, participants may better determine the impact of their work.

360-degree feedback.

The already useful 360-degree feedback approach can become even more so if given a results orientation—simply by asking the "so that" question for each item. Such feedback may have significant impact on leadership development, especially if every leader's 360 is tailored to the unique results required of a particular job. All leaders, for example, should be oriented to the future, as indicated by how well they shape their group's vision, understand customers, and anticipate technology changes. Generally a 360 instrument reflects the need for these skills and behaviors (see the example of General Electric's instrument in the appendix to Chapter 1). But while all leaders in a firm may need to shape the vision of a group, this task differs for the leader at the top of the organization, the first-line supervisor, and every level in between. By focusing on results—by including "so that" statements in the individually tailored 360 instruments, leaders at every organizational level will get the most information and value from the process.

Specific skill training.

A burgeoning market exists for specific skill training around topics, including interviewing, coaching, performance management, leading a meeting, feedback, positive discipline, and so on. This training tends to be practical, job related, concrete, and easy to implement; in many cases, leaders and aspiring leaders find it very helpful. With a results focus, however, it could be even more so. This would require that every module, workshop, or role-play activity begin and end with the explicit statements of the intended results for the organization of the skill being taught. "So that" queries and statements, again, can provide skill training with a result. For example, managers attending interview training should know that this skill, when put into practice, should lead to employee capability. The purpose of training is not just to interview better, but to produce measurable improvement through interviewing in employee, organization, customer, or investor results. Trainers often believe they are doing this. But when participant evaluations of the training indicate satisfaction with the congeniality of the instructor, the quality of the materials, or the comfort and attractiveness of the physical setting, the skill training has not adequately focused on results. A results measure of participants' learning experiences would emphasize how they feel the skills mastered will affect their organization's balanced results.

Performance appraisal.

Results-based leadership connects tightly to performance appraisals. The standard set for results-based leaders should focus on both the results, or ends, and the attributes, or means, needed to achieve them.

Results-based leaders should participate in developmental experiences and should be able to connect those experiences to the performance standards set on the job. Such an awareness can help avoid or reduce any gap between what leaders are held accountable for on the job and the skills they acquire through development.

Roles for Leaders Developing Leaders

The responsibility for leaders developing results-based leaders is shared. Current leaders who are senior managers have the ultimate challenge of preparing a next generation of leaders, every one of whom should be more capable than themselves. Traditional training managers, and more senior chief learning officers, often have direct responsibility for developing leaders. Ultimately, each leader in an organization must assume responsibility for developing future leaders. Each of these roles will be discussed in turn.

SENIOR LINE MANAGERS

Thom Nielson, chief executive officer of Baladyne and an ecclesiastical leader, learned an important lesson in senior leadership from what he calls his "button the coat" experience. Nielson discovered that, if he wore and buttoned his suit coat for three or four weeks, his subordinates would soon do the same. If he left his suit coat unbuttoned, so would they. If he did not wear a coat, neither would they. His simple lesson suggests the most important role senior leaders play in building leaders: lead by example.

If senior leaders want results-based leaders to follow in their footsteps, they must be results-based leaders themselves. They must pay attention to, talk about, continually emphasize, and strive to define and deliver results. The ultimate test for leaders is the quality of the leaders they produce. This should impel all senior leaders to invest in the next generation. Here are some specific actions and techniques for modeling—and producing—results-based leadership:

- SPEND TIME ON RESULTS. Leaders must define clearly the few focused results required for the organization to succeed. They should do regular calendar checks to ensure that they use their time effectively to achieve these results. They should move people, as needed, to give them experience in making the various results happen. They should teach results to other leaders in the organization through workshops and forums, to all employees through videos and other communications, to customers through visits and direct contact, and to investors through shareholder meetings and written communications.

- **HAVE PASSION FOR RESULTS.** Employees easily understand and feel the passions of a senior leader. At Harley-Davidson, for example, former CEO Rich Teerlink talked openly and often about his commitment to the Harley lifestyle, his feeling for the motorcycle, his affection for Harley owners who generously donate to charities, and his hopes for the company's future. He felt, communicated, and believed in the firm equity at the center of Harley's results—and he thus furthered those results for the company and with its future leaders. Real leadership passion must be congruent with leaders' behavior and consistent over time, however, or employees will quickly replace commitment with cynicism.

- **HAVE A FOCUS ON RESULTS.** Senior leaders wanting to build the next generation of results-based leaders must continually *focus on results*. Telling results-oriented stories, tracing and celebrating successes, and finding stimulation through new metaphors for the results message become critical for leaders trying to build results-based leaders.

- **ASK RESULT-BASED QUESTIONS.** Senior leaders building results-based leaders must continually ask future leaders results-based questions. The following questions, for example, have proved useful to many leaders trying to foster a results focus:

What results are you trying to attain?

How balanced are the results you are after? Do you have the right balance for your business strategy?

How able are you to attain these results?

What do you bring to these results that will help you attain them?

What do you lack that would help make these results happen?

What do you need to learn more about or do differently to get the results you desire?

Using these questions, in both public forums and private conversations, senior leaders can help instill a results mind-set in the next generation of leaders.

CHIEF LEARNING OFFICER

The relatively new corporate title "chief learning officer (CLO)" signifies a role at a growing number of companies that goes beyond that of the training manager as traditionally conceived. Chief learning officers bring to the task of building the next generation of leaders four mutually enhancing sets of skills:

- **BUSINESS.** The CLO knows, appreciates, and influences business strategy, including customer relationships and financial performance.

- **CHANGE.** The CLO appreciates the nuances of making change happen and can apply change principles throughout the organization.

- **KNOWLEDGE MANAGEMENT AND LEARNING.** The CLO understands the essence of information and knowledge management and can create an organization in which learning occurs.

- **HUMAN RESOURCES.** The CLO maintains a focus on training and development but is sensitive to the entire array of HR practices, including staffing, compensation, communication, and so on.

The success of chief learning officers should be measured less by the number of people attending training than by the extent to which employee capability and commitment increase. They are concerned less with curriculum design (what courses are taught) than with culture-change methods of creating firm equity. They ensure not only the personal growth of individual employees, but the clear definition and reliable delivery of organizational capabilities. They help organizations to build a management equity that investors would pay for.

Responsibility for building the next generation of results-based leaders falls heavily on CLOs. They must institute and maintain the right mix of formal training programs, job experiences, coaching, best-practice sharing forums and technologies, and personal development experiences. Worksheets like that in Figure 8-4 can help chief learning officers work with aspiring leaders to develop personal leadership plans. The most successful of these plans start with results: what results in each of the four categories does the aspiring leader need to learn to create? The plan then lays out a number of alternative ways in which aspiring leaders may master these results; for example, through training, experience, coaching, feedback, sharing best practices, and so on. Then, for each designated time period—often, as in the example, in a quarter— leaders fill in the appropriate cells to show what leadership development has occurred. Such a completed worksheet becomes both a blueprint and a record of achievement for individual leaders' development.

These individual leadership plans may be collapsed and integrated into the corporate learning agendas by the CLOs. This enables the CLO to identity the critical next generation of leaders (often about 1 percent of all employees or 10 percent of all managers). Chief learning officers may then sponsor and propose activities in each of the rows of the leadership template in Figure 8-4 to build leadership depth, with cells representing the percentage of targeted leaders involved in each development activity each quarter. The discipline of compiling such a template helps chief learning officers integrate leadership development on results, as derived through leadership investment.

ALL LEADERS

Ultimately, all leaders in an organization have the responsibility of investing in their successors, so the next generation of leaders can achieve even better results. Once aspiring leaders master results and how to achieve them, their work is not done. They must engender similar discipline in the next generation. This sounds like a tall order, but concrete techniques exist to promote the process.

Help the next generation of leaders to define their results.

Results-based leaders constantly help the next generation by asking, talking about, coaching on, and emphasizing results. At its simplest level, this might mean maintaining an ongoing dialogue about what results the organization needs and how they can be achieved. One executive continually asks his subordinates two questions: "What are you trying to accomplish?" and "How will that affect the business two to three years from today?" These two questions help clarify for next-generation leaders how current results tie into future results.

FIGURE 8-4

TEMPLATE FOR NEXT-GENERATION LEADERSHIP
(Personal or Organizational)

RESULTS REQUIRED:

Employee:

Organization:

Customer:

Investor:

LEADERSHIP DEVELOPMENT ACTIVITY	QUARTER				QUARTER			
	1	2	3	4	1	2	3	4
Formal training: In-company								
Formal training: Off-company								
Job experience: Permanent								
Job experience: Temporary								
Mentoring/coaching								
360° feedback								
Personal growth								
Technology-based best practice								
Action learning								
Other								

Offer the next generation opportunities to deliver results.

Results-based leaders give the next generation's leaders chances to lead, to risk, and, at times, to fail. One of the few characteristics common to all results-based leaders is the occasional failure. For the results-based leader, failure intensifies learning and tests the will to try again. Preparing the next generation of results-based leaders requires giving these future leaders opportunities to lead. These opportunities may be scaled back to avoid large risks, but they must be real and serious. Senior leaders can almost always think back to a job or assignment for which they were not fully prepared, but which contributed significantly to their leadership development. When asked if they would willingly give the next generation of leaders a similar opportunity, however, some say no, indicating that avoiding failure has a higher priority for them than does promoting the professional growth of the upcoming leadership generation.

Be a teacher by learning from failures and successes.

Results-based leaders build the next generation by helping them learn from their experiences, whether the experience is a win or a loss. The next generation of leaders needs the support provided by senior management's humility in victory and courage in defeat. When the next generation fails, a results-based leader turns it into a learning experience by probing: "What worked?" "What didn't work? "Why?" "Why not?" "What would you do differently next time, knowing what you know now? "How can you make sure you apply these lessons in the future?" When the next generation succeeds, a results-based leader celebrates—but also probes, "What made this work?" "Who helped?" "What were the antecedents or conditions that helped this succeed?" "How can you find ways to re-create those conditions?" "If those condition don't exist, how could you apply your lessons in a new situation?" Results-based leaders thus build learning organizations. By constantly teaching, results-based leaders turn activities into experiences and single events into ongoing repeatable patterns. The critical activities here for building the next generation of results-based leaders are cheerleading by enthusiastically supporting the work of others and coaching by giving quiet, consistent, and honest feedback.

Let go.

Finally, and perhaps most importantly, results-based leaders must be prepared to step aside, let go, and allow the next generation to lead. When leaders linger—staying on boards, keeping offices, consulting, and in other ways continuing their active involvement in a company— very often these well-intentioned efforts to transfer knowledge to the next generation backfire, undermining the next leaders' ability to define and deliver results. Allowing the next-generation leader to invite input from the former leader allows the information to be more timely and useful. Results-based leaders realize that their achievements and methods may not and should not be imposed on someone else.

If 50 percent of current leaders were to work with 50 percent of the next generation of leaders to make them results-based leaders, leadership quality in almost all organizations would rise dramatically.

The final test of any leader lies in the preparation and success of the next generation. Even after physically leaving an organization, results-based leaders will have instilled in the next generation of leaders a mind-set predisposed to deliver results.

Notes

CHAPTER 1

1. Louis Csoka, "Bridging the Leadership Gap," Report #1190-98-RR, Conference Board, New York City.
2. Human Resource Institute, *Major Issues Impacting People Management* (St. Petersburg, Fla.: Human Resource Institute, Eckerd College, 1997).
3. The Human Resource Planning Society has published a number of studies on the theme of "future challenges facing global business." The following two publications also offer useful explications: Robert Eichinger and Dave Ulrich, "It's Deja Future All Over Again: Are You Getting Ready?" *Human Resource Planning Journal* 20, no. 2 (1997): 50–61; and Robert Eichinger and Dave Ulrich, "Are You Future Agile?" *Human Resource Planning Journal* 18, no. 4 (1995): 30–41.
4. Society for Human Resource Management, *The SHRM Task Team Review on the Future of HR* (Alexandria, Va.: Society for Human Resource Management, 1998).
5. Floyd Kemske, "HR 2008: A Forecast Based on Our Exclusive Study," *Workforce* (January 1998): 47–60.
6. McKinsey & Company, a consulting firm, did a 1998 study called "The War for Talent."
7. See, for example, Peter F. Drucker, "The Shape of Things to Come," *Leader to Leader* 1, no. 1 (1996): 12–19; and Peter F. Drucker, "Toward the New Organization," *Leader to Leader* 2, no. 3 (1997): 6–8.
8. Some of the more popular books on leadership include Warren Bennis and Patricia Biederman, *Organizing Genius: The Secrets of Creating Collaboration* (Reading, Mass.: Addison-Wesley, 1997); Noel Tichy and Eli Cohen, *The Leadership Engine: How Winning Companies Build Leaders at Every Level* (New

York: Harper Business, 1997); Morgan W. McCall, Jr., *High Flyers: Developing the Next Generation of Leaders* (Boston: Harvard Business School Press, 1997); Colin Powell, *On Leadership* (New York: Random House, 1998); Lynne Joy McFarland, Larry E. Senn, and John R. Childress, *21st Century Leadership* (New York: Leadership Press, 1994); and John P. Kotter, *Leading Change* (Boston: Harvard Business School Press, 1996).

9. Michael Lombardo and Robert Eichinger, "What Characterizes a HiPo? Ferreting Out the True High Potentials," working paper, Lominger, Minneapolis, 1997; Michael Lombardo and Robert Eichinger, *Twenty-two Ways to Develop Leadership in Staff Managers* (Greensboro, N.C.: Center for Creative Leadership, 1990); and Personnel Decisions, *Successful Manager's Handbook* (Minneapolis: Personnel Decisions, Inc., 1992).

10. Many articles describe why General Electric is highly regarded as a repository of leadership talent and development. See, for example, Deborah Keller, "Building Human Resource Capability: General Electric," *Human Resource Management Journal* 31, nos. 1 and 2 (1992): 102–126; Stephen Kerr, "GE's Collective Genius," *Leader to Leader* 1, no. 1 (1996): 30–35; and Jennifer Reingold and John Byrne, "Wanted: A Few Good CEOs," *Business Week*, 11 August 1997, 64–70.

11. S. D. Friedman and T. P. Levino, "Strategic Appraisal and Development at General Electric," in *Strategic Human Resource Management*, ed. Charles J. Fombrun, Noel M. Tichy, and Mary Anne Devanna (New York: Wiley, 1984).

12. See, for example, Dave Ulrich and Dale Lake, *Organizational Capability: Competing from the Inside/Out* (New York: Wiley, 1990).

13. Interview with Warren Bennis, *Human Resource Executive*, December 1996.

14. See James Kouzes and Barry Posner, *The Leadership Challenge: How to Keep Getting Extraordinary Things Done in Organizations* (San Francisco: Jossey-Bass, 1995); and James Kouzes and Barry Posner, *Credibility* (San Francisco: Jossey-Bass, 1993).

15. See, for example, Stephen Covey, "The Habits of Effective Organizations," *Leader to Leader* 2, no. 3 (1997): 22–28; Stephen Covey, *The Seven Habits of Highly Effective People: Implementation Model* (Provo, Utah: Covey Leadership Center, 1991); and Stephen Covey, *The Seven Habits of Highly Effective Leaders* (New York: Simon & Schuster, 1989).

16. Richard E. Boyatzis, *The Competence Manager* (New York: Wiley, 1980); and Morgan W. McCall, Jr., Michael Lombardo, and Ann Morrison, *The Lessons of Experience: How Successful Executives Develop on the Job* (Lexington, Mass.: Lexington Books, 1988).

17. For a thorough review of the 360 instrument, see the special issue on 360-degree management, Walter W. Tornow, guest editor, *Human Resource Management Journal* 32, nos. 2 and 3 (1993); and Walter W. Tornow, Manuel London, and CCL Associates, *Maximizing the Value of 360-Degree Feedback: A Process for Successful Individual and Organizational Development* (San Francisco: Jossey-Bass, 1998).

18. A wonderful book on how CEOs see their firms is G. William Dauphinais and Colin Price, eds., *Straight from the CEO: The World's Top Business Leaders Reveal Ideas That Every Manager Can Use* (New York: Simon & Schuster, 1998).

19. Steven Kerr, "Substitutes for Leadership: Some Implications for Organization Design," *Organization and Administrative Sciences* 8 (1977): 135–146; and

Steven Kerr and John Jermier, "Substitutes for Leadership: Their Meaning and Measurement," *Organization Behavior and Human Performance* 23 (1978): 374–403.

CHAPTER 2

1. A warning about our criteria. They are not intended to induce guilt. True, the criteria are comprehensive; but a leader achieving truly excellent results in all of these areas would, we recognize, be superhuman. It is axiomatic that any leader evaluating him- or herself against these criteria will be found wanting in some area or areas. These comprehensive results criteria, however, provide a standard, making possible an assessment of strengths and weaknesses alike. The clear picture thus attained, vis-à-vis the ideal state, empowers leaders and potential leaders to choose how they will improve.

2. For more on stakeholder theory, see Edward Freedman, *Strategic Management: A Stakeholder Approach* (Boston: Pitman, 1985); Robert Kaplan and David Norton, "Putting the Balanced Scorecard to Work," *Harvard Business Review*, September–October 1993, 134–147; and Robert Kaplan and David Norton, "Using the Balanced Scorecard as a Strategic Management System," *Harvard Business Review*, January–February 1996, 75–87.

3. For more on Martinez's position and its effects, see Anthony Rucci, Steven Kirn, and Richard Quinn, "The Employee-Customer-Profit Chain at Sears," *Harvard Business Review*, January–February 1998, 82–98.

4. The role of customer and investor results at Sears is covered in James O'Shea and Charles Madigan, "Taming 'The Monster of the Midway,'" in *Dangerous Company: The Consulting Powerhouses and the Businesses They Save and Ruin* (New York: Random House, 1997), 109–145.

5. For further discussion of the elemental forms of business focus, see Lee Tom Perry, Randall G. Stott, and W. Norman Smallwood, *Real Time Strategy* (New York: Wiley, 1993); Michael Treacy and Fred Wiersema, "Customer Intimacy and Other Value Disciplines," *Harvard Business Review*, January–February 1993, 84–96; and Michael Treacy and Fred Wiersema, *The Discipline of Market Leaders* (Reading, Mass.: Addison-Wesley, 1995).

6. For comments on the drawbacks of a short-term perspective, see, for example, Gary Hamel and C. K. Prahalad, *Competing for the Future* (Boston: Harvard Business School Press, 1994).

7. The concept of "satisficing" is described in more detail in the following articles: H. A. Simon, "A Behavioral Model of Rational Choice," *Quarterly Journal of Economics* 69 (1955); and H. A. Simon, "Bounded Rationality and Organizational Learning," *Organization Science* 2, no. 1 (1955): 125–134.

8. See Morgan McCall, Jr., and Michael M. Lombardo, "What Makes a Top Executive," *Psychology Today*, February 1983, 28.

9. See Morgan McCall, Jr., *High Flyers: Developing the Next Generation of Leaders* (Boston: Harvard Business School Press, 1998).

10. Gene Dalton and Paul Thompson, *Novations: Strategies for Career Management* (Glenville, Ill.: Scott, Foresman, 1986), 207.

11. See, for example, Susan Mohrman, Susan Cohen, and Allan Mohrman, Jr., *Designing Team-Based Organizations: New Forms of Knowledge Work* (San Francisco: Jossey-Bass, 1995); Jon R. Katzenbach and Douglas Smith, *The*

Wisdom of Teams: Creating the High-Performance Organization (Boston: Harvard Business School Press, 1993); and Richard Guzzo, Eduardo Salas, and Associates, *Team Effectiveness and Decision Making in Organizations* (San Francisco: Jossey-Bass, 1995). John Zenger, Ed Musselwhite, Kathleen Hurson, and Craig Perrin, *Leading Teams, Mastering the New Role* (Homewood, Ill.: Business One Irwin, 1994); Jack Orsburn, Linda Moran, Ed Musselwhite, and John Zenger, *Self-Directed Work Teams: The New American Challenge* (Homewood, Ill.: Business One Irwin, 1990).

12. This principle is discussed further in Jay Galbraith, *Designing Organizations: An Executive Briefing on Strategy, Structure, and Process* (San Francisco: Jossey-Bass, 1995); and H. O. Armour and D. J. Teece, "Organization Structure and Economic Performance: A Test of the Multidivisional Hypothesis," *Bell Journal of Economics* 9 (1978): 106–122.

CHAPTER 3

1. For more on intellectual capital, see Scott Snell, David Lepak, and Mark Youndt, "Managing the Architecture of Intellectual Capital: Implications for Strategic Human Resource Management," in *Research in Personnel and Human Resources Management*, ed. Patrick Wright, Lee Dyer, John Boudreau, and George Milkovich (Greenwich, Conn.: JAI Press, 1998); Thomas Stewart, *Intellectual Capital* (New York: Doubleday, 1997); James Brian Quinn, "Leveraging Intellect," *Academy of Management Executive* 10, no. 3 (1996): 7–27; and Hubert Saint-Onge, "Tacit Knowledge: The Key to the Strategic Alignment of Intellectual Capital," *Strategy and Leadership*, March–April 1996, 10–16.

2. See the following for more on human capital: Gary S. Becker, *Human Capital: A Theoretical and Empirical Analysis, with Special Reference to Education* (New York: National Bureau of Economic Research, 1964); and S. Snell and J. Dean, "Integrated Manufacturing and Human Resource Management: A Human Capital Perspective," *Academy of Management Journal* 35, no. 3 (1992): 467–504.

3. The following sources describe knowledge management: Karl Erik Sveiby, *The New Organizational Wealth: Managing and Measuring Knowledge-based Assets* (San Francisco: Berrett-Koehler, 1997); Robert J. Hiebeler, "Benchmarking Knowledge Management," *Strategy and Leadership*, March–April 1996, 22–29; and I. Nonaka, "The Knowledge-Creating Company," *Harvard Business Review*, November–December 1991, 96–104.

4. See the following for more information on the learning organization: Robert Aubrey and Paul Cohen, *Working Wisdom: Timeless Skills and Vanguard Strategies for Learning Organizations* (San Francisco: Jossey-Bass, 1995); C. Argyris, "Teaching Smart People How to Learn," *Harvard Business Review*, May–June 1991, 99–109; C. Argyris and D. A. Schon, *Organizational Learning, A Theory of Action Perspective* (Reading, Mass.: Addison-Wesley, 1978); and Arthur Yeung, Dave Ulrich, Stephen Nason, and Mary Ann Von Glinow, *Learning Capability* (New York: Oxford University Press, 1998).

5. Nobel prize–winning economist James Tobin called market to replacement value "Tobin's q," defining it as a global measure of the value a firm creates from its present assets. For further information, see Scott Snell, David Lepak, and Mark Youndt, "Managing the Architecture of Intellectual Capital: Implica-

tions for Strategic Human Resource Management, in Wright, Dyer, Boudreau, and Milkovich, *Research in Personnel and Human Resources Management.*

6. Thomas Stewart's work on intellectual capital includes definitions of human capital measures; see Stewart, *Intellectual Capital*, 229–234.

7. See James Brian Quinn, *Intelligent Enterprise* (New York: Free Press, 1992).

8. For more on the "volunteer" employee, see David E. Bowen and Caren Siehl, "The Future of Human Resource Management: March and Simon (1958) Revisited," *Human Resource Management Journal* 36, no. 1 (1997): 57–64; and Peter F. Drucker, "Toward the New Organization," *Leader to Leader* 2, no. 3 (1997): 6–8.

9. For more on the distance between the employee's and the executive's work situation, see Frederick F. Reichheld, *The Loyalty Effect* (Boston: Harvard Business School Press, 1996).

10. See, for example, Dave Ulrich, Richard Halbrook, Dave Meder, and Mark Stuchlik, "Employee and Customer Attachment: Synergies for Competitive Advantage," *Human Resource Planning* 14, no. 2 (1991): 89–102; Benjamin Schneider and David E. Bowen, *Winning the Service Game* (Boston: Harvard Business School Press, 1995); and Bill Fromm and Len Schlesinger, *The Real Heroes of Business and Not a CEO Among Them* (New York: Doubleday, 1993).

11. See Stewart, *Intellectual Capital.*

12. For more on the underlying processes of commitment, see C. R. Schwenk, "Information, Cognitive Biases, and Commitment to a Course of Action," *Academy of Management Review* 2 (1986): 298–310; B. M. Staw, "The Escalation of Commitment to a Course of Action," *Academy of Management Review* 6 (1981): 577–587; and R. E. Walton, "From Control to Commitment in the Work Place," *Harvard Business Review*, March–April 1985, 77–84.

13. For more on competitive pressure and worker commitment, see Robert Johansen and Rob Swigart, *Upsizing the Individual in the Downsized Organization* (Reading, Mass.: Addison-Wesley, 1994).

14. See B. Joseph Pine II, *Mass Customization: The New Frontier in Business Competition* (Boston: Harvard Business School Press, 1993).

15. For more on generation X workers as harbingers of the worker of the future, see Jay Conger, "How 'GenX' Managers Manage," *Strategy and Organization* 10 (1998): 21–31; N. Zill and J. Robinson, "The Generation X," *American Demographics*, April 1995, 24–33; Bruce Tulgan, "Generation X: Slackers? Or the Workforce of the Future?" *Employment Relations Today*, Summer 1997, 55–64; and Bruce Tulgan, *Manager's Pocket Guide to Generation X* (New York: HRD Press, 1997).

16. A profile of this new worker-management relationship appears in Nina Munk, "The New Organization Man," *Fortune*, 16 March 1998, 62–68.

17. For more information, see J. L. Cotton and J. M. Tuttle, "Employee Turnover: A Meta-Analysis and Review with Implications for Research," *Academy of Management Review* 11 (1986): 55–70; and J. E. Sheridan, "Organizational Culture and Employee Retention," *Academy of Management Review* 35 (1992): 1036–1056.

CHAPTER 4

1. For more on the Kodak transformation, see Stephen Frangos, *Team Zebra* (Essex Junction, Vt.: Oliver Wright Publications, 1993).

2. McKinsey and Company, a consulting firm, first developed and used the 7-S model. Its subsequent evolution and current use are described in Richard Tanner Pascale, *Managing on the Edge: How the Smartest Companies Use Conflict to Stay Ahead* (New York: Simon & Schuster, 1991).

3. Jay Galbraith best describes the "star" model of organization diagnosis. See, for example, J. R. Galbraith, E. E. Lawler III, and Associates, *Organizing for the Future* (San Francisco: Jossey-Bass, 1993); Jay Galbraith, *Designing Complex Organizations* (Reading, Mass.: Addison-Wesley, 1973); Jay Galbraith, *Designing Organizations: An Executive Briefing on Strategy, Structure, and Process* (San Francisco: Jossey-Bass, 1995); and J. R. Galbraith, *Organization Design* (Reading, Mass.: Addison-Wesley, 1977).

4. Descriptions of other organization models as systems appear in the following: David Nadler, Marc Gerstein, Robert Shaw, and Associates, *Organizational Architecture: Designs for Changing Organizations* (San Francisco: Jossey-Bass, 1992); and David Nadler and Michael Tushman, "A Model for Diagnosing Organizational Behavior: Applying a Congruence Perspective," *Organizational Dynamics* 9, no. 2 (1980): 35–51.

5. The organizations-as-capabilities approach has been synthesized as *cultributes* in work by Lominger. This work summarizes the research from these six disciplines and identifies eighty *cultributes* (or capabilities). Copies of this work are available from Bob Eichinger at (612) 377-0122.

6. See Brian E. Becker, Mark A. Huselid, Peter S. Pickus, and Michael F. Spratt, "HR as a Source of Shareholder Value: Research and Recommendations," *Human Resource Management Journal* 36, no. 1 (1997): 39–48.

7. Dave Ulrich, Mike Lombardo, and Bob Eichinger propose the term *cultributes* for *capability*. In work appearing as part of the series Organizational Architect, they show leaders how to assess the capabilities their organizations require, given their particular business strategies, and then how to turn those capabilities into leadership competencies.

8. The sixteen cultributes (capabilities) identified by Lombardo, Eichinger, and Ulrich here become the four most common, through a three-step process. First, the original sixteen included capabilities necessary for results other than organization results. Some, for example, link to increasing intellectual capital (employee results), to building intimacy with customers (customer results), or to predictable profitability (investor results). This chapter treats only capabilities tied to organization results. Second, a content analysis of recent literature on organizational capabilities needed to win revealed an emphasis on the four capabilities identified here. Third, dozens of capability assessments done in organizations of all types suggest that the four capabilities covered here are those most widely recognized as critical to success. Other organizational capabilities can certainly be identified and even defined as critical. These four, however, adequately, even fully, illustrate how results-based leaders focus on and achieve organization results.

9. See Arthur Yeung, Dave Ulrich, Stephen Nason, and Mary Ann Von Glinow, *Organization Learning Capability: Generating and Generalizing Ideas with Impact* (New York: Oxford University Press, 1998); and Dave Ulrich, Mary Ann Von Glinow, and Todd Jick, "High-Impact Learning: Building and Diffusing Learning Capability," *Organizational Dynamics*, Winter 1993, 52–66.

10. The learning index in Figure 4-5 and the research supporting it are reported more fully in Ulrich, Von Glinow, and Jick, "High-Impact Learning."

11. For more on the leader's role in learning, see Yeung, Ulrich, Nason, and Von Glinow, *Organization Learning Capability*.

12. For more on change at General Electric and Sears, see Dave Ulrich, *Human Resource Champions: The Next Agenda for Adding Value and Delivering Results* (Boston: Harvard Business School Press, 1997).

13. The importance of speed and what leaders need to do to make things happen quickly are further described in Richard Pascale, Mark Millemann, and Linda Gioja, "Changing the Way We Change," *Harvard Business Review*, November–December 1997, 126–139.

14. Further information on the removal of boundaries at General Electric can be found in Ron Ashkenas, Steve Kerr, Todd Jick, and Dave Ulrich, *The Boundaryless Organization: Breaking the Chains of Organization Structure* (San Francisco: Jossey-Bass, 1995).

CHAPTER 5

1. For more on the influence of product brands, see David Aakers, *Managing Brand Equity* (New York: Free Press, 1997); Vijay Vishwanath and Jonathan Mark, "Your Brand's Best Strategy," *Harvard Business Review*, May–June 1997, 123–132; and David Aakers, "Should You Take Your Brand to Where the Action Is?" *Harvard Business Review*, September–October 1997, 135–145.

2. For a good general look at product brand studies, see David Aaker and Alexander Biel, eds., *Brand Equity and Advertising* (Hillsdale, N.J.: Lawrence Erlbaum Associates, 1993). This excellent book of readings focuses on advertising, but the essays also deal with issues such as how brand affects categories, the global role of brands, brands and performance, and how to build brand identity.

3. See, for example, J. Barney, "Organizational Culture: Can It Be a Source of Sustained Competitive Advantage?" *Academy of Management Review* 11, no. 3 (1986): 656–665; Edgar Schein, "Leadership and Organizational Culture," in *The Leader of the Future*, ed. Frances Hesselbein, Marshall Goldsmith, and Richard Beckhard (San Francisco: Jossey-Bass, 1995), 59–70; and Dave Ulrich, "Culture Change: Will We Recognize It When We See It?" in *Managing Strategic and Cultural Change in Organization*, ed. Craig Schneier (New York: Human Resource Planning Society, 1995).

4. For more information on this relationship, see John Kotter and James Heskett, *Corporate Culture and Performance* (New York: Free Press, 1992).

5. *Firm equity* should be distinguished from *customer equity*, as described by Robert C. Blattberg and John Deighton, "Manage Marketing by the Customer Equity Test," *Harvard Business Review*, July–August 1996, 136–144. Customer equity focuses on the customer's perception of a brand and deals with issues such as how to get current customers to buy more of an existing product. Firm equity focuses on the customer's perception of the firm and deals with issues such as how to create common ground for the customers and firms.

6. For more on this relationship, see Dave Ulrich, "Tie the Corporate Knot: Gaining Complete Customer Commitment," *Sloan Management Review*, Summer 1989, 19–28.

7. A useful discussion of customer intimacy appears in Michael Treacy and Fred Wiersema, "Customer Intimacy and Other Value Disciplines," *Harvard Business Review*, January–February 1993, 84–96.

8. See also Joseph Wayne Brockbank and Dave Ulrich, "Avoiding SPOTS: Creating

Strategic Unity," in *Handbook of Business Strategy 1990*, ed. H. Glass (New York: Gorham, Lambert, 1990).

9. The Southwest Airlines story appears in greater detail in Jeffrey Pfeffer, *Competitive Advantage through People* (Boston: Harvard Business School Press, 1994).

10. For more on segmentation by channel, see Regis McKenna, "Real-Time Marketing," *Harvard Business Review*, July–August 1995, 87–98.

11. This example of segmentation comes from earlier work first described in Brockbank and Ulrich, "Avoiding SPOTS."

12. For more on customization, see B. Joseph Pine II, *Mass Customization: The New Frontier in Business Competition* (Boston: Harvard Business School Press, 1993).

13. For more insight into customer satisfaction, see Thomas O. Jones and Earl Sasser, Jr., "Why Satisfied Customers Defect," *Harvard Business Review*, November–December 1995, 88–99.

14. For more on guarantees, see Christopher Hart, "The Power of Unconditional Service Guarantees," *Harvard Business Review*, July–August 1988, 54–62; and Christopher Hart, "The Power of Internal Guarantees," *Harvard Business Review*, January–February 1995, 64–74.

15. For more information, see Regis McKenna, "Real-Time Marketing."

16. Michael Hammer and Steven Stanton, "The Power of Reflection," *Fortune*, 24 December 1997, 291–294.

17. Steve Kerr, "On the Folly of Hoping for A while Rewarding B," *Academy of Management Journal* 18 (1975): 769–783.

18. Gene Dalton and Paul Thompson, *Novations: Strategies for Career Management* (Glenville, Ill.: Scott, Foresman, 1986), 207–208.

19. See, for example, Michael M. Lombardo and Robert W. Eichinger, "HR's Role in Building Competitive Edge Leaders," *Human Resource Management Journal* 36, no. 1 (1997): 141–146; Michael Lombardo and Robert Eichinger, *Twenty-two Ways to Develop Leadership in Staff Managers* (Greensboro, N.C.: Center for Creative Leadership, 1990); and Morgan W. McCall, Jr., Michael Lombardo, and Ann Morrison, *The Lessons of Experience: How Successful Executives Develop on the Job* (Lexington, Mass.: Lexington Books, 1988).

20. See, for example, Dave Ulrich and Hope Greenfield, "The Transformation of Training and Development to Development and Learning," *Journal of Management Development* 1, no. 2 (1995): 11–22.

CHAPTER 6

1. Alfred Rappaport, *Creating Shareholder Value: The New Standard for Business Performance* (New York: Free Press, 1986), 11.

2. "Behind Oxford's Billing Nightmare," *Business Week*, 17 November 1997.

3. "New Technology Was Oxford's Nemesis," *Wall Street Journal*, 11 December 1997.

4. Arthur C. Martinez, "Transforming the Legacy of Sears," *Strategy and Leadership* 25, no. 4 (July–August 1997): 30–35.

5. See, for example, Dwight L. Gertz and Joao Baptista, *Grow to Be Great: Breaking the Downsizing Cycle* (New York: Free Press, 1995); and Gary Hamel

and C. K. Prahalad, *Competing for the Future* (Boston: Harvard Business School Press, 1994).

6. Michael Price (of Mutual Shares), cited in Peter Tanous, *Investment Gurus* (New York: New York Institute of Finance, 1997), 38.

7. Mario Gabelli (of Gabelli Funds), cited in Tanous, *Investment Gurus*, 80.

8. Laura Sloate (of Sloate, Weisman, Murray, and Company), cited in Tanous, *Investment Gurus*, 136, 143.

9. Scott Sterling Johnson (of Sterling Johnson Capital Management), cited in Tanous, *Investment Gurus*, 158.

10. John Ballen (of MFS Emerging Growth Fund), cited in Tanous, *Investment Gurus*, 290.

11. Jonathan Low and Tony Siesfeld, "Measures That Matter: Wall Street Considers More Than You Think," *Strategy and Leadership*, March–April 1998, 24–30.

12. Bruce Jensen, an associate at Novations, was extremely helpful during the preparation of this research.

13. "Jack's Men," *Industry Week*, 7 July 1997, 13.

14. "Fifty-two Fiefdoms' No More," *Industry Week*, 20 January 1997, 59.

15. Alan L. Wilkins, *Developing Corporate Character* (San Francisco: Jossey-Bass, 1989).

CHAPTER 7

1. The argument that most training does not produce a measurable return was first stated in Fred Fiedler, "The Trouble with Leadership Training Is That It Doesn't Develop Leaders," *Psychology Today*, February 1973, 31–35.

2. James Collins and Jerry Porras, *Built to Last: Successful Habits of Visionary Companies* (New York: Harper Business, 1995), 91–115.

3. For more on this subject, see Dave Ulrich and Hope Greenfield, "The Transformation of Training and Development to Development and Learning," *Journal of Management Development* 1, no. 2 (1995): 11–22.

CHAPTER 8

1. The term *virtuous cycle* is adapted from work on the service chain by J. Heskett, T. Jones, G. Loveman, E. Sasser, and L. Schlesinger, "Putting the Service Profit Chain to Work," *Harvard Business Review*, March–April 1994, 164–174.

2. The Career Architect, a product of Lominger, illustrates how competencies may be sorted and derived for any organizational unit. A summary of this work may be found in Michael M. Lombardo and Robert W. Eichinger, "HR's Role in Building Competitive Edge Leaders," *Human Resource Management Journal* 36, no. 1 (1997): 141–146.

3. See, for example, Morgan W. McCall, Jr., Michael Lombardo, and Ann Morrison, *The Lessons of Experience: How Successful Executives Develop on the Job* (Lexington, Mass.: Lexington Books, 1988); and Morgan W. McCall, Jr., *High Flyers: Developing the Next Generation of Leaders* (Boston: Harvard Business School Press, 1997).

4. See Dave Ulrich and Hope Greenfield, "The Transformation of Training and Development to Development and Learning," *Journal of Management Development* 1, no. 2 (1995): 11–22.

Index

About the Authors

Dave Ulrich is a professor of business administration at the University of Michigan, where he is on the core faculty of the Michigan Executive Program and codirector of Michigan's Human Resource Executive Program. He has published more than 90 articles and book chapters. He has also coauthored a number of books, including *Organizational Capability: Competing from the Inside/Out, The Boundaryless Organization: Breaking the Chains of Organization Structure, Human Resource Champions: The Next Agenda for Adding Value and Delivering Results,* and *Tomorrow's (HR) Management.*

Dave is the editor of *Human Resource Management Journal,* a fellow in the National Academy of Human Resources, and a cofounder of the Michigan Human Resource Partnership. He has been listed by *Business Week* as one of the world's "top ten educators" in management and the top educator in human resources. He has consulted and done research with over half of the Fortune 200.

Jack Zenger is president of Provant, Inc., a group of companies in the organizational performance improvement industry. He was previously chairman of the Times Mirror Training Group, which, prior to Provant, was the world's largest group of training companies. In 1977 he cofounded Zenger-Miller, a leading leadership and management development company, and served as its president and CEO until 1991.

He has also served on the faculty at USC and taught at the Stanford Graduate School of Business.

Jack is a coauthor of the bestselling books *Self-Directed Work Teams: The New American Challenge, Leading Teams: Mastering the New Role,* and *Keeping Teams on Track,* and the author of *Not Just for CEOs: Sure-Fire Success Secrets for the Leader in Each of Us,* and *22 Management Secrets to Achieve More with Less.* In 1994, Jack was inducted into the Human Resources Development Hall of Fame.

Norm Smallwood is CEO of Results-Based Leadership, a Provant company in Boston, MA. He has devoted his career to the development and clarification of business strategies and their implications for organizational design. He began his career at Procter & Gamble and Esso Resources Canada, Ltd., and in 1985 became a founding partner of Novations Group, Inc., a change management firm helping companies increase individual and organizational effectiveness. An advocate of effecting strategic change at the total business scale, Smallwood continued his work as coauthor of *Real-Time Strategy: Improvising Team-Based Planning for a Fast-Changing World.* He has published articles in the business press and technical journals, including the *Wall Street Journal, Organization Dynamics,* and *Infosystems.*

The Results-Based Leadership Company provides training and consulting services based on the ideas contained in this book. For more information, contact Results-Based Leadership at 877-725-4764 or visit www.rbl.net.